EDUCATION AND
THE CULTURAL PROCESS

PAPERS

PRESENTED AT SYMPOSIUM COMMEMORAT-
ING THE SEVENTY-FIFTH ANNIVERSARY
OF THE FOUNDING OF FISK UNIVERSITY
APRIL 29–MAY 4, 1941

Edited by CHARLES S. JOHNSON

Fisk University

NEGRO UNIVERSITIES PRESS
NEW YORK

Originally published in 1943
by The American Journal of Sociology

Reprinted in 1970 by
Negro Universities Press
A Division of Greenwood Press, Inc.
Westport, Connecticut

SBN 8371-3596-6

Printed in United States of America

TABLE OF CONTENTS

EDUCATION AND THE CULTURAL PROCESS: INTRODUCTION TO SYMPOSIUM

I

The importance of education, as we commonly recognize the term in our modern society, needs no emphasis. It is this very sense of urgency that has been responsible for the rapid multiplication of its methods and for the elaboration of its technology. Although sociologists and anthropologists have dealt occasionally with the subject, it has not been regarded as their province. As a matter of fact, the development of American formal education into such a highly involved system has made it seem appropriate to refer all problems of the field to a class of specialists known as "educators."

The assumption is, usually, that formal education is merely a rational procedure for further carrying on and completing in the schoolroom a task begun with the child in the home. But the problem of education in America is by no means so simple as this, for the reason that the process of cultural transmission and renewal, as John Dewey describes it, is complicated by the diverse cultural origins of the population and by the continued isolation of many groups in more or less closed communities. This is a contingency that does not adjust satisfactorily to the necessity for meeting educational needs by methods of mass production. Dewey's conception of education is that it is not only a process by which a cultural heritage is transmitted from one generation to another but a process by which, through the medium of communication, a society renews and perpetuates itself as a society. Communication, as Park, the sociologist, interprets it, is not merely a means of transmission but a means of participation in a common experience and a common culture.

The experience of the younger generation of immigrants in America emphasizes the vital role of cultural succession in educational development. As Park points out, to this second generation of immigrants, because the new world which is strange and foreign to their parents is the only world they know, strange things happen of which they are scarcely aware—things the significance of which only a psychiatrist would fully understand. Strange things happen to the older generation, too, for that matter. An interruption of the cultural process has profound consequences which involve the whole educational process, not only that which goes on normally in the home but also that which goes on in the schoolroom and on the street. These problems that arise, in the course of such cultural diffusion and acculturation, are usually thought of as problems of personality. Whether they arise in the home or in the school, they are pedagogical problems that grow out of the difficulties of transmitting a cultural tradition from one generation to another or from one unit to another. In the schoolroom it is the problem of "rote learning"; in the home it is that of the "problem child."

What has been described by reference to the immigrant is true of any other group that is culturally isolated in any degree in the American society. It is even possible for changes in our modern world to bring about breaks in the cultural succession so pronounced that one generation may lose touch with the one that preceded it.

II

One indication of the maturity of the modern world is the present disposition of philosophers and others who have time for such things to characterize the epoch in which we are living, and so put it in its place in history. One of the most obvious char-

acteristics of this modern world is the remarkable advance in technology and in the
application of science to all sorts of human
affairs, from agriculture to education. Under the influence of this impulse, fashion, or
trend, activities that in the past have been
traditional and customary have been analyzed, rationalized, reformed, and revolu-
tionized until education, if not agriculture,
seems in many cases to have lost contact
with the spontaneous interests and traditional forms in which it was carried on before its methods became rational and scientific.

The methods and technology of education have multiplied so extensively that the
schools have almost ceased to exist in the
original sense of that term and have instead
become laboratories in which teachers, operating under the direction of experts, are engaged in trying out some new apparatus or
experimenting with some new methods of
teaching or speeding up and making more
efficient the educational processes, as they
are carried on under the artificial conditions
that are imposed by the classroom and the
necessities of mass education. This mass-
production method has permitted the
schools frequently to make fairly effective
use of teachers of inferior mentality. At the
same time, the rationalization and standardization of the process have discouraged
initiative in the more competent ones. Originally education was carried on informally
in the family or in the tribe as part of, and
indistinguishable from, the whole matrix of
living. Now one of the problems of formal
education grows out of the fact that it has
lost touch with the family and the education
in the school is frequently in conflict with
that imparted informally in the family. Under these circumstances it has become, para-
doxically, the task of the school, through its
education of children, to reform the families.

The vast accumulation of historical and
technical knowledge in recent years and the
rapid changes in the conditions of life during
the same period have put the knowledge required to carry on the tasks of modern life
beyond the reach of any but the experts, and

the experts themselves have to struggle to
keep up with events. It is a situation that
has been aptly characterized by the statement that knowledge has become "more and
more about less and less."

The interesting relationship of these educational problems to the fundamental process of acculturation itself suggested the possible profit of inviting sociologists and anthropologists to address themselves to the
issue. Having no technical or professional
interest in education but with a familiarity
with methods of education as carried on traditionally among nonliterate and folk peoples, they might be presumed to be able to
discuss education in its broader aspects, as a
part of the cultural process by which tradition is transmitted and its continuity maintained.

The papers here presented were prepared
for a seminar conducted by the Department
of Social Sciences of Fisk University on the
occasion of the celebration of the Seventy-
fifth Anniversary of the institution. The
seminar was concerned with the practical
problem of examining the method for the
transmission of and diffusion of an existing
cultural tradition within a society like that
in the United States, composed of divergent
cultural and racial stocks.

There has been one outstanding precedent for this seminar in the New Education
Fellowship Conference held at Capetown
and Pretoria, in South Africa, in 1934. This
conference, the sessions of which occupied a
month and were attended by more than four
thousand persons, was enlivened by some
three hundred formal addresses by such persons as John Dewey, of New York, the late
Bronislaw Malinowski, then of London, and
K. S. Cunningham, of Australia, chief exec-
utive officer of the Australian Council for
Educational Research at Melbourne.

What made the proceedings of the South
African conference in some respects comparable with the present seminar was less
the technical aspects of education, which
came up for consideration, than the fact
that the educational problems of South
Africa are so largely determined, as they are

in the United States, by the complexity of the racial and cultural diversities of South African peoples.

South Africa, like the United States, is a country where there are peoples who are very poor, as are the sharecroppers and mountaineers of the Appalachian Mountains, in a country with vast natural resources. It possesses fabulous wealth in the gold mines and diamond fields but has, nevertheless, a "poor-white" problem and a diversity of racial stocks, including a mixed-blood population of Cape Colony, a native population, and an Indian population, each living in a condition of more or less complete segregation from every other. This factor complicated the educational as well as the political problem of the conference. However, added to these ethnic problems was the persistence of a smoldering conflict between the British and the Boers, the aftermath of the Boer War, involving issues not unlike those existing between the northern and southern states of America.

The existence of this conflict imposed upon South African education not only the necessity of a dual school system, as in the southern states, but a problem of bilingual education in African and English. As might be expected, all these problems were reflected in the papers and even more in the discussions as indicated in the extensive report of the conference published under the title of *Educational Adaptations in a Changing Society.*

In South Africa, as in the United States, the problem and process of education seemed to be more than the transmission of a cultural tradition from one generation to another. Quite as important among the problems, educational and otherwise, were the difficulties encountered in the processes by which different races and peoples were being slowly but inevitably welded into a workable cultural and political unity. As we are realizing in this war, there is no more important problem of education in the United States today than that which is traditionally assigned to the school.

III

The contributions to this symposium raise many serious questions for education and at the same time offer some significant suggestions. The papers dealing with the special cultures clearly describe the process of "education without schools." The papers dealing with the educational procedure under our highly rationalized system describe what might almost be called "schools without education."

Attention may be called illustratively to Professor Redfield's discussion of culture and education in the midwestern highlands of Guatemala. Here is a society composed of former Europeans, natives, and mixed-bloods. There is no apparent "race consciousness" and no caste; there are merely class distinctions dividing the three racial and cultural groups. Yet there are no "marginal men." The secularization of the culture in the case of the Ladinos is striking. Most of what is "religion" in the case of the native has become "art" in the case of the Ladinos. Professor Redfield's observations suggest how ideas are transmitted informally; how new ideas are held in suspense if they seem novel or dubious; how they are checked on by repetition or observation as opportunity is offered when any question is raised. This is what one may see anywhere if one is interested and observant enough.

In the American Indian culture described by Dr. Scudder Mekeel it is possible to observe the role of education as an attempt to solve the everyday problems which every society faces. When culture is conceived as an operational totality and a dynamic entity, the significance of its effect upon the individual, and particularly the individual of different background, is far reaching. He raises the question of the role of self-consciousness in education. Why do some peoples seek to maintain their independence and their cultural identity and individuality while others seek to submerge their identity in that of a dominant group?

Professor Malinowski's paper concerns itself with the complex problems of education of native African peoples under conditions that have been changing the meaning of life for the native African. He asks how the African is to learn to appreciate his native culture and preserve that which suits his present needs in a situation of conflicting group aims and imperatives. The evolution of Bantu nationalism seems to be "nature's remedy." Where there are, obviously, such divergent interests as between the Africans and the Europeans in Africa, the most important education must be gained through competition and co-operation, as individuals and as groups, with other persons and peoples with whom they are in more or less association. The problem is how to make this competition and co-operation fruitful so that individuals and races may profit from it. This merely emphasizes more strongly, through the experiences of widely divergent peoples, the basic problems of cultural transmission.

Professor Herskovits' contribution is no less significant for its insights into the role of the educative process in maintaining cultural stability.

On the other hand, there are the examples of formal schools without education, or much of it, in the discussion of the plantation economy by Dr. Thompson, in which rote learning becomes an almost inseparable incident, in some of the implications of the case study of the Negro colleges provided by Dr. Bond, and in Dr. Ruth Benedict's penetrating analysis of the methods of the American school system with reference to the transmission of our democratic heritage. Dr. Margaret Mead points out, further, the shift in education generally from its original point of view as an effort to gain, though not to discover, knowledge to the point of view where it becomes an effort to impose something that is not wanted except as a means of acquiring status or of maintaining an existing social order or imposing a new one.

The difficulties and possibilities of acculturation, which in the American society involve alike the immigrant, the Jew, the Oriental, the American Indian, the religious sect, and various other culturally isolated groups, appear in clearest outline in the case of the American Negro who is more overtly segregated.

The essence of this cultural process may be stated briefly as follows: When peoples of different cultures come together, there is acculturation, in which there is a constant struggle between disintegration and integration. Basically this is education. Education, thus, is more than the transmission of culture from one generation to another. It is this transmission and it is also transformation of peoples who are more or less in conflict. Under these circumstances the whole process may become painful, because it may lead to the disintegration of the culture of one or more of the groups in contact. Technical knowledge can be transmitted with relative ease. Ideas are more difficult to communicate. Implicit in the process of acculturation is solidarity of the society. In times of change, as in the present, the moral solidarity of the society itself may be undermined. One aspect of acculturation appears in the constant struggle to get a new society and a new solidarity.

In the papers that follow we are able to see our own system through the eyes of anthropologists and sociologists who have observed the process of education in a context in which it is not rationalized. A comprehension of the natural process may help the rationalized system by providing a fresh perspective and a new realism.

FISK UNIVERSITY

OUR EDUCATIONAL EMPHASES IN PRIMITIVE PERSPECTIVE[1]

MARGARET MEAD

ABSTRACT

Modern conceptions of education are contrasted with the primitive emphasis upon the need to learn that which was fixed and traditional, based primarily on the child as the learner. Today, owing to the meeting and mingling of peoples among whom superiority was claimed by one as over against another, our concepts of education have been shaped by the will to teach, convert, colonize, or assimilate adults. From the observation of this process in the next generation we have come also to believe in the power of education to create something new, not merely perpetuate something old. But not until the dogma of superiority of race over race, nation over nation, class over class, is obliterated can we hope to combine the primitive idea of the need to learn something old and the modern idea of the possibility of making something new.

In its broadest sense, education is the cultural process, the way in which each newborn human infant, born with a potentiality for learning greater than that of any other mammal, is transformed into a full member of a specific human society, sharing with the other members a specific human culture. From this point of view we can place side by side the newborn child in a modern city and the savage infant born into some primitive South Sea tribe. Both have everything to learn. Both depend for that learning upon the help and example, the care and tutelage, of the elders of their societies. Neither child has any guaranty of growing up to be a full human being should some accident, such as theft by a wolf, interfere with its human education. Despite the tremendous difference in what the New York infant and the New Guinea infant will learn, there is a striking similarity in the whole complicated process by which the child takes on and into itself the culture of those around it. And much profit can be gained by concentrating on these similarities and by setting the procedure of the South Sea mother side by side with the procedure of the New York mother, attempting to understand the common elements in cultural transmission. In such comparisons we can identify the tremendous potentialities of human beings, who are able to learn not only to speak any one of a thousand languages but to adjust to as many different rhythms of maturation, ways of learning, methods of organizing their emotions and of managing their relationships to other human beings.

In this paper, however, I propose to turn away from this order of comparison—which notes the differences between human cultures, primitive and civilized, only as means of exploring the processes which occur in both types of culture—and to stress instead the ways in which our present behavior, which we bracket under the abstraction "education," differs from the procedures characteristic of primitive homogeneous communities. I propose to ask, not what there is in common between America in 1941 and South Sea culture which displays in 1941 a Stone Age level of culture, but to ask instead: What are some of the conspicuous differences, and what light do these differences throw upon our understanding of our own conception of education? And, because this is too large and wide a subject, I want to limit myself still further and to ask a question which is appropriate to this symposium: What effects has the mingling of peoples—of different races, different religions, and different levels of cultural complexity—had upon our concept of education? When we place our present-day concept against a backdrop of primitive educational procedures and see it as influenced by intermingling of peoples, what do we find?

I once lectured to a group of women—all of them college graduates—alert enough to be taking a fairly advanced adult-education course on "Primitive Education" delivered

[1] This paper is an expression of the approach of the Council on Intercultural Relations.

5

from the first point of view. I described in detail the lagoon village of the Manus tribe, the ways in which the parents taught the children to master their environment, to swim, to climb, to handle fire, to paddle a canoe, to judge distances and calculate the strength of materials. I described the tiny canoes which were given to the three-year-olds, the miniature fish spears with which they learned to spear minnows, the way in which small boys learned to calk their canoes with gum and how small girls learned to thread shell money into aprons. Interwoven with a discussion of the more fundamental issues, such as the relationship between children and parents and the relationships between younger children and older children, I gave a fairly complete account of the type of adaptive craft behavior which was characteristic of the Manus and the way in which this was learned by each generation of children. At the end of the lecture one woman stood up and asked the first question: "Didn't they have any vocational training?" Many of the others laughed at the question, and I have often told it myself as a way of getting my audience into a mood which was less rigidly limited by our own phrasing of "education." But that woman's question, naïve and crude as it was, epitomized a long series of changes which stand between our idea of education and the processes by which members of a homogeneous and relatively static primitive society transmit their standardized habit patterns to their children.

There are several striking differences between our concept of education today and that of any contemporary primitive society;[2] but perhaps the most important one is the shift from the need for an individual to learn something which everyone agrees he would wish to know, to the will of some individual to teach something which it is not agreed that anyone has any desire to know. Such a shift in emphasis could come only with the breakdown of self-contained and self-respecting cultural homogeneity. The Manus or the Arapesh or the Iatmul adults taught

[2] This discussion, unless otherwise indicated, is based upon South Sea people only.

their children all that they knew themselves. Sometimes, it is true, there were rifts in the process. A man might die without having communicated some particular piece of ritual knowledge; a good hunter might find no suitable apprentice among his available near kin, so that his skill perished with him. A girl might be so clumsy and stupid that she never learned to weave a mosquito basket that was fit to sell. Miscarriages in the smooth working of the transmission of available skills and knowledge did occur, but they were not sufficient to focus the attention of the group upon the desirability of *teaching* as over against the desirability of *learning*. Even with considerable division of labor and with a custom by which young men learned a special skill not from a father or other specified relative but merely from a master of the art, the master did not go seeking pupils; the pupils and their parents went to seek the master and with proper gifts of fish or octopus or dogs' teeth persuaded him to teach the neophyte. And at this level of human culture even close contact with members of other cultures did not alter the emphasis. Women who spoke another language married into the tribe; it was, of course, very important that they should learn to speak the language of their husbands' people, and so they learned that language as best they could—or failed to learn it. People might compliment them on their facility or laugh at them for their lack of it, but the idea of *assimilating* them was absent.

Similarly, the spread of special cults or sects among South Sea people, the desire to *join* the sect rather than the need to make converts, was emphasized. New ceremonies did develop. It was necessary that those who had formerly been ignorant of them should learn new songs or new dance steps, but the onus was again upon the learner. The greater self-centeredness of primitive homogeneous groups (often so self-centered that they divided mankind into two groups —the human beings, i.e., themselves, and the nonhuman beings, other people) preserved them also from the emphasis upon the greater value of one truth over another which is the condition of proselytizing. "*We* (human beings) do it this way and *they* (other people) do it that way." A lack of a desire to teach *them* our ways guaranteed also that the *we* group had no fear of any proselytizing from the *they* groups. A custom might be imported, bought, obtained by killing the owner, or taken as part of a marriage payment. A custom might be exported for a price or a consideration. But the emphasis lay upon the desire of the importing group to obtain the new skill or song and upon the desire of the exporting group for profit in material terms by the transaction. The idea of conversion, or purposely attempting to alter the ideas and attitudes of other persons, did not occur. One might try to persuade one's brother-in-law to abandon his own group and come and hunt permanently with the tribe into which his sister had married; physical proselytizing there was, just as there was actual import and export of items of culture. But, once the brother-in-law had been persuaded to join a different cultural group, it was his job to learn how to live there; and you might, if you were still afraid he would go back or if you wanted his cooperation in working a two-man fish net, take considerable pains to teach him this or that skill as a bribe. But to bribe another by teaching him one's own skill is a long way from any practice of conversion, although it may be made subsidiary to it.

We have no way of knowing how often in the course of human history the idea of Truth, as a revelation to or possession of some one group (which thereby gained the right to consider itself superior to all those who lacked this revelation), may have appeared. But certain it is that, wherever this notion of hierarchical arrangements of cultural views of experience appears, it has profound effects upon education; and it has enormously influenced our own attitudes toward education. As soon as there is any attitude that one set of cultural beliefs is definitely superior to another, the framework is present for active proselytizing, unless the idea of cultural superiority is joined with some idea of hereditary membership,

as it is among the Hindus. (It would indeed be interesting to investigate whether any group which considered itself in possession of the most superior brand of religious or economic truth, and which did not regard its possession as limited by heredity, could preserve the belief in that superiority without proselytizing. It might be found that active proselytizing was the necessary condition for the preservation of the essential belief in one's own revelation.) Thus, with the appearance of religions which held this belief in their own infallible superiority, education becomes a concern of those who teach rather than of those who learn. Attention is directed toward finding neophytes rather than toward finding masters, and adults and children become bracketed together as recipients of conscious missionary effort. This bracketing-together is of great importance; it increases the self-consciousness of the whole educational procedure, and it is quite possible that the whole question of methods and techniques of education is brought most sharply to the fore when it is a completely socialized adult who must be influenced instead of a plastic and receptive child.

With social stratification the possibility of using education as a way of changing status is introduced, and another new component of the educational idea develops. Here the emphasis is still upon the need to learn—on the one hand, in order to alter status and, on the other, to prevent the loss of status by failure to learn. But wherever this possibility enters in there is also a possibility of a new concept of education developing from the relationship between fixed caste and class lines and education. In a static society members of different caste or class groups may have been teaching their children different standards of behavior for many generations without any essential difference between their attitudes toward education and those of less complex societies. To effect a change it is necessary to focus the attention of the members of the society upon the problem, as conditions of cultural contact do focus it. Thus, in present-day Bali, the high castes are sending their daughters to the

Dutch schools to be trained as schoolteachers because it is pre-eminently important that learning should be kept in the hands of the high castes and profoundly inappropriate that low-caste teachers should teach high-caste children. They feel this strongly enough to overcome their prejudices against the extent to which such a course takes high-caste women out into the market place.

As soon as the possibility of shift of class position by virtue of a different educational experience becomes articulately recognized, so that individuals seek not only to better their children or to guard them against educational defect but also to see the extension of restriction of educational opportunity as relevant to the whole class structure, another element enters in—the relationship of education to social change. Education becomes a mechanism of change. Public attention, once focused upon this possibility, is easily turned to the converse position of emphasizing education as a means toward preserving the status quo. I argue here for no historical priority in the two positions. But I am inclined to believe that we do not have catechumens taught to say "to do my duty in that state of life into which it has pleased God to call me" until we have the beginning of movements of individuals away from their birth positions in society. In fact, the whole use of education to defend vested interests and intrenched privilege goes with the recognition that education can be a way of encroaching upon them. Just as the presence of proselytizing religions focuses attention upon means of spreading the truth, upon pedagogy, so the educational implications of social stratification focus attention upon the content of education and lay the groundwork for an articulate interest in the curriculum.

Movements of peoples, colonization, and trade also bring education into a different focus. In New Guinea it is not uncommon to "hear" (i.e., understand without speaking) several languages besides one's own, and many people not only "hear" but also speak neighboring languages. A head-hunting people like the Mundugumor, who had

the custom of giving child hostages to temporary allies among neighboring peoples, articulately recognized that it was an advantage to have members of the group be well acquainted with the roads, the customs, and the language of their neighbors, who would assuredly at some time in any given generation be enemies and objects of attack. Those who took the hostages regarded this increased facility of the Mundugumor as a disadvantage which had to be put up with. But the emphasis remained with the desirability of learning. Today, with the growth of pidgin English as a lingua franca, bush natives and young boys are most anxious to learn pidgin. Their neighbors, with whom they could trade and communicate more readily if they knew pidgin, are not interested in teaching them. But the European colonist is interested. He sees his position as an expanding, initiating, changing one; he wants to trade with the natives, to recruit and indenture them to work on plantations. He needs to have them speak a language that he can understand. Accordingly, we have the shift from the native who needs to learn another language in order to understand to the colonist who needs someone else to learn a language so that he, the colonist, may be understood. In the course of teaching natives to speak some lingua franca, to handle money, to work copra, etc., the whole focus is on teaching; not, however, on techniques of teaching, in the sense of pedagogy, but upon sanctions for making the native learn. Such usages develop rapidly into compulsory schooling in the language of the colonist or the conqueror, and they result in the school's being seen as an adjunct of the group in power rather than as a privilege for those who learn.

Just as conquest or colonization of already inhabited countries brings up the problems of assimilation, so also mass migrations may accentuate the same problem. This has been true particularly in the United States, where education has been enormously influenced by the articulate need to assimilate the masses of European immigrants, with the resulting phrasing of the public schools as a means for educating other peoples' children. The school ceased to be chiefly a device by which children were taught accumulated knowledge or skills and became a political device for arousing and maintaining national loyalty through inculcating a language and a system of ideas which the pupils did not share with their parents.

It is noteworthy that, in the whole series of educational emphases which I have discussed here as significant components of our present-day concept of "education," one common element which differentiates the ideas of conversion, assimilation, successful colonization, and the relationship between class-caste lines and education from the attitudes found in primitive homogeneous societies is the acceptance of discontinuity between parents and children. Primitive education was a process by which continuity was maintained between parents and children, even if the actual teacher was not a parent but a maternal uncle or a shaman. Modern education includes a heavy emphasis upon the function of education to create discontinuities—to turn the child of the peasant into a clerk, of the farmer into a lawyer, of the Italian immigrant into an American, of the illiterate into the literate. And parallel to this emphasis goes the attempt to use education as an extra, special prop for tottering continuities. Parents who are separated from their children by all the gaps in understanding which are a function of our rapidly changing world cling to the expedient of sending their children to the same schools and colleges they attended, counting upon the heavy traditionalism of slow-moving institutions to stem the tide of change. (Thus, while the father builds himself a new house and the mother furnishes it with modern furniture, they both rejoice that back at school, through the happy accident that the school is not well enough endowed, son will sit at the same desk at which his father sat.) The same attitude is reflected by the stock figure of the member of a rural school board who says, "What was good enough for me in school is good enough

for my children. The three *R*'s, that's enough."

Another common factor in these modern trends of education is the increasing emphasis upon change rather than upon growth, upon what is done to people rather than upon what people do. This emphasis comes, I believe, from the inclusion of adults as objects of the educational effort—whether the effort comes from missionaries, colonizers, conquerors, Old Americans, or employers of labor. When a child is learning to talk, the miracle of learning is so pressing and conspicuous that the achievement of the teachers is put in the shade. But the displacement, in an adult's speech habits, of his native tongue by the phonetics of some language which he is being bullied or cajoled into learning is often more a matter of triumph for the teacher than of pride for the learner. Changing people's habits, people's ideas, people's language, people's beliefs, people's emotional allegiances, involves a sort of deliberate violence to other people's developed personalities—a violence not to be found in the whole teacher-child relationship, which finds its prototype in the cherishing parent helping the young child to learn those things which are essential to his humanity.

We have been shocked in recent years by the outspoken brutality of the totalitarian states, which set out to inculcate into children's minds a series of new ideas which it was considered politically useful for them to learn. Under the conflicting currents of modern ideologies the idea of *indoctrination* has developed as a way of characterizing the conscious educational aims of any group with whom the speaker is out of sympathy. Attempts to teach children any set of ideas in which one believes have become tainted with suspicion of power and self-interest, until almost all education can be branded and dismissed as one sort of indoctrination or another. The attempt to assimilate, convert, or keep in their places other human beings conceived of as inferior to those who are making the plans has been a boomerang which has distorted our whole educational philosophy; it has shifted the emphasis from one of growth and seeking for knowledge to one of dictation and forced acceptance of clichés and points of view. Thus we see that the presence of one element within our culture—a spurious sense of superiority of one group of human beings over another, which gave the group in power the impetus to force their language, their beliefs, and their culture down the throats of the group which was numerically, or economically, or geographically handicapped—has corrupted and distorted the emphases of our free schools.

But there has been another emphasis developing side by side with those which I have been discussing, and that is a belief in the power of education to work miracles—a belief which springs from looking at the other side of the shield. As long as the transmission of culture is an orderly and continuous process, in a slowly changing society, the child speaks the language of his parents; and, although one may marvel that this small human being learns at all, one does not marvel that he learns French or English or Samoan, provided that this be the language of the parents. It took the discontinuity of educational systems, purposive shifts of language and beliefs between parents and children, to catch our imagination and to fashion the great American faith in education as creation rather than transmission, conversion, suppression, assimilation, or indoctrination. Perhaps one of the most basic human ways of saying "new" is "something that my parents have never experienced" or, when we speak of our children, "something I have never experienced." The drama of discontinuity which has been such a startling feature of modern life, and for which formal education has been regarded in great measure as responsible, suggested to men that perhaps education might be a device for creating a new kind of world by developing a new kind of human being.

Here it is necessary to distinguish sharply between the sort of idea which George Counts expressed in his speech, "Dare the Schools Build a New Social Order?" and the idea of education as creation of something new. Dr. Counts did not mean a new social

order in the sense of an order that no man had dreamed of, so much as he meant a very concrete and definite type of society for which he and many others believed they had a blueprint. He was asking whether the teachers would use the schools to produce a different type of socioeconomic system. His question was still a power question and partook of all the power ideas which have developed in the long period during which men in power, men with dominating ideas, men with missions, have sought to put their ideas over upon other men. His question would have been phrased more accurately as "Dare the schools build a different social order?" The schools of America have these hundred years been training children to give allegiance to a way of life that was new to them, not because they were children to whom all ways were new, not because the way of life was itself one that no man had yet dreamed of, but because they were the children of their parents. Whenever one group succeeds in getting power over the schools and teaches within those schools a doctrine foreign to many of those who enter those doors, they are building up, from the standpoint of those students, a different social order. From the standpoint of those in power, they are defending or extending the old; and, from the moment that the teachers had seriously started to put Dr. Counts's suggestion into practice, they would have been attempting by every method available to them to extend, in the minds of other people's children, their own picture, already an "old" idea, of the sort of world they wanted to live in.

It is not this sort of newness of which I speak. But from those who watched learning, those who humbly observed miracles instead of claiming them as the fruits of their strategy or of their superior teaching (propaganda) techniques, there grew up in America a touching belief that it was possible by education to build a new world—a world that no man had yet dreamed and that no man, bred as we had been bred, could dream. They argued that if we can bring up our children to be freer than we have been—freer from anxiety, freer from guilt and fear, freer from economic constraint and the dictates of expediency—to be equipped as we never were equipped, trained to think and enjoy thinking, trained to feel and enjoy feeling, then we shall produce a new kind of human being, one not known upon the earth before. Instead of the single visionary, the depth of whose vision has kept men's souls alive for centuries, we shall develop a whole people bred to the task of seeing with clear imaginative eyes into a future which is hidden from us behind the smoke screen of our defective and irremediable educational handicaps. This belief has often been branded as naïve and simple-minded. The American faith in education, which Clark Wissler lists as one of the dominant American culture traits, has been held up to ridicule many times. In many of its forms it is not only unjustified optimism but arrant nonsense. When small children are sent out by overzealous schoolteachers to engage in active social reforms—believed necessary by their teachers—the whole point of view becomes not only ridiculous but dangerous to the children themselves.

Phrased, however, without any of our blueprints, with an insistence that it is the children themselves who will some day, when they are grown, make blueprints on the basis of their better upbringing, the idea is a bold and beautiful one, an essentially democratic and American idea. Instead of attempting to bind and limit the future and to compromise the inhabitants of the next century by a long process of indoctrination which will make them unable to follow any path but that which we have laid down, it suggests that we devise and practice a system of education which sets the future free. We must concentrate upon teaching our children to walk so steadily that we need not hew too straight and narrow paths for them but can trust them to make new paths

through difficulties we never encountered to a future of which we have no inkling today.

When we look for the contributions which contacts of peoples, of peoples of different races and different religions, different levels of culture and different degrees of technological development, have made to education, we find two. On the one hand, the emphasis has shifted from learning to teaching, from the doing to the one who causes it to be done, from spontaneity to coercion, from freedom to power. With this shift has come the development of techniques of power, dry pedagogy, regimentation, indoctrination, manipulation, and propaganda. These are but sorry additions to man's armory, and they come from the insult to human life which is perpetuated whenever one human being is regarded as differentially less or more human than another. But, on the other hand, out of the discontinuities and rapid changes which have accompanied these minglings of people has come another invention, one which perhaps would not have been born in any other setting than this one—the belief in education as an instrument for the creation of new human values.

We stand today in a crowded place, where millions of men mill about seeking to go in different directions. It is most uncertain whether the educational invention made by those who emphasized teaching or the educational invention made by those who emphasized learning will survive. But the more rapidly we can erase from our society those discrepancies in position and privilege which tend to perpetuate and strengthen the power and manipulative aspects of education, the more hope we may have that that other invention—the use of education for unknown ends which shall exalt man above his present stature—may survive.

AMERICAN MUSEUM OF
NATURAL HISTORY

CULTURE AND EDUCATION IN THE MIDWESTERN HIGHLANDS OF GUATEMALA

ROBERT REDFIELD

ABSTRACT

Education is here identified with "the process of cultural transmission and renewal." Rural Ladinos of midwestern Guatemala are, with respect to education, intermediate between tribal and urban society. Schools exist, but they have little importance. On the other hand, ceremony and myth do not play a large part in the transfer of tradition. The attention of the investigator is therefore drawn to the more elementary and universal aspects of education: the informal day-to-day situations in which tradition is communicated or modified. Such a situation is analyzed, and the educational importance of these occurrences remarked, in this Guatemalan society where schools represent regulation largely external to the culture and where important traditional ceremonials are lacking.

When education is considered as it occurs in a modern society, we think first of the school. In a primitive society there are neither schools nor pedagogues; yet we speak of the "education" of the primitive child. In so doing we are, of course, recognizing a conception of education much wider than the domain of the school; we are thinking of it as "the process of cultural transmission and renewal"—a process present in all societies and, indeed, indistinguishable from that process by which societies persist and change.

When we describe education in such school-less and bookless societies, we are likely to fix attention upon other institutions which obviously and formally express and communicate the local tradition. Such are ceremony, myth, tribal and familial symbols and stories, initiation ceremonies, and men's houses. In these we recognize a certain fixity and emphasis of major elements of culture, and we see that in their perpetuation and repetition these elements receive restatement and are communicated to the young. Indeed, we have come to think of primitive societies as providing a well-organized and self-consistent system of institutions by which children are brought up to think and act as did their fathers. In such societies we connect education with traditional forms expressive of a rich content. In comparison with the educational effect of a katchina dance upon a Hopi child, a chapter in a civics textbook seems pretty thin, educationally speaking.

To the invitation to give an account of the educational process, I respond from a point of view of certain rural communities in the midwestern highlands of Guatemala which are neither modern nor primitive but in many respects intermediate between a simple tribe and a modern city. Educational institutions among these rural mountain-dwellers do not quite conform to either the primitive or civilized type. These people have schools, but the schools are of small importance. They have ceremonies and legends, but these forms do not have so much content as one might suppose. In these Guatemalan societies schooling is far from accomplishing what our educational experts claim generally for schools. On the other hand, ceremony and myth do not come up to the standard set by many primitive societies. In this part of the world there are no central and powerful educational institutions around which an essay can conveniently be written.

The situation is not without value, however, for students of the cultural process. In recognizing in this part of Guatemala the limited educational influence of schools, on the one hand, and of traditional forms, on the other, one is brought to see aspects of education which underlie all formal institutions. People in Guatemala do get educated (in the sense that the heritage is transmitted) with adjustments to meet changing circumstances, even though many of them never go to school and even though there are no great puberty ceremonies, with revelations of the sacred *alcheringa* and narrations of totemic myths, such as occur among Australian aborigines. In this paper I shall make some observations on certain features of these highlands societies in so far as the educational process is concerned; and I shall, in particular, call attention to aspects of that process which are probably to be encountered in every society. I call attention to them because education is ordinarily studied without much reference to them.

As I look at the school in the little village where I once was resident, it appears to me to play a greater part in changing the culture of the people than in handing it on from one generation to the next, although its influence in the direction of change is indirect. Nearly all the time in the school is given to learning to read and to write and to calculate. Some children acquire a fair command of these arts; others do not. The arts of literacy have many practical uses, and their possession carries some prestige. They improve the opportunities for gainful employment, and their possession disposes the individual to seek his fortune in the town or in the city. In some cases success in school leads to higher education in the city and so to participation in urban civilization.

The majority of people of this community are Indians; a minority are a Spanish-speaking people of mixed ancestry known as Ladinos. The cultures of the two groups are identical in many areas of experience; in others they are still notably different. Where both kinds of people live in the same settlement, both attend the same school. The school makes more change for the Indian than for the Ladino, because through association with the Ladinos in the school he learns Spanish and in not a few cases is disposed to put off Indian dress, to live in the manner of the Ladinos, and so to become a Ladino. There is here no obstacle of prejudice or law to prevent this not infrequent occurrence. The school is one important institution, therefore, through which the Indian societies tend to lose members to the Ladino society and so ultimately to disappear.

As such an instrument of acculturation and culture change, the school is only one among a number of effective institutions. The penitentiary deserves mention, for, although its liberalizing influence is less widely distributed than in the case of the school, not a few individuals profit by this form of widened experience and return to the village with a new song, a new trade, and a less parochial view of life. The common custom of bringing up other people's children is also effective, as when the child is an Indian brought up in a Ladino household. Of such individuals it may later be said that "that Ladino is really an Indian," but the ethnic origin of the individual carries little or no social disadvantage and is quickly forgotten.

Considered as an institution helping to preserve the local culture, the role of the school is small. I venture the assertion that the abolition of schools in these highlands would leave the culture much as it is. Except for the texts of prayers recited on many occasions, little of the rural Ladino heritage depends on literacy. And, furthermore, it is only necessary that a few individuals in each society be literate so as to preserve access to written or printed sources. Indeed, for generations the Indian cultures in the more isolated societies have got along with a semi-professionalization of literacy. A few individuals in each village or group of villages were trained to read the Mass; the central government sent from the city a literate person to deal with the written communications of formal government. The more pagan religious ritual was, and still is, stored, unwritten, in the memories of a small number of professionals. Their knowledge is highly specialized and is little understood by the layman.

The village school in this area devotes little time to instruction other than the purely technical; and the little "cultural" instruction which it gives has small support in other branches of the village life. Some instruction is given in Guatemalan history and geography. What is taught is not reinforced by books in the homes, because there are almost no books in the homes. Nor is the instruction closely related to the content of oral tradition. The knowledge that Columbus discovered America is perpetuated in the school and is possessed by most Ladinos as an item of information, but few people whom I interrogated were able to tell me that that discovery was the event commemorated by the little celebration which the government orders to occur each year in the village municipal building on October 12. (Of course the more sophisticated townsman understands the meaning of the occasion.) At any rate, Columbus is no tribal or village legendary hero.

As not a great deal is accomplished by formal instruction in the school, one might suppose the lack to be made up by a great deal of deliberate inculcation and discipline in the home. At least with regard to the rural Ladino society, I am sure that this is not the case. Children are taught to do what they are expected to do chiefly as an aspect of coming to perform the tasks of adults. Moments of instruction are not segregated from moments of action. Boys are taught to farm and girls to cook as they help their elders do these things. Along with instruction in the practical arts, parents comment on conduct, saying what is "good" and what is "bad." The word *pecado* is applied to innumerable interdicted acts, from those which are regarded as mildly unlucky to those to which some real moral opprobrium attaches. Some parents will select a serious and special moment in which to convey sex instruction, and sometimes other subjects will be somewhat formally inculcated; but on the whole I should say that instruction in the home is casual and unsystematized.

Certainly it is not characteristic of this Ladino culture that the young gather around the knees of the old to listen reverently to a solemn exposition of the holy traditions and sacred memories of the people. Indeed, in this society, as in our own, it is hard to find the holy traditions, let alone to get anyone

to listen while they are expounded. Most instruction that occurs in the home or outside it is connected with the practical arts of life.

It seems to me interesting that, while few of these Ladinos are today teaching their children the prayers of their Catholic tradition, they do take pains to teach them the traditional forms of address and salutation, which in these cultures are complicated and elaborate. It is characteristic of this people that requests and other communications are not abruptly and directly presented but are wrapped in highly conventional preliminary and terminal utterances; also, in general, among them polite language is regarded as seemly conduct.

It also seems to me that this formal language is a way in which people preserve their personal lives from too easy invasion and that it is therefore a useful art. It is, moreover, one which every man must practice for himself. The case is different with the prayers. Apparently it is not thought sufficiently important that every child have formal language in which to talk with God. It is, however, thought important that the prayers be recited by someone on the occasions of novenas for the saints and following a death. But all that is necessary is that one or a few persons be available to recite the prayers. It would not greatly surprise me if in these villages the reciting of Catholic prayers became a paid profession, as are now the reciting of a Mass by priest or layman, the teaching of the spoken text of a dance-drama, or the playing of the little flageolet which accompanies processions bearing images of the saints.

This observation about the teaching of prayers and of mannerly speech may be generalized into two wider characterizations of these Guatemalan cultures. The point of view on life is practical and secular rather than religious or mystical; and formal activity is more than usually large, it seems to me, in proportion to the content of symbolic meaning which underlies it. This statement I am disposed to make about both the Indian and the Ladino cultures, although there are differences of degree or kind in these respects between the two.

For the rural Ladinos it may be safely asserted that religious pageantry and mythology do not play a large part in the education of the individual. The Christian epic is known very incompletely; it exists in the form of many unco-ordinated fragments of lore, and it is not vividly presented in any coherent or impressive way. These country people read very little sacred literature; they very rarely hear sermons; and there is no important traditional ceremony or drama in which it might be expressed. An exception in part must be made for the ninefold repetition at Christmas time of the journey of Mary and Joseph and for the little enactment of the birth of the child. The effigies of and stories about Christ, and in less degree and importance of and about the saints, do constitute a body of lore in which significant traditional conceptions are perpetuated. But these ceremonials occupy a very small part of the time and interests of the Ladinos, and the element of mere entertainment in them is very large.

For the Indian, more is to be said as to the contribution of ceremony and myth to the educational and cultural process. The cult of the saints is more elaborate, and ritual observances are more extensive. Justification for the statement that the culture of the Ladinos is more shallow or less integrated than that of the Indians is in part to be found, it seems to me, in the fact that most stories told among Ladinos—and they like to tell and to hear stories—deal chiefly with fairies, witches, talking animals, and the adventures of picaresque personages, and that these stories are not regarded as true and are not thought of as describing the world in which the individual lives. They are recognized as fanciful creations that serve to entertain. The Indian, on the other hand, is disposed to regard the stories which he tells as true. Taken as a whole, the Indian's stories deal with men and animals and supernatural beings that he believes to exist

about him, and their telling helps to define and redefine the conventional world in which the Indian lives.

A story well known in the Indian village of San Antonio tells how St. Anthony was once a man who dwelt in that village as other men, and how, counseled by his friend, Christ, whom he sought to rescue when our Lord's enemies were after him, he took the form of a saint so as to help the village where he lived and worked. The story offers an explanation for the origin of every significant element of costume and accouterment in the effigy of St. Anthony as customarily fashioned and as it exists in the village church; and it explains and justifies by reference to the saint's divine will many of the elements in the cult now customary: the marimba, the masked dancers, the fireworks, incense, and candles. Indeed, except that the content of the story is of Old World origin, the story in feeling and form is quite like many origin or hero myths that are told among non-Europeanized Indians.

A study of the educational process among these Indians would certainly have to take into account the existence of these stories and the circumstances under which they are told. It is plain that their telling helps to communicate and perpetuate the tradition of the group. It is significant that in the Indian villages every man passes through a series of public services; that in the course of many of these employments he spends long hours sitting in company with his age-mates and his elders, and that the elders at such times tell stories and relate episodes. The Ladino society is almost entirely without such an institution.

The existence of such a story as the one about St. Anthony is another evidence of the power within a culture to make itself, if such an expression may be employed. We may be sure that no priest set out to teach just this story to the Indians of the village. The story has grown in the course of generations of speculation upon an effigy and a ritual already sanctified and mysterious. Indeed, we catch glimpses of this process today when we hear of Indians who have found new explanations for some element of decorative design in church, or when an ethnologist's informant begins to offer speculations of his own.

Yet I am struck with the fact that even in the case of the Indian cultures there is more form than content in their collective life. In this same village of San Antonio there is performed every year in Holy Week a series of ceremonies occupying several days. It is generally understood that these ceremonies are a representation of the Passion of our Lord, and a general air of gravity attends them. But in my notes is a list of elements of the ritual for which none of my informants has been able to offer any explanation at all. Structures are erected and taken down, and effigies are used to which no meaning is assigned other than mere custom. One could fill many hundreds of pages with a detailed account of the goings and comings, the processions, the handing-over of effigies, the ritual drinking and bowing and the like, which custom provides must be carried on each year in one of these Indian villages among the groups of men in whose custody rest the images of the saints. On the other hand, even making liberal allowance for the relative difficulty of getting trustworthy information on the meanings of these acts, I feel sure that little could be said about the symbolic connections these acts have with the content of tradition. Yet, even in so far as these rituals have no symbolic meaning, they do maintain traditional ways within which behavior is regulated, and, therefore, they have their place in a broad investigation of the educational process in these communities.

The relatively formal or external aspect of much of the Guatemalan cultures is conspicuously illustrated in the dance-dramas. These are performed by Indians at most Indian festivals and very infrequently are performed by Ladinos at Ladino festivals. The observer sees a score of men dressed in brilliant and fantastic costumes, carrying highly specialized objects in their hands, and dancing, gesturing, and reciting long lines of

set speech. The performance might be an enactment of some centrally important holy myth. It is, as a matter of fact, nothing of the sort. There are about a dozen dance-dramas known in Guatemala. Most of these have spoken text. Specialists possess these texts and at festival time are hired to teach groups of Indians to speak them and to perform the accompanying dances. The texts are in oratorical Spanish, and it is rare that an Indian understands well what he is saying. The general theme of the drama is known: if the dance called "The Conquest" is danced, the combat between Alvarado, the Spanish invader, and the pagan Indians is understood. But the tradition means little to the dancers; they will just as well enact Cortes' triumph over Montezuma, if that dance is cheaper to put on or provides a better show. The dance is performed, indeed, because a group of men is willing to put money and time into doing something lively for the festival. It may be compared to putting on a minstrel show in another culture, or hiring a merry-go-round. The comparison is not quite fair, but it suggests the truth.

In these societies of which I write, then, the educational process is not greatly dependent upon institutions organized for pedagogical purposes or upon organized and deliberate instruction within the family or other primary group. The ceremonial and other expressive customs which we find in every society are significant educationally here in Guatemala, too; but at least this one observer finds that, compared with some other societies, there is a great amount of formal machinery for the regulation of activities without corresponding symbolic content. To a marked extent the transmission of culture takes place within a complex of regulations: the traditional machinery of government and of ritual observances, the superimposed police control of the Guatemalan national government, the general traditional emphasis upon forms of utterance and conduct.

Nevertheless, an investigation of the educational process in these communities would be far from complete if it were to consider only institutions, pedagogic or ceremonial, as elements in that process. Here, as elsewhere, the heritage of the group is communicated and modified in situations much less clearly defined than any of which mention has so far been made in this paper. I refer to that multitude of daily situations in which, by word and gesture, some part of the tradition is communicated from one individual to another without the presence of any formal institution and without any deliberate inculcation. This class of situations corresponds in a general way with what Spencer called the "primary forms of social control."

Let us imagine that we are standing unseen outside a house in the village where I am living. Within the house some Ladino women are praying a novena, and outside it six men and two boys stand around a little fire and talk. Someone compares the heaping-up of pine cones made ready for this fire to the heaping-up of twigs by Indians at certain places on hilltops where, by Indian custom, the traveler strokes away the fatigue from his legs with a twig and then adds the twig to a growing pile. As soon as the comparison has been made, one man of those beside the fire expresses derision at this Indian belief, which is well known to all present. Others briefly indicate similar disbelief in the custom. Another man then makes a remark to the effect that what does in fact serve to relieve tired legs is to rub rum on the ankle-bones. A younger man—apparently unfamiliar with this remedy—asks how this can be effective, and the older man explains that the rum heats the nerves that run near the ankle-bone and that the heat passes up the body along the nerves and so restores strength. The explanation is accepted; the apparent physiological mechanism provides a warrant for accepting the worth of rum as a remedy.

After a short period of silence, conversation begins about snakes, one man having recently killed a large snake. A young boy, apparently wishing to make an effective contribution to a conversation in which he has

as yet played no part, remarks that the coral snake joins itself together when cut apart. The man who laughed at the Indian belief about tired legs scornfully denies the truth of the statement about coral snakes. Another older man in the group comes to the support of the boy and in a tentative way supports the truth of the belief as to coral snakes. A younger man says that it is not true, because he cut apart such a snake without unusual result. The skeptical man appeals to the company; another witness offers testimony unfavorable to the belief. The boy has not spoken again; the other man who ventured to support him withdraws from the argument. But this man wishes, it seems, to restore his damaged prestige. With more confidence he offers the statement that some animals *can* do unusual things: the monkey, when shot by a gun, takes a leaf from the tree in which he is sitting and with it plugs the wound. The smaller of the two boys, who has not yet spoken, adds that the jaguar can do this also. Discussion breaks out, several persons speaking at once; the trend of the remarks is to the effect that, although undoubtedly the monkey can do as described, the jaguar is unable to do so. The quick statements of opinion break out almost simultaneously, and very quickly thereafter the matter is dropped. The bystander recognizes that there is substantial consensus on the points raised; the boy is apparently convinced.

We may safely assume that in such a situation as this the states of mind of the participants in the conversation with reference to the points at issue differ from one another less at the conclusion of the conversation than they did at the beginning. The matter is not ended for any one of them, of course; subsequent experiences and conversations about fatigue, snakes, and monkeys will again modify their conceptions, or at least redeclare them. We may suppose also that the outcome of this particular conversation —an apparent consensus in favor of rum and against twigs, supporting the belief about monkeys and unfavorable to the beliefs about coral snakes and jaguars—will not be duplicated exactly in the next conversation that occurs among similar men on these subjects. We are not so simple as to suppose that by attending to this little talk we have discovered "the belief" of the Ladinos on these points. The personalities of the influential men, the accidents of recent experiences had with monkeys or snakes, and, indeed, probably also the general tone of the moment, which may or may not have been favorable to the serious reception of a marvelous story, are among the factors that have entered into the situation. They have brought about, not a conclusive conviction, but a sort of temporary resting-place of more or less common understanding. We may think of the outcome of such little exchanges of viewpoint as the component of many forces. Because each man's state of mind at the time of the conversation is itself the component of many such forces, most of which have been exerted within the same community of long-intercommunicating men and women, it is likely to be not greatly different from that of his neighbors. Still, there are always individual differences; and it is largely in such little happenings as that which took place around the pine-cone fire that these differences are made influential and that they come to be adjusted one to another.

The episode may be recognized as one of that multitude by which the heritage is transmitted. It was a tiny event in the education of the people. Some part of the heritage with reference to the treatment of fatigue and with reference to the behavior of certain animals passed from older people to younger people—and, indeed, it passed also from younger people to older people, for oral education is a stream that flows through all contemporaries, whatever their ages.

At the same time it was a small event in which the culture of the group underwent a change. Some old people in the community tell me that when they were young they heard about the ability of the coral snake to join itself together and did not doubt its truth.

Perhaps the boy who advanced the belief received his first knowledge of it from such a grandfather. After this evening around the pine-cone fire he will treat grandfather's remarks with a new grain of skepticism. Some of the men who took part in this conversation have traveled and have lived in the city among men whose tradition disposed them more readily to laugh at the story of the coral snake, and the effects of such experiences were also registered in the outcome of the evening's conversation. The result of these various influences was to shift, though ever so slightly, the center of gravity of the community beliefs on these points.

Furthermore, the trifling occurrence was also an event in the transmission of tradition from one group to another. No Indian took part in the conversation, but one man, who was born an Indian but had lived long among Ladinos, stood silent in the dark edges of the group. As an ethnologist who has talked with Indians, I know that the belief about getting rid of fatigue by brushing the legs with twigs is by them generally accepted, and great credence is given to beliefs as to the ability of injured animals to treat themselves. Now there has impinged upon that silent Indian a set of forces tending to shift the center of his belief; and now, when he takes part in a similar discussion among Indians, he is more likely to be on the skeptical side of the center of consensus than if he had not been here this evening. It is largely by the accumulating effect of innumerable such occurrences that the culture of the Indians and that of the Ladinos are becoming more and more alike.

We are not to suppose that it is always the Indian who is disposed to change his mind so that it becomes more like that of the Ladino. For certain reasons the predominating trend tends to substitute Ladino tradition for that of the Indians. But the Ladino has in four hundred years taken on a great deal from the Indians—the techniques of maize-farming and the use of the sweat bath, to mention just two elements—and he still learns from the Indian. The episode around the pine-cone fire could be matched by an episode in which Indians, showing Ladinos the nicked ears of wild animals, by this evidence tended to persuade the Ladinos that these animals were indeed under the domestication of a supernatural protector inhabiting the woods.

It is a fair guess that in any society the process of education depends more on such events as represented in the conversation I have reported than it does upon all the formal pedagogical devices which exist in the society. In the speech and gestures which take place in the home, in the play and work groups, and wherever people talk naturally about matters that are interesting to them, the tradition is reasserted and redefined. In these situations the culture is not merely spoken about; it is acted out; it happens before the eyes and even through the persons of children, who by this means, in large degree, are educated. This basic part of the educational process takes place in every society and probably to such an extent that societies are greatly alike in this respect. Upon the flow of such experience are erected those more clearly defined institutions of the folk traditions, as well as the deliberate enterprises of pedagogy and propaganda. As to these, societies will be found greatly to differ.

Comparing these particular Guatemalan societies with—let us say, that of the French-Canadian villages—I should say that here education is more secular and more casual. These Guatemalan societies seem to me relatively meager with respect to organized moral convictions and sacred traditions. What the Indians tell me about the times of their grandfathers suggests strongly that the Indian societies have lost in ceremonial richness, as I suspect they have lost in the moral value and the integration of their local traditions. Because I have observed the influence of priests in other communities in maintaining a sacred tradition and in explaining symbolic significance of traditional rituals, I think it likely that, if, indeed, these societies

have been becoming more casual and more secular, the lessened influence of the Catholic priests has been one factor in this change. The Guatemala of today is well regulated by secular government in the interests of public order and hygiene. My guess—which is to be tested by historical investigation—is that secular external regulation (important probably even in pre-Columbian times) has grown in later years, while that control dependent upon moral conviction and instruction and upon local tradition has declined. The school, for these rural people, is another form of external regulation rather than an expression of local tradition.

Whatever study of the history of this part of rural Guatemala may in fact show, the present situation in these societies suggests the question of whether a rich culture is compatible with a society in which the mechanisms for education consist chiefly of formal regulations and of casual conversation. The comparison between Indian and Ladino societies—alike though they are in their generally secular character—indicates a correspondence between certain characteristics of culture and certain characteristics of education. The Indian beliefs and tales have relation to current life, and more of them have moral content or depth than is the case with Ladino beliefs and tales. And, second, in the Indian societies there is a social-political-religious organization—a system of progressive public services through which all males pass—that is largely native to the community, that is a force in social control, and that involves relatively sacred things. This organization is largely lacking in the Ladino societies. These differences may be stated in terms of differences in the educational institutions of the two peoples: To a greater degree than is the case with the Ladinos, the Indians hear and tell stories that express and justify traditional beliefs; and by passing through the hierarchy of services the individual learns the ritual that is the inner and relatively sacred side of the formal civic organization. Emphasizing characteristics of those Guatemalan societies which are more evident in the case of the Ladinos than of the Indians, this paper concludes, then, with the suggestion that an education which is made up, on the one side, of practical regulation and instruction without reference to tradition and, on the other, has nothing much more compulsive and expressive in which to exert its influence than the casual contacts of everyday life is not likely to educate with reference to any greatly significant moral values.

University of Chicago

THE PAN-AFRICAN PROBLEM OF CULTURE CONTACT

BRONISLAW MALINOWSKI[1]

ABSTRACT

The young African of today lives in two worlds and belongs fully and completely to neither. European education has alienated him from native traditions and imbued him with the values and expectations of European culture. At the same time European interests exclude him from the white community and deny him the material basis for the style of life he has been taught to aspire to. Education must be transformed to close rather than perpetuate this vicious gap between expectation and reality. African schools should train their pupils for adaptation to the African environment. Respect for native values should be maintained along with the equipment for co-operation with the European community. European wealth should be used to provide the basis for fulfilling the claims and needs which Western education has developed.

THE PROCESSES OF SCHOOLING AND OF CULTURAL TRANSMISSION

I want to start from the axiom that education is something much wider and more comprehensive than schooling. By education I mean the integral process of transmission of culture. Schooling is that somewhat restricted part of it which is professionally given by teacher to pupil, by the professional educator to those who come under his tutelage in an organized institution of learning.

In every society, whether it be simple or complex, the infant is born naked, untutored, endowed only with his innate qualities of mind and body; and even those have still to be gradually developed in the process, not only to acquire the skills and the ideas of his culture, but also to develop those moral values, social attitudes, and beliefs which constitute citizenship and personality in the widest sense of the term. In primitive cultures this integral process of education is carried on by the family, by the play group, through initiation ceremonies, and by apprenticeship given by every professional group into which the individual is adopted.

In communities which boast of a more highly differentiated civilization the child is taken away from home, from playmates and occupations, and has to enter a specialized institution, the school, which concentrates, first, on giving him the elements of general knowledge and skills and then, gradually, on

[1] This was the last article written by Dr. Malinowski before his decease last fall.

developing (in a few cases at least) professional abilities, manual or mental. We know that around us, in all the branches of our hypertrophied Western civilization, there is a rift between school and home, between schematized teaching and the direct influence of life and its unregimented pursuits. This rift has probably assumed pathological forms under the new wave of totalitarian regimes. There the state, controlling school, or juvenile regiment is trying to mold the child into a very specific type of personality —into what, in fact, is nothing more or less than an interchangeable part or cog in a vast human mechanism subjected to the centralized control of the totalitarian party in rule. Even in democratic communities, however, there is a serious problem of harmonizing the influences of school and home, of book learning and the real, effective apprenticeship to life.

All these difficulties and dangers increase immensely when education is given from one culture to another, as is the case at present in Africa. Under such conditions the school is based on systems derived from a highly mechanized, capitalistic, and sophisticated European civilization, while the life of the people still runs largely on the tribal basis.

We must remember that most (practically all) education was started in Africa by the Christian missionaries and that even up to the present it still remains almost exclusively in missionary hands. For this the Africans and their friends and partisans must express a deep debt of gratitude. The fact, however, has some important consequences. The missionary, even more than the professional educator, is endowed with strong faith. He not only believes in the value of education—which would be bad enough—but he also believes in the saving virtue of spiritual uplift. He is deeply convinced that, by implanting the seeds of the right faith in a man's heart, you not only transform him spiritually but also give him most (maybe all) of the privileges of freedom, happiness, and, indeed, of wealth and welfare. Now, however sympathetically we might turn to the point of view of the faithful, enthusiastic, and zealous, the hard facts of human life and human relationships contradict this easy solution of human problems.

The anthropologist has to state, at this point, that human culture is a hard and heavy reality. Man lives in his culture, for his culture, and by his culture. To transform this traditional heritage, to make a branch of humanity jump across centuries of development, is a process in which only a highly skilled and scientifically founded achievement of cultural engineering can reach positive results.

We shall, in a moment, have a closer look at the general principles of this cultural transformation—or transculturation, as we might call it—following the great Cuban scholar, Dr. Fernando Ortiz, whose name may well be mentioned here, for he is one of the most passionate friends of the Africans in the New World and a very effective spokesman of their cultural value and sponsor of their advancement.

Let us see how this process of transculturation was managed at the beginnings of European contact in Africa. The onslaught of white civilization on native cultures was carried out, we may say, by two columns. There was a column of "good will" toward the African, represented by the missionary and the educator and often also by some of the more sympathetic and enlightened administrative officials. There was also the column of "good gain." This was represented by the predatory elements—by the slave raiders in the bad old days when the Dark

Continent was subject to this shameful pursuit, and later on by those who wanted to exploit the native resources of Africa, as well as the native labor, which was indispensable to the exploitation. The column of good will was prepared to give the native unstintingly of our knowledge and our Christianity, of our sport and our predilections for cotton and linen, for soap and water. But the other part of the white community was not prepared to grant any of the privileges and consequences of education or of Christianity, still less any advantages in terms of political power, personal independence, and material gain.

Thus we had, on the one hand, the theory that by exorcisms and exhortations the level of African life could be raised up to that of a European gentleman—that is, an educated Christian. The exorcisms were directed against witchcraft and polygamy, against tribal warfare and cannibalism, against going around naked, and also against such innocent practices as dancing, beer-drinking, or unusual forms of courtship. The African had to be "freed from his fear of sorcery and supernatural terrors." He had to be "clothed in the garb of Christian cleanliness." He was promised "to live in perpetual peace and satisfaction." In this, administrative ruling, evangelization, and schooling went hand in hand. The anthropologist should immediately register here that a great deal of African culture was destroyed or undermined in the process. The exorcisms produced a negative effect.

What was given instead? First and foremost, the principles of Christianity. The native was taught to believe in the Trinity and in the Gospels instead of in his tribal ancestors, his nature divinities, or the beneficent powers of constructive magic and totemism. Christianity, however, means, in its essence, not merely the affirmation that God exists; it implies also the principle that all men are the children of God. And here at once there came the profound clash due to the two-column approach of the Europeans. The African might become a fervent believer in all the dogmas. He might pay all the price to be paid, giving up his wives and concubines, his pleasant customs of courtship, his dances, and his beer drinks. Yet gradually he became aware that he could not worship his White God in the same churches with the pale-skinned children of Christ. He was made aware that, on path or pavement, in public assembly or in private converse, he was not the brother of his white fellow-Christian—not even the younger brother, but rather someone to be shoved aside at the white Christian's fraternal pleasure and convenience.

Thus the process of uplift and education, started with strong hopes and convictions, did not lead to the results desired by missionary and native alike. The African lost a great deal of his cultural heritage, with all the natural privileges which it carried of political independence, of personal freedom, of congenial pursuits in the wide, open spaces of his native land. He lost that partly through the predatory encroachments of white civilizations, but largely through the well-intentioned attempts of his real friends. At the same time he did not gain any foothold in white citizenship in the social and cultural world of European settlers, officials, and even missionaries and educators—a foothold the promise of which was implicit in the very fundamental principles of Christianity and education alike.

In order to understand more fully the reasons for all those thwarted and wrecked attempts at uplift, in order to appreciate the nature of the process and its consequence, let us turn to our little anthropological workshop and consider more fully the nature of human civilization and the place of the educational mechanisms within its context.

EDUCATION AS A CULTURAL PROCESS

We can define culture as the body of material appliances, the types of social organization, customs, beliefs, and moral values which man needs and wields as an instrumentality in the adjustment to his environment and the satisfaction of his needs. Every culture, simple or highly differentiated, must, first and foremost, provide man with his nutritive maintenance, allow him to reproduce, provide him with bodily comforts and with safety against the forces of environment and against animal or human foes. Culture, however, raises man above his mere animal needs.

Culture thus satisfies first the organic standard of living and then adds an increased artificial standard of enjoyment, in which aesthetic pleasures, joys of companionship, and creative achievements can be developed. In all this, culture is an organic unit. The anthropologist recognizes more and more fully how dangerous it is to tamper with any part or aspect of culture, lest unforeseeable consequences occur. To educate one community out of its culture and to make it adopt integrally a much more highly differentiated civilization can be done only in a gradual, well-considered, and extremely well-informed way. Thus, for instance, the change from one type of sexual ethics to another may be desirable from the theological or moralistic point of view. But such a change invariably implies the reorganization not only of courtship and marriage but also of the family and the kinship system.

Again, to abolish the belief in sorcery seems a very simple and invariably desirable achievement. If we remember, however, that the belief in sorcery is not the cause but the consequence of the hard, inescapable facts of human misfortune, disease, and death, matters cease to be so simple. The Africans do not accuse one another of sorcery wantonly, out of malice or superstition. This belief has grown up through ages and in response to conditions in which the knowledge of medicine and pathology is rudimentary and of preventive medicine, nonexistent. Examined carefully, scientifically and sympathetically, the belief in sorcery appears as a very crude but sometimes very effective means of managing misfortune, disease, and the threat of death in terms of human machinations or the influence of manageable spiritual anger rather than in terms of inexorable decrees of destiny.

If you think of African witchcraft, spirit doctrine, or magic as an almost exact parallel to certain modern religious or even scientific forms of treatment, you will see the point more clearly. The Christian Scientist, who affirms and apparently believes that misfortune and illness are effluvia of evil thoughts pouring out from within the soul or from the social environment, handles the threats to human welfare very much as does the African witch doctor. The famous Nancy school of mental therapy, which established both a preventive hygiene and a psychological increase of organic resistance by the simple formula of autosuggestion, proceeds on the same lines as does the Bantu Iñanga, who tells his patient that the evil influences have been removed and the bad substrata of sorcery counteracted.

The real cure for the belief in witchcraft and sorcery must go to the root of the evil and not to its innocuous psychological consequences. Give the Africans better nourishment, better housing, systems of preventive medicine, and adequate medical care, and then, but then only, will they stop bothering about sorcerers, flying witches, or ancestral spirits.

We can already see from these one or two examples that transculturation—the transformation of living conditions, of ideas, beliefs, and social forms—is something very much more comprehensive than the process of education. This, again, should not proceed by destroying first and then wondering what can be put in its place. It ought to be accomplished by the positive building-up, first and foremost, of sound living conditions and then of ideas and principles adequate to this cultural improvement.

We can see now the theoretical scheme which our brief analysis of culture and of education suggests to us. Education, under normal conditions, is the transmission of culture from one generation to another. Under conditions of culture change or transculturation it implies not merely the transmission of one system but the welding-together of two. And here, when in addition to cultural differences there enter two more complicating factors—that of race and of difference in level of development—the situation becomes both complex and fraught with dangerous, (not to say tragic) possibilities.

THE THREE PHASES OF EDUCATION: BIRTHRIGHT, MOLDING, AND CHARTER OF CITIZENSHIP

In order to introduce some clarity into the confusion which interracial education always implies, let us first consider the process as one of supply and demand. In each community, simple or mixed, there is a demand for new members. Education in the form of schooling and apprenticeship to life is the process of supply which ought to meet the demand. When we have two strata or two groups divided by race, cultural level of development, and type of citizenship, the meeting-point between supply and demand becomes complicated. There is the need or the demand for new citizens. Immediately, however, there arises a question: Citizens of what type? Citizens prepared for which tasks? Citizens endowed with what kind of status?

It becomes clear at once that if we introduce a type of schooling which normally is organized and meant to produce European citizens, with a lifework, a status, and a set of privileges adapted to white European conditions, such schools may not meet the specific demand of the mixed community, which obviously is divided by such elements as the Color Bar, race prejudice, and the unwillingness to grant educated Africans the position and status which education implies.

We might formulate our scheme even more in detail. Like all processes of production, education implies the raw materials, the mechanisms of molding or fashioning, and the open market for the finished product. To translate these somewhat metaphorical terms into concrete concepts, we can say that all education, taken in its widest cultural context, presents three definite phases: birthright, molding of personality, and the charter of citizenship. On each of these points we shall have important differences to register when we approach interracial and intercultural education as opposed to the simple transmission of traditional skills, ideas, and values within a homogeneous group.

As regards birthright, a human being is born with a biological endowment and also with his social and cultural destiny largely defined by the fact of his birth. Thus birthright is determined partly by biological heredity, partly by cultural inheritance. In our own civilization we have recognized this fully; and the second phase of education—that of schooling or molding—takes definite cognizance of the health, the I.Q., and also the original social and cultural endowment of the child. The type of schooling and teaching has to be definitely adapted to birthright. The better this adjustment is weighed, planned, and effected, the more certain will be the charter of citizenship received by the human product at the end of his education. Obviously this charter is the demand for a trained individual; for the place which society is ready to grant him in the body politic; for the duties and also the economic rewards and privileges implicit in his cultural performance.

As regards birthright, we obviously are faced in Africa, as elsewhere where two races coexist, with the vexed problem of race. I shall state here only epigrammatically my anthropological conviction that no grading of races into "inferior and superior," into "dominant and subordinate," has any scientific basis whatsoever. To this I should like to add immediately that in my opinion we need not assume a complete identity in all racial characters. It is, indeed, my conviction that certain differential abilities, certain specific contributions of one variety of the human species as against another, ought to be appreciated, developed, and regarded as an essential asset in interracial co-operation.

Pretentious but only pseudoscientific conclusions often have been drawn concerning the character of a race, its abilities, and its cultural possibilities from physical measurements. Even in Africa, and fairly recently, we had attempts made at a depreciation of African intelligence and capacity by reference to a smaller volume of the skull. Since,

however, there is no way whatsoever of inferring from the material substratum of intelligence to its pragmatic value in performance, such attempts are completely worthless.

The application of intelligence tests, especially when these are used with reference to two groups who live under different cultural conditions, seems also inconclusive. A yardstick to measure human intelligence or personal character is not easy to devise. Tests and examinations may be of some use when applied to very specific cultural situations and as a measure of concrete specific processes of learning. To assess the general character of one race as against another, they probably will never serve any useful purpose.

The only means of effective rating of races is the principle that race is as race does. And here I should like once more to quote from a lecture, one which was not delivered before an African audience but was addressed to a white community who have shown the greatest tendency to discriminate against their African fellow-citizens:

The African race . . . . shows signs of developing strongly in the New World, as well as in its own home. The birthright, that is, the innate capacity of the Africans, and the limits of these, have not yet been explored. All evidence points to the conclusions that the African child responds as well to any type of schooling as does the European.[2]

So much for the innate birthright of the Africans. As regards the cultural birthright, the native in Africa has been profoundly affected by the encroachments of European colonists and colonial agencies. Today, in any part of Africa, the child is born no more

[2] I am quoting this from an address given in 1934 before a South African white audience at Johannesburg, with the present prime minister, Jan Smuts, in the chair. At that time, as on many other occasions, I have been able to expatiate upon the incredible strides made by Africans in the New World; to point out the leadership of New World Africans in art, in literature, and in scholarship; indeed, to mention among others, the achievements of this very university at which I have now the privilege of speaking [Fisk University].

to a world of freedom where the integral territory belongs to him and his people; where he can choose among the careers which, though limited, were well adapted to his cultural interests and personal inclinations. The modern African on his continent lives in a world which is politically subject, economically dependent, culturally spoon-fed, and molded by another race and another civilization.

The young African of today has to make a living, and in this he has two worlds, as it were, to depend upon. He belongs to neither of these fully and completely—that is, after he has undergone the process of European training. For he becomes, through this, partly alienated from pure tribal tradition but never completely adopted into the white community. His clear and unquestionable cultural birthright has been taken from him. What does he receive instead?

This brings us to the process of schooling, or molding. Education, in the sense of school training, is a key word used by all those whites who are sincerely in sympathy with the natives, who represent and lead the column of good will. Everywhere we find as the panacea for all the troubles "education and more education, better education and higher education." And as the second theme in this counterpoint of good will, we find the exhortation that the native should give up his tribal system and his superstitions, his heathen ways and his own cultural outlook.

Obviously, no one in his senses would nowadays try to belittle the value of schooling. The point which I am trying to make here is that education in the sense of schooling is but one phase of a process. It is a means to an end. You teach or train a man or a woman to better skills or greater efficiency, to moral or intellectual abilities. The end is to use these abilities and also to gain the advantages in terms of income, influence, and privilege. To put it crudely, I would suggest that for every pound or dollar spent in training there ought to be ten budgeted for the improvement of native conditions of life, for the purchase of more soil for the native,

and for the creation of opportunities in manual and intellectual work, of which the Africans now are almost completely deprived.

THE PRINCIPLES OF TECHNICAL SCHOOLING IN AFRICA

The technique of conducting elementary and higher schooling in Africa is not a subject which can be discussed in detail in a few pages. Indeed, it would not be easy to undertake a treatise on it, since we have but a limited documentary evidence on the subject. This in itself is not very reliable. Part of the work consists of programs, ideals, and expressions of good will but little related to what actually happens. There is also some literature containing more or less pertinent criticism.

The anthropology of culture contact and change—that is, of transculturation—is in its infancy. During my association with the International Institute of African Languages and Culture, I have attempted to train a number of young workers in the methods and problems of anthropological field work directed frontally toward the study of what actually happens in native schools, on mission stations and labor compounds, and in so-called detribalized African communities. Some of this work has already been published, mostly in the journal *Africa*. Some still awaits the light of day.

We have also to remember that under the various colonial systems the education of Africans has divergent aims, techniques, and implications. The French colonial school, largely political and antireligious, aims at the production of African Frenchmen. Portuguese schooling, as far as it exists, is largely carried out by foreign missions, partly under government control devoid of any definite constructive program. In the Belgian Congo, schooling is largely dominated by industrial and commercial interests. In the British colonies most teaching is still done by missions and is only supervised by educational departments.

Through all this, however, there run two or three general problems or principles; and we shall have to confine ourselves to these, having primarily the British colonial areas, as well as the Union of South Africa, in view. Here we find perhaps the greatest problem raised by the coexistence of two principles or slogans: "The Africans must be given the best European education," and "The Africans must be developed on African lines."

It is clear that each principle represents one side of the problem and that each remains an empty slogan unless analyzed more fully and formulated more clearly. To give an African child the best type of European education would mean to prepare him for the best type of European life. But if you give a young African all the best European interests and values and raise in him the expectations, hopes, and claims which you can satisfy in your own children, and then send him back to his tribe or compel him to work on the other side of the Color Bar, you obviously not merely waste your time and his but also inflict on him a grievous injury. He has been educated to a life-task which he will never be allowed to exercise. Instead, he is compelled to accept a remuneration in terms of money, standard of living, and status, which profoundly clashes with the expectations raised.

As regards the principle of educating the African on African lines, this is hardly less fallacious. First of all, such an education can obviously best be given the African in his home, among his playmates, and by his elders. A school conducted by Europeans is perhaps the worst agency for imparting genuine African education. The slogan can only mean, as it often does, to educate Africans to an inadequate and inferior position within the lower caste of a mixed community. Again, the African today needs something more than merely to be brought up to the ways and traditions of his own community, tribal or detribalized. His education must prepare him to face the realities of European encroachment. He is necessary within the compounded community, for the European depends upon him. He must know something about European ways of behavior, about the manner in which law and justice will be administered to him, about the way in which he will be treated or ill-treated.

We must, therefore, draw the simple conclusion that African education has to proceed on two fronts. The child has to receive a type of schooling which will prepare him— and prepare him advantageously—for his contacts, his contests, and his co-operation with Europeans. He has to be taught subjects and skills which give him the maximum chance as regards European employment. And he has to be forewarned and forearmed against all the dangers and discriminations which he will suffer. Tragic and depressing as this sounds, it obviously means that realism is safer than wishful thinking and that the school might as well face squarely the end of the road on which it is leading the child and not impart hopes and illusions which are bound to be shattered.

The second front of African education must be based on the principle that schooling should not in any way increase the disintegration and the rift which is very often created between the educated African and his fellow-tribesmen.

All this means, obviously, that the education which we organize and give to the African child in the special schools cannot proceed alone. It has to be somehow welded and harmonized with such apprenticeship to file as the child receives at home and in the village and which makes him a member of his own community, tribe, race, and culture. The two important principles here implied are that whatever the child learns in school should not estrange him or her from membership in his own society. He should not merely be prevented from developing a contempt for his own traditional heritage and his own race; he ought also to be taught the meaning, the value, and the importance of such African customs, ideas, and institutions which still survive. This would teach him to respect his own culture and to be proud of being a member of the African race. That this is not an empty phraseology will be shown briefly; it is common knowledge to those acquainted with present conditions in Africa.

On the other hand, pure African education is not a task to be undertaken by the European school. It is a reality to be respected by the teachers but not a subject to be directly imparted by them. The preparation for work under the modern African conditions—a preparation which may consist merely of literacy, appreciation of what European culture means, and an acquaintance with the best ways of gaining employment within the new framework of change— is also indispensable. As regards this part of education, however, it should be given not in order to satisfy European aims or ideas of uplift but rather so as to prepare the African for his own tasks, in his own interests, and from a genuine and realistic point of view.

Through all this the three principles mentioned above run clearly: respect for African birthright; the clear vision of the charter of citizenship implied—that is, the opportunities and advantages to be gained from education; and the adjustment of the specialized phase, that of teaching and molding of character to both birthright and charter. Indeed, the fuller and better founded the charter of citizenship, the more we shall find that the birthright of the African, which in its native, natural form we have taken away from him, will be at least partly replaced by something new, yet of substantial value.

EDUCATION ON AFRICAN LINES

We have dismissed this principle when it functions merely as a vague slogan. We have now to reformulate it as a reality. As such, it refers rather to what happens outside the school, which should affect the school only in so far as actual teaching should neither interfere with nor destroy native training but, on the contrary, respect it and become adjusted to it.

The question might be raised, especially when we consider the so-called detribalized parts and sections of modern Africa, as to whether African education is not impossible and unnecessary. Facts prove that, on the contrary, African education is still urgently necessary and that it is in existence—hence, certainly possible. The African, because of

the European attitudes toward him, has to live among people of his own color. After his term of service in a European-managed mine or plantation, he returns to his tribe and continues to live a largely tribal life. The detribalized sections on farms or in native townships are efficiently "segregated" and must rely on their own companionship and on a new type of culture—a culture which certainly is not typically European. If we were to study the conditions among the civilized and even highly educated Bantu classes of South Africa, we should find that the custom of *lobola*, or bride-price, is still practiced. The language spoken is often the vernacular. The kinship code in matters of obligations, attitudes, and taboos still rules supreme. A new African nationalism or conservatism on the rebound is rapidly forming.

Not only are many old customs and traditions retained, but a new African culture is being developed. We have, for instance, the increasing growth of independent African Christian churches. In these churches, dogma, ritual, and ethics are in an interesting way a new creative development of African genius. Sometimes such independent churches even incorporate certain old customs, such as polygamy, and the Bantu marriage law; elements of initiation rites and of ancestor-worship. They are always a reformulation of Christianity in terms of the new needs of the detribalized or partly detribalized African community.

As regards economics, we have a new independent type of Bantu trade-unionism and socialism. The Africans in the Union and in other parts of East Africa are also developing their own mutual aid associations, their own clubs and own forms of entertainment. New dances, new games, and new types of licit or illicit liquor-brewing satisfy the needs for entertainment, amusement, and nonreligious uplift.

The reasons for this formation of a new African culture (which is not so much a mixture of African traditionalism with European elements as it is a creative reinterpretation in which many entirely new ideas, principles, rules, and even devices are improvised) are not difficult to find. The African has to create his own ways of life because he is not allowed to participate fully; indeed, he is not admitted to any participation in white citizenship and in white life.

Culture can be effectively transmitted only by the full admission of those who have to adopt it into the community which practices it. The Africans are constantly exhorted by teachers and missionaries alike to become "civilized"; that means, to assimilate as far as possible to the white community. They are effectively prevented from doing it by the system of segregation, by the Color Bar legislation, by being excluded from most of the benefits and privileges which must accompany the status of an educated, civilized man or woman. They have, obviously, to fall back on their own resources. In many regions and in many respects they go back to their own system of kinship, to their laws of marriage, to their initiation practices, and to some of their own entertainments. When this is not possible because they have been too strongly transformed (as in religion, for instance), they have to devise new forms of it adapted to their political, economic, and social position. They have to cling either to the old kinship system or to new forms of kinship solidarity; since, when out of work or in financial trouble or in illness, they are not provided by the European with systems of insurance, they cannot become members of friendly societies run by whites, and they often do not even have adequate hospital facilities. They would probably adapt readily to the European Christian family if they were given the means of adequate housing and if they were received by their European neighbors as guests in friendly intercourse. Since, however, the economic, technical, and social means of establishing a European household are not there, something new has to be created.

I have attempted to show that even the detribalized portion of the African community does not and cannot live within the framework of European civilization. Large portions of Africa, however, are still under tribal conditions. The Africans are fed by their own primary production, and it can be proved that even the detribalized natives receive a large portion of their wealth from the tribal areas. In many areas the political organization is still a going concern, whether recognized by the Europeans or not. African religion is still alive, and it works, even when driven underground.

In both regions—that is, in the tribal portions and in those areas where a new African culture is gradually developing—part of the educational process has to be given to the African child by his African setting. The concept of education developed by modern functional anthropology implies that training must exist in every culture. The tradition and the organization within every community has to be preserved by being handed down from one generation to another. If we were to take the African culture as it stands now, we should have, obviously, to consider what the child learns in his domestic setting; how he is affected by initiation ceremonies and the apprenticeship to technical skills, by a knowledge of custom and principle which is given to him as he enters the various institutions of which he is a part.

I cannot here enter more fully into the details of the African educational agencies. Here, again, it must be remembered that we have a field of ethnographic research which has been somewhat neglected by official anthropology. I have elsewhere summed up the salient points of African education as it happens at home, within the group of playmates, at initiation ceremonies, through age-grade organizations, and the institution of Bantu regiments.[3]

These processes ought to be known and appreciated by the missions and teachers and the educational departments of colonial administrations. The school ought to take cognizance of these processes in giving the scholars at least a full understanding of what the function, the importance, and the value of African traditional customs and institu-

[3] "Native Education and Culture Contact," *International Review of Missions*, October, 1936, pp. 480–515.

tions are. The details as regards skill, knowl-edge, and instructions cannot be given in the school. In this the European or the Euro-pean-trained native teacher is not compe-tent. But he could, and he ought to, explicit-ly show and state his appreciation of African family life and marriage law. He ought to teach the children to respect their tribal el-ders and parents and even to be aware of the value of ancestor-worship. The teacher might show that initiation ceremonies are not an evil heathen custom but that they are an important agency in imparting respect for tradition. The young African must be made aware of the significance and value of his tradition instead of being taught to de-spise it, as it happens mostly at present.

Another practical point which can be made here is that a definite co-operation between tribal elders or the important mem-bers of a detribalized community and the scholastic authorities should be established. When working in tribal areas or in the native townships of South Africa and the Rhodesi-as, I constantly come across complaints from both sides. The school has a permanent grievance that no co-operation is given by domestic or local authorities of the African race and that, instead, the children are con-stantly compelled to take part in some eco-nomic pursuits or tribal festivities or domes-tic events. The Africans, on the other hand, resent the time which the children have to give to schooling, which in one way they appreciate yet in many ways they have not been made to understand. A co-operation between parents and schools, a system which we are now trying to introduce in our own educational institutions, is even more neces-sary under interracial conditions.

These practical suggestions are not just armchair dreams of an enthusiastic anthro-pologist. I could adduce evidence of such tendencies and movements from the writ-ings of enlightened missionaries, from educa-tional reports, and even from actual occur-rences in various parts of Africa.[4]

[4] I should like to refer here to the important vol-ume, *Essays Catholic and Missionary*, ed. E. R. Mor-gan (1926), especially to the article, "The Christian

TRAINING IN EUROPEAN SCHOLARSHIP

Even if we were to confine ourselves here to the British colonies and the Union of South Africa, the technicalities of the prob-lem would escape any brief summary. We should have to discuss the missionary point of view under government supervision; the elementary schools in the Bush and co-ordinating educational attempts, such as the Joanes movement, and technical schools and native colleges giving an equivalent of university training.

Instead of a detailed analysis of such facts (which would take up a volume and for which we have only scanty and scattered data), I shall quote an experienced teacher and organizer of education—a convinced Christian, and one who is in sympathy both with our religion and culture and with the interests of the Africans.

It is a common criticism of our educational policy in Africa that education, from the African point of view, has come to mean unrelated in-formation, the acquiring of literary skill and languages, but that it has had singularly little influence in the life of the masses of the people. It has not resulted, as we hoped, in the adoption of improved habits in elementary matters of food and clothing, the care of babies and the practice of agriculture by the communities around the school. Schools have been isolated centres of "learning" rather than centres of training for a life of action. Their influence has been strangely confined to the individuals who have there learned to read, write or do sums in arithmetic. To them the tools of learning have been primarily decorative or profitable to them-selves rather than practical and useful in their familiar social background.[5]

_____

Approach to Non-Christian Customs" by the Rt. Rev. W. V. Lucas, Bishop of Masasi. A notable ex-periment in a co-operative school, which has been started by W. B. Mumford at Malangali, is described by the originator in "Malangali School," *Africa*, III (July, 1930). In Swaziland, the paramount chief, Sobhuza II, has successfully transformed the nation-al school of his Protectorate into a co-operative in-stitution, very much on the lines advocated here.

[5] J. W. C. Dugall, "School Education and Native Life," *Africa*, III, 51.

In commenting on this, I would say only that some elements of ordinary European knowledge are necessary for the African and that these, on the whole, are given to him. For many—though by no means all—of the natives, reading and writing, the elements of arithmetic, of bookkeeping, and of the skills necessary in running European tools or even machines, are very useful. But here one or two important principles might be laid down. The differentiation of European schools for Africans is at present based on the interests of Europeans and not on those of the African community. It is a differentiation according to whether the teaching is given by the Roman Catholics or the Dutch Lutherans, by groups who believe in Indirect Rule or those who are convinced that the African must be assimilated as rapidly as possible.

The fundamental principle here advocated is that some comprehensive planning of African schools, if possible for the continent as a whole, should be made—and made in the interests of the population and not of those who are guiding the system, very often to satisfy their own ideals, predilections, tastes, or even vested interests. Thus, for instance, in completely tribal regions, especially such as Nigeria or Tanganyika Territory or Northern Rhodesia, where Indirect Rule has been granted, the schools ought to be very much more adjusted to tribal life. Indirect Rule, as is well known, is the preservation of African institutions—political, social, and even religious—with a considerable latitude in autonomy and self-determination. In such regions schools which primarily aim at estranging the child from his own tradition and cultural setting become an absurdity. In many parts of Africa even the acquisition of the European language is a mere waste of time.

An entirely different type of school might be advocated for regions where a great deal of autonomy is combined with a progressive political administration and African response. We have tribes such as the Chagga on the Kilimanjaro; the Kikuyu living round Mount Kenya; and many other communi-

ties in Uganda and round the Lakes where cotton, coffee, sisal hemp, and other cash produce are being developed by native enterprise, very often with native capital. There, obviously, a different type of training is necessary. To compete with European planters, the native must know how to organize into co-operatives; how to carry on accountancy or control white accountants; how to appreciate economic factors at home and abroad. In such regions not only must the three R's be taught, as well as a good knowledge of English, but also schools for well-trained technical and business management ought to be developed. This is, again, not a mere fantasy. Such movements have been set into motion by the inevitable pressure of facts. Yet there is no comprehensive planning, no full map of Africa, with its cultural necessities and its educational instrumentalities plotted out systematically.

There are other regions where the native depends economically upon European enterprises. This, obviously, refers primarily to the Union, to the Protectorates, and to large parts of Portuguese Africa as well as the Rhodesias. In such regions I would suggest that the schools ought to prepare the young boy or girl for the very tasks and conditions under which he or she will have to work. There is no doubt for me that the vexed question of the linguistic medium of teaching ought to be solved in such regions by adopting definitely the dominant European language of the area. In the earliest grades there ought to be teachers conversant in the vernacular who can impart the knowledge of English or French, maybe also Portuguese and Afrikaans. Later on, however, teaching ought to be given in the dominant European language of the region. I would like to see the cultivation of the several substitute, semi-African languages, such as Swahili, Hausa, or Arabic, gradually eliminated.

As regards higher types of teaching, the most important point here refers to the final phase of the process—that is, to the character of citizenship. It is hard on a community if opportunities for professional development are granted but opportunities for the exercise of a profession are withheld.

It is hardly necessary for me to frame an indictment of many features of the present system. Associated as education has usually been either with missionary uplift or with a direct attempt at refashioning the African into the guise of a civilized Frenchman or Belgian, the religious and the lay education alike has produced the effect of estranging the scholar from his own community, of making him dislike and despise his parental home, his village, and his tribe. The church elders or the members of the "civilized élite" in French or Belgian Africa have been made into the stronghold of anti-African feeling and opinion.

Were it possible to extend the élite to all the tribesmen, or the privileges enjoyed by the few wealthier and better-established African teachers or elders to the whole community, there would be no serious objection to a transition from things African to things European. But it has been stated here, again and again, that a complete transition of the whole of Africa to European standards would involve, first, the complete withdrawal of Europeans from Africa so as to restore the land, the political power, and opportunities which are now usurped at the African's expense. Not only that. It would be necessary to pour capital from Europe and the whole Western world into the Dark Continent, and the fruits of this should not be garnered, as now, by European capitalists but presented to the Africans. As long as we are not prepared to do this, the worst we can do to the Africans is to make them despise their own conditions of life and, at the same time, prevent them from adopting the new conditions which we teach them to appreciate and value.

The disparagement of ancestor-worship and beer drinks, of African interests and pursuits, is, therefore, a most undesirable by-product of the one-sided European-controlled and European-aimed education on European lines. The only thing which we ought to give them from this point of view is the maximum preparation for contact with the white community. The African ought to be taught what are his rights and his claims, and also his duties and liabilities. He ought to obtain a clear idea from the outset of how much he will be allowed to claim politically, economically, and socially. He ought to be shown also where the artificially imposed disabilities, which differ from one area to another but are never absent, will cut across his career and those hopes and expectations which education always induces. The schooling we give him should never be subversive of his respect for his own tribal dignity or racial characteristics.

THE CHARTER OF CITIZENSHIP

This concept has been the leitmotiv of all our argument. Ideally and normally, the higher the education obtained by an individual, the better his position in a community ought to become. This is, obviously, not fully at work even among ourselves. A movie star, a successful bootlegger, a fraudulent stockbroker, a political boss—whether his name be Adolf Hitler or Mayor Plague or anything else—receives a finer and fuller reward in income, respect, and social position than the most learned rabbi, professor, of pundit. But, by and large, education—especially in the wider sense of development or abilities, personality, and foresight—does raise the standard of living, of personal influence, and of social importance.

Under conditions of interracial teaching, however, almost the reverse is true. At times even elementary education received by a child becomes a mere waste of time, a handicap in the learning of really useful skills through tribal apprenticeship, and an injury through partial estrangement from tribal ways. Cases could be quoted, from some parts of Africa, where a technical school had been opened for the training of skilled labor and African engineers while soon after its establishment discriminating legislation forbade, in the same area, skilled African labor to be used. Colleges and universities train people for professions in which there are but few openings, with definitely inadequate rewards. Again, the highly educated African is put at a disadvantage in that his hopes and expectations have been raised, his sensitivity increased, and then his person submitted to all the discriminations, pass-laws, and indignities which are lavished on any and every African.

The charter of citizenship, which is perhaps the most sacred and inalienable right of an educated man, is set at naught in Africa for an African because of the policy of segregation, the laws of Color Bar, and the facts of political disabilities, the absence of rights to organize, and the absence of full, impartial justice. I add to this the artificial restrictions on the freedom of movement, the exclusion from equal comradeship in places of entertainment, parks, and other means of public amenity; and you will see what agencies cut at the charter.

Let us have a look at the economic opportunities given by education. In so far as we still have tribal areas run by old African tradition, European education has added but little to the native charter of citizenship. In fact, as we have seen, it detracts from it. In detribalized parts of the Union and other colonies we have to distinguish. In some areas where African skilled labor is admitted and where natives are encouraged to develop their own natural resources by their own capital, labor, and enterprise, education has a value and gives a charter with its advantages and privileges. As soon, however, as the Color Bar enters, in the form of either enacted laws or customary restrictions or unfair competition, the battle for education once more has to be fought with reference to its last phase—that is, the opportunities given.

Let us have a look at what is usually defined as the policy of segregation. This is very often erroneously and hypocritically described as means of "independent development for the Africans." Segregation could be equitable. It could be so if it allowed the African a sufficiency in territorial expansion; that is, if we granted him enough land to build comfortable villages and townships, to develop his farms, and even to produce lucrative cash crops and raise cattle on a com-

mercial basis. Certain remedies have been instituted in the Union of South Africa by the passage of the Herzog laws. Had these laws not demanded such a high price in other native prerogatives, they could have been regarded as a great benefit. Even here, however, we have to wait until the laws are effectively implemented. Equitable segregation would also demand a full range of economic opportunities. For the time being, the native can engage in a labor contract in mines and factories in which his income is artificially restricted and in which he is neither encouraged nor helped to economize and accumulate capital. Segregation would mean an equal share in services, amenities, and institutions. We should have to demand independent African banks, means of transport, parks, and business organizations. Obviously, nothing of the sort exists. Political autonomy is a goal of which, in many parts of Africa, it is now fantastic to speak. This, obviously, refers to precisely those areas where education is necessary and where it ought to give also this political charter. Political autonomy exists only within restricted tribal areas which enjoy Indirect Rule.

What "segregation" as we find it amounts to is a complete political and legal control of Africans by whites. It means economic dependence, the complete absence of suffrage or any other mechanism for political influence, and a treatment under law and court systems which is neither segregated nor equitable.

The result of all this is that as soon as we approach the detribalized phases of African society—and these are the only ones in which the problem of education is really relevant—we find the complete absence of that even, well-balanced structure necessary to a healthy development of a community and of a culture. A sound society must be based on the even distribution of occupational groups —manual, skilled, and professional. It must have an independent, self-sufficient economy of food production and the production of primary necessities. This is absent as regards the detribalized sections of Africa. A sound society must also produce an artisan class, people in small business, small employees, and professional men. And here we have the most unfortunate fact—that the great bulk of African wage-earners do not and cannot give employment either to small business, such as shopkeepers, nor yet to African professionals. Most of the wage-earners, such as mine labor and factory employees, are supervised and spoon-fed by organized European institutions. There is no room for an African doctor, for an African lawyer, for an African nurse, for an African retailer, as regards custom drawn from the three-hundred-thousand-odd colored workers who live on Witwatersrand. All the profits which these professional Africans might gain are gathered by European employees and officials on the mines.

There is no progress or development possible in such a society, hampered and handicapped at every point. What is actually occurring now in those parts of Africa where large sections of previously self-contained communities have been thrown into the melting-pot or temporarily weaned from tribal life, is the formation of a rigid caste system. This new caste division is determined by the congenital social status, in which every member is born to a predestined course of existence. The rigid laws against intermarriage and interbreeding have also a definite caste character. The strict definition—or, more correctly, limitation—of power, privilege, and wealth places members of the caste within a system of economic bondage.

This concept of caste system with which I have approached the problem of detribalized Africa some twelve years ago supplies in many ways the *tertium comparationis* between the problems of Africa and a number of problems on our own continent.

CONCLUDING REMARKS

I have already mentioned that in my opinion all the studies on transculturation and interracial relationships between Europeans and Africans ought to be placed within a framework of Pan-African theory. The reason for this is that here, as in every com-

parative research, we ought to consider the widest range of evidence available. The process of contact and change is essentially the same, whether it happens round the Kalahari, in the jungles of the Congo, in Brazil, the West Indies, or the southern states of the American Union. It is the same as long as the main determinant factors are similar or comparable. There are, obviously, profound differences as between the Latin and the Anglo-Saxon attitude, the principle of Indirect Rule and the Grondwet (which stipulates racial inequality as a lasting norm). But both similarities and differences can be brought into relief only when we have a genuine Pan-African framework of reference.

All the theoretical considerations, as well as all planning, organizing of evidence, and practical efforts, should be referred to such a framework. This has a great value also in that it allows us to discover and establish historical trends by the evidence of comparative analysis within contemporary conditions. There are regions in Africa where the process of transculturation has but recently started. There are areas such as the Union of South Africa, some islands in the West Indies, and the southern states of this federation where we can observe, study, and define the *terminus ad quem*, the ultimate goal toward which the process seems to be moving. This ultimate goal is in some cases, as in the British West Indies or the island of Cuba, one of relative freedom, equality, and identical or at least similar opportunities for all. In the Union of South Africa and in some parts of the United States we have, on the other hand, the beginnings of a rigid caste system.

I should like once more to quote from a previous publication of mine, at some length, especially since it is found in an inaccessible and nonspecialist periodical.

.... the most dramatic, not to say tragic, configuration of racial relationships occurs where neither race displaces the other, where whatever mixture takes place is socially degraded, and where, in consequence, a rigid caste system comes into being. In such cases, the result is a stratified society, such as we find in its classical formation in pre-European India, and as we see now rapidly being formed in South Africa and in the United States of America. There we have groups of different racial stock living in the same territory, yet socially segregated, subject to legal and political discrimination, forced into different occupations, and prevented, more or less effectively, from mixing with each other in marriage.

Wherever caste has been stabilized, wherever the network of rules, prohibitions and restrictions has been accepted by lower and higher alike and has led to permanent adjustment, the system shows no glaring evils—on the surface at least.

In reality, however:

It is inevitably a source of weakness, it prevents the community as a whole presenting a united front, it leads to brutality and abuses from above, to servility and deceitfulness from below. The social disabilities weigh heavily on the lower and demoralize the higher stratum. Practical and legal discrimination is a perpetual source of abuse, dishonesty, and graft. Sexual relations between the two strata are essentially unsound, leading to bastardization of the lower caste and to preventive taboos with lynching and draconic laws meant to protect the women of the higher caste; while on the economic side, as we have abundantly proved, the caste system in its modern setting leads to forced labor with all its inherent evils. The point need not be labored, however, because everything which has been said in this article about the maladjustments and difficulties in the relations between black and white is an indictment of the caste system.[6]

That I was correct in my anticipatory historical diagnosis in suggesting the caste concept as the principal framework of reference has been proved since by the independent discovery of this principle by such American sociologists and anthropologists as Professor Lloyd Warner, Dr. H. Powdermaker, Dr. John Dollard, and Dr. Allison Davis.[7]

[6] *Listener*, Suppl. No. 8 (July 16, 1930), published by the British Broadcasting Company, London.

[7] See H. Powdermaker, *After Freedom* (1939); J. Dollard, *Caste and Class in a Southern Town* (1937); A. Davis and J. Dollard, *Children of Bondage* (1940).

In the present argument the recognition of the two-caste constitution of the society in the southern states is of some consequence. It gives us, as mentioned, a legitimate basis for comparison and the drawing of parallels. As soon as a community becomes split into two genuine castes, we are faced not merely with an interracial but also with an intercultural situation. Two castes really mean two cultures. For culture is an instrumentality in which man has to find the full range not merely for the satisfaction of his organic needs but also for the expression of his personality. Where the caste system deprives one of the component cultures of such fundamental necessities of a civilized human being as political rights, full legal protection, a full range of economic opportunities, and also the indispensable social and aesthetic amenities of life, the underprivileged culture differs fundamentally from its counterpart on the other side of the Color Bar line. Read the books quoted, which are among the most recent contributions to the problem; read the many volumes and periodicals published by the American Negro in scientific terms or in a political mood or as direct statements of his grievances; and you will find every word of what has been said here confirmed and fully documented.

Since we are, however, here discussing facts in a dispassionate scientific spirit, it will be better if I return to the problem of interracial education. I should like to restate the conclusions drawn directly with reference to the education in Africa and briefly to comment upon their validity as regards the problem on this continent.

1. Education is bigger than schooling.

2. We are supplying the schooling somewhat artificially; for full education the African child has still to rely on his social and cultural milieu.

3. European schooling, if divorced from the African background, contributes toward the breakdown of tribal life and cultural continuity.

4. African education is not dead, even in detribalized areas; it lives in family life, in the structure of kinship and community, in

the special setting of native economic pursuits, old and new.

5. European schooling and African education have to be harmonized and carried on simultaneously, with conscious direction and adjustment. The alternative is conflict within the individual and chaos in the community.

6. The focusing of this adjustment lies in respect for African values and an equipment to meet the impact of European civilization, as well as to co-operate with the European community. Education must proceed on these two fronts simultaneously.

7. The addition of European schooling, as part of our culture impact, raises the African above his own standard of living; it develops his ambitions and needs, economic, political, and cultural. To pour all the money, energy, and zeal into schooling and "developing" without any wherewithal to satisfy the resulting claims is the royal road to a social catastrophe.

We have started a process which cannot now be checked. The Africans are on the move. They will not return to the old groove of tribal life, though they will not abandon all their heritage rapidly and completely for some time to come. Their capacities and desires have been awakened. They need more land than we have left them, more economic opportunities than we have opened up for them, and greater political autonomy. There must take place a revision of the Color Bar policy; sooner or later better conditions in towns and more breathing space in the reserves will have to be given. These are the cornerstones of a sound educational policy.[8]

How far do these conclusions apply to conditions in the southern states? Points 1 and 2 obviously are general points of view

[8] The last paragraph obviously refers to the conditions in Africa, more especially in the Union of South Africa. The statements just made appeared not only in a missionary periodical but also in the daily papers of Johannesburg and Cape Town and provoked hostile protests (cf. *International Review of Missions*, October, 1936, and the daily press of Capetown, July 10, and of Johannesburg, July 26, 1934). Since they were uttered, some improvement has already taken place in the Union of South Africa.

which hold good with reference to the situation here and now.

3. Since we are agreed that the Negro lives within a different cultural setting and has to rely on his own community here in America, even as in the detribalized parts of Africa, there is no doubt that the school should not be divorced from the home and the community background in our area exactly as in Africa. Indeed, here as in Africa, we might speak of education on two fronts, in that a type of schooling which would undermine the respect and the appreciation of one's own race is dangerous under any caste system.

4. In discussing the new civilization which the Africans have to reconstruct or, more correctly, to create under conditions where tribal control has ceased, we pointed out the reasons for this fact. The same reasons hold good with reference to the southern states, even though we might not agree with some enthusiastic anthropologists who still find a good deal of genuine African background in the culture of the American Negro. In so far, however, as they are right, our conclusions are even better validated.

5. We would rephrase the above by saying that schooling and the education at home and through community life ought to be carried out harmoniously without adding to the inevitable conflicts and rifts which exist in every caste system.

6. Here, once more, education on two fronts is necessary in our communities here, in so far as it must prepare the young man of African descent for collaboration with the white community while he remains a good citizen of his own group.

7. This point implies the principle that improvement of education ought to be supplemented by an economic, social, and even political action for the raising of status. Indeed, to put it even more explicitly, the informed and wise statesmanship of white and African alike must face (the sooner the better) the problem of how the caste system can be broken down.

Some of the suggestions contained in the

present article might be briefly stated. There is a possibility of developing an equitable system of segregation, of independent, autonomous development, which yet would have nothing whatsoever in common with the caste division. Speaking as a European, and a Pole at that, I should like to place here as a parallel and paradigm the aspirations of European nationality, though not of nationalism. In Europe we members of oppressed or subject nationalities—and Poland was in that category for one hundred and fifty years, since its first partition, and has again been put there through Hitler's invasion—do not desire anything like fusion with our conquerors or masters. Our strongest claim is for segregation in terms of full cultural autonomy which does not even need to imply political independence. We claim only to have the same scale of possibilities, the same right of decision as regards our destiny, our civilization, our careers, and our mode of enjoying life.

This is, I think, a perfectly feasible charter for interracial co-operation or intercultural relations alike. It leaves untouched some of the ineradicable prejudices on either side of the dividing-line. We do not need to be all alike in order to be happy. Differentiation—cultural, racial, religious, intellectual, and aesthetic—is fully compatible with the democratic structure of civilization. The main evils which every sane, decent and wise man or woman physically, as well as intellectually, must oppose are discrimination in terms of slavery, caste, subjection, injustice, and the limitation of the inalienable rights of every man and woman.

THE WEST AFRICAN "BUSH" SCHOOL

MARK HANNA WATKINS

ABSTRACT

Education, in its widest significance, is identical with the cultural process. In the least elaborated societies the cultural heritage may be learned adequately by direct participation in daily life, while more complex social orders require specialized educational institutions. The "bush" school in West Africa is considered here as having the function of inculcation in a society which, in degree of complexity, is of intermediate type. Studied in its own cultural milieu, the "bush" school appears to be genuinely educative.

The social anthropologist and the sociologist consider education in its broadest aspects to be coterminous with the cultural process in which, over successive generations, the young and unassimilated members of a group are incorporated by their sharing of the social heritage. Education from this point of view thus is directed by the group in the daily interaction of its members as well as by specialized functionaries or subgroups, and in the process the cultural patterns are transmitted and the socially accepted values realized.

The social values of a group are those phenomena which it recognizes as constituting the active or potential factors in the promotion of its welfare or which, when not properly controlled, create dysphoric conditions. Thus there are, on the one hand, positive social values, as food, shelter, health, and the fundamental necessities of life, as well as other socially desirable ends defined by the culture, and, on the other hand, negative social values, as crime, disease, death, witchcraft. These constitute in a large measure the social environment and determine the characteristic activities of a society. It is in relation to them that we may therefore speak of the function of education. This function is not to be confused with purpose, although in social life the two are often closely related; for the function of anything is simply what it does, and we speak of the function of objects which have no purposes, as, for example, that of the sunlight. Moreover, in attempting to achieve the goals which are proposed, a people often attain quite different ends, as in the case of the teacher who, desirous of creating friendship, makes two boys embrace after a fight, but only intensifies their enmity; or of the Volstead Act, which created a wave of vice and crime instead of a nation of temperate citizens.

Hence, while the function of social life, in general, is that of passing on the cultural heritage, it may be recognized that not every social example is worthy to be copied and preserved. Every group struggles to maintain only its ideals, along with the technology and skills needed for providing subsistence. Thus, while education is identical with life in a particular society, it is obligatory that in every group there should be imposed upon certain institutions the duty of making deliberate efforts toward fostering the best in the cultural heritage, in regard both to the objective world of materials and techniques and to their subjective counterpart of sentiments, interests, and attitudes. In short, the incidental educative function of social life is supplemented by a more or less self-conscious purpose, superimposed upon one or more fundamental institutions or carried out by a special educational organization. This purpose involves the conservation, extension, and transmission of all the culturally accepted values and ideals to the succeeding generations so as to insure their continuity as they are defined in the local group and thus to perpetuate its life. There generally is required a more or less special emphasis determined by national or local aims. There also are the problems of adjusting the group to the larger world in which it lives and of accommodating the individual so that his efforts to realize his wishes may not conflict too seriously with the needs of his society.

The formulation of an educational program for any group therefore is dependent upon two general factors: the nature and needs of the child, which determine the methods of procedure, and the nature and needs of the society, which determine the goals.

In the very simplest societies, as that of the Andaman Islanders, the Sakai of the Malay Peninsula, an Eskimo village, or other similar groups, informal education, in which the individual learns incidentally by direct participation and imitation, is relatively adequate for social continuity. The learning that goes on under such conditions is genuine; for the patterns of life are presented to the individual in their immediate setting, and what he learns is close to his interests and put into direct use; in fact, he learns by doing. In such a society where there is only a meager differentiation of vocations, with no complex technology, and in which the system of beliefs and practices is comparatively simple, the gap between the growing child and the adult world is relatively narrow and may be spanned without a long period of special preparation. Here the inculcation of the social values is achieved with a minimum of self-conscious purpose; that is to say, it is not abstracted from the daily life. In more complex social orders, where only the general designs of life are accessible to the young, the educative process must take on some degree of specific and separate organization; the social heritage must be broken up into assimilable portions and simplified, so that education as a purposive endeavor becomes differentiated from the educative function of daily life. Some form of specialized educational institution develops, and the passing-on of selected social ideals takes place in a relatively distinctive and artificial environment. But this differentiation entails certain problems, for the social values tend to become somewhat impersonal to the learner, are not immediate and vital in character, and are likely to be hidden in symbols. In such a situation learning may degenerate to mere acceptance of performulated matter, to rote memory without understanding or responsibility. It becomes more and more difficult to relate the experiences acquired under such formal circumstances to those obtained in direct association, to distinguish between intrinsic and mediate values, and for the learner to understand the mediate values associated with his contemporary activity.

From the foregoing remarks it would appear that the adequacy of any deliberate and formalized educational system may be tested by considering the extent to which it is representative of the cultural heritage and its achievement in so relating the activities of the more or less specialized environment to those of the practical social world of which it is a part that the two may be contiguous.

It seems permissible and profitable to describe and study the "bush" school of West Africa on the basis of this framework, although that educational system may not be regarded as formal on a par with the schools among westernized peoples. The "bush" school, as will be seen, has the characteristics of a deliberate and purposive procedure in a specialized environment.

The training of youth in West Africa is accomplished through one of the types of secret societies common in the area. In these societies, as in many other affairs, the sexes are segregated. The name which is now in general usage for the boys' society is *poro*— in the Vai language, *pólò* or *pórò* (with open *o*).[1] This form, or some dialectic variant of it, is found over a relatively wide area in Li-

[1] For sake of economy, the few native (Vai) words included have not been transcribed in phonetic script, with the exception that the tones are shown by the grave accent (for low) and the acute accent (for the high register). There are at least three significant tonal distinctions (tonemes) in this language, but the middle tone does not appear in any of the words employed here. The vowel qualities have been described briefly in parentheses following the first occurrence of each word. The Vai *a* is invariably a low back vowel, while *i*, *e*, and *o* may be open or closed. A colon following a vowel indicates that the vowel is long. The consonants have practically the same qualities as in English.

beria, Sierra Leone, and other areas over which the Mandingo languages are spoken. The name for the corresponding girls' society is *bondo*, Vai *bòndò* (*o* closed), or, more correctly, *sàndì* (with open *i*). There is little variation in the organization and activities of these societies as they occur among the Mende, Vai, Kpelle, Krima, Gola, and other related groups. The description given here refers to them as they are established among the Mende and Vai, the data being obtained primarily from Miss Fatima Massaquoi, a native Vai student at Fisk University, including notes in correspondence with her brother, Mr. S. Ciaka Massaquoi, of Pendembu, Sierra Leone. *Poro* seems to be a generic term which once was and still may be applied to the societies without regard to the sex of the participants and which includes similar associations among men and women, the adult groups being political and civic rather than distinctively educational in aim.

The most widely distributed and probably also the oldest name of the society is *poro*, strictly speaking, *polo*, thus with open *o* in both instances. Dapper, in the seventeenth century, called it *paaro*, so that perhaps the stem originally contained an *a*.[2]

The adult groups are not strictly germane to the subject presented here and therefore may be omitted.

The original meaning of the word *poro* is not known clearly. Westermann, quoting two other authors, makes the following statement:

Wallis (p. 183) says *poro* means literally "law" or "one word"; also Alldridge, *A Transformed Colony* (p. 194), speaks of "the order of the Poro or law." If this translation is not etymologically correct, it is nevertheless expressive of the power of the *poro* for legal discipline.[3]

These societies are of fundamental importance in the local culture, and every

[2] Diedrich Westermann, *Die Kpelle* (Göttingen, 1921), p. 236.

[3] *Ibid.*, p. 236 n. The writers quoted are Braithwaite Wallis, "The Poro of the Mendi," *Journal of the African Society*, IV (1904–5), 181–89, and T. J. Alldridge, *A Transformed Colony: Sierra Leone as It Was and Is* (London, 1910).

youth, male or female, must receive such training before being considered worthy to assume the responsibilities of an adult. With the growing influence of Mohammedanism, Christianity, and European culture, the significance of the *poro* in native life is waning, along with detribalization and the general modification of aboriginal culture.

The boys' society or school may be described first. In the Vai language, the specific name for this institution is *bélì*, and a person who has been inducted into it is known as a *bélì kàì*, "initiated man." (The *e* of *bélì* is open, the *i* closed; in *kàì* the *a* is a low back vowel and the *i* is closed.)

The sessions of this school are not held in the towns or villages proper, but a permanent place is selected in the forest not far distant from the principal or capital town of a chiefdom or district. This special section of forest is called *bélì fìlà* (*fìlà* pronounced with closed *i*, low back *a*), "*bélì* forest," and is never used for other purposes, although all the structures are burned at the close of each term. Every district or subchiefdom has its own school and special reserved forest for the purpose.

Once boys have entered the forest, they are at no time allowed to return to the towns until their training is complete; nor under any circumstances are female visitors tolerated. No one except members of the society is permitted entrance to the area. If uninitiated persons approach it, they must make their presence known so that none of its secrets will be exposed. If a man trespasses, he will be initiated, while a woman under such circumstances will be killed. During the period in which the school is in session the forest is said to be the special possession of the principal official of the institution, and not even the chief is permitted to enter without the permission of this man. Thus, in a physical and spatial sense, the "bush" school is a special or distinctive environment.

The principal official of the school is the *dá zò:* (*a* low back, *o* closed and long), "the leader who stands at the mouth or head," who is endowed with wisdom and mystic power in a superlative degree. He has a majestic status in the society, is respected by the chief and elders of the tribe, and is honored with intense devotion by the youth of the land. In personal characteristics he must be chivalrous, courteous, public-spirited, law-abiding, and fearless. He must have a full knowledge of all the native lore, arts, and crafts, must be well versed in the history and traditions of his people and an authentic judge of all matters affecting their welfare. Other men of good repute who are specialists in various fields of activity serve as his assistants and as teachers of the novices.

For the institution among the Kpelle the characteristics and role of the leader have been described in the following words:

The grandmaster, *namū*, is, of course, a human being and is known as such by the members. At the same time, he possesses attributes which raise him above the merely human. He himself is immortal; that is, his death is kept a secret, and the choice of the successor takes place in the strictest secrecy and in the narrow circle of the outstanding members; and he has the power to kill people and restore them to life. This refers, of course, actually to the secret sojourn of the *poro* youths in the *poro* bush and their later re-entrance into the community of village companions. They are thought of as having been dead and restored to life, actually swallowed by the grandmaster and reborn, which, however, the usual popular opinion quite generally conceives of as the ability of the *namū* to revive the dead.

It is only natural that the imagination of the folk is vigorously occupied with the *namū* and attributes to him the supernatural. He is seen surrounded by the beings [people] in the village, since he moves about just as other people, but he also flies through the air. Thus near Densu [place name] there is pointed out a large, slender tree with fantastically projecting boughs, on which the *namū* takes rest when on his journeys through the air or on which he meets the grandmistress of the *sande* society.

On his visits to the towns the grandmaster always makes his appearance surrounded by a group of initiated, who protect him from strange glances [glances of the uninitiated]. He generally goes unclothed. Only to the initiated is he visible: upon his appearance in the village all the uninitiated—women, children, and strangers—must retire to the huts and close the doors.

On festive occasions the *namū* wears a gala costume which consists of wide trousers extending over the knees; a short-sleeved, close-fitting waistcoat; and a headdress which is a type of cylindrical hat made of small metal plate, ornamented on the upper portion of the front with the head of a plumed raven [*Hornraben*], and trimmed with cowrie shells and white otter or ape fur; over the brow a white band; around the neck a large ruffle made of projecting leather pieces (leopard and antelope skin), three to five centimeters wide and ten centimeters long, trimmed with white fur and cowrie shell; a medicine bag and other magic hung around the neck; in one hand a large fan decked with many pieces of skin underneath and little bells above and in the other hand a horsetail or cowtail.

A *namū* can conduct several schools at the same time—as many as three—which often are located some distance apart. In this case he spends alternately some time in each one and intrusts the remaining part of the development to his assistants, one of whom always carries out the inspection of a school. The journeys of the *namū* from one school to another are kept secret, and the students learn hardly anything of his absence; therefrom originates the belief that he may be in several places simultaneously and is bound to no locality. Often agreements are made between various headmasters for the purpose of conducting a course interchangeably. The headmasters then hold a conference in the capital of the oldest, and the latter presides.[4]

The period during which a session is to be held is determined by a council consisting of the leader, his assistants, and the elders of the tribe. The term in length varies from group to group. Among the Gola, in the old days, the session is said to have had a duration of from four to eight years; among the Krima, or Krim, it was three to five years; while among the Mende and the Vai the time was from two to three years. Westermann gives the length of the term as recorded by himself and others for a number of tribes. His figures vary from two months among the Kru to ten years for the Temne, although he adds the statement that "many

[4] Westermann, *op. cit.*, pp. 238–40.

of the figures given above may be more ideal than actual."[5]

At present, under the influence of new ideas and the gradual Europeanization of the region, there is a general desire for opportunity to acquire knowledge which the "bush" school alone cannot provide, so that the periods have been progressively reduced. Thus the term among the Vai and the Mendi is now approximately eighteen months only, while it is about two years among the Krima and from two to three years among the Gola.

When the time arrives for the school to convene, parents who wish their boys to be initiated make known their desires to the tribal elders, who in turn inform the paramount chief. The latter passes the information on to the leader and other officials of the school. Then the news circulates rapidly throughout the land, and the boys begin to gather, coming in from all parts of the chiefdom. There is no established regulation covering the age limits for membership. However, it is generally believed that human beings are more tractable and teachable when young than when fully mature, so that boys are expected to enter usually between the ages of approximately seven to nineteen years. In exceptional cases, however, the authorities do not generally object.

At the beginning of the session all the boys who have not been circumcised already are given this treatment. The number of boys who are circumcised at this time is dependent upon the age distribution, as the older ones will have received the operation prior to entrance. It appears that in years before the influence of the West was so great, most of the novices were quite young and consequently were uncircumcised at the opening of the term.

Circumcision constitutes a sanitary measure, although there were no social diseases before the coming of the Europeans. It is thought, however, that less dirt will be accumulated when the skin of the male organ has been excised. An uncircumcised man, moreover, is considered to be a weakling and is despised as an inferior being.

[5] *Ibid.*, pp. 234–35.

After the circumcision rites a period of time is allowed for the healing of the wounds. Then a feast is celebrated so that the boys may be given opportunity to know one another as well as to become acquainted with the teachers. The women prepare food for this festival, but they are not permitted to bring it into the school.

Now begin the specific forms of training. The boys are divided into groups according to their ages and aptitudes and receive instruction in all the arts, crafts, and lore of native life, including a variety of games and sports, such as swimming, canoeing, hunting, trapping, acrobatic stunts, dancing, singing, drumming and the playing of other musical instruments, wrestling, climbing, etc. These are for the purpose of physical development, the acquisition of fundamental skills, the sharpening of the wits, and appreciation for native art. It is by this means that the character is molded and a youth is prepared to take his place among the generation of adults. Moreover, the continuation of all these traits is insured. The first instruction involves a series of tests in order to determine individual differences, interests, and ambitions (to see what the boys can do) and an acquisition of the fundamental knowledge which every adult is supposed to know. Later, opportunity for demonstration of special ingenuity, skills, and originality is afforded. A youth who shows special aptitude for weaving, for example, is trained to become a master of the craft; while those who show distinctive skill and interest in carving, leatherwork, dancing, "medicine," folklore, etc., likewise are developed along these specialized lines. This early training also includes work in the erection of the structures which are used while the session lasts. The buildings constructed for the school are sufficiently numerous to constitute one or more towns. All the laws and traditions of the tribe are taught, as well as duty to the tribal chief, tribe, and elders, and the proper relations to women. Training is given in the recognition and use of various medicinal herbs, their curative powers, and various antidotes. Also, the secrets of wild animals are taught—how they live, how to recognize their spoor, and how to attack them.

All this training is tested out in the laboratory of "bush"-school life. For example, instruction in warfare is accompanied by actual mock battles and skirmishes. The boys are separated into various "towns" similar in location and arrangement to those in which the general population is or has been distributed. These towns must be barricaded, defended, and attacked. Previous wars in which the tribe has been engaged are re-enacted, the boys of one group playing the role of the people under attack at a certain time, while those of another act the parts of the enemies. The ruses which the enemy employed are gone over carefully, and the attackers must carry them out with precision and dexterity. Some of the attacks are made on rainy nights, when the inhabitants are asleep; others are made when there are festivals, when the "men" are in the fields, the actual situation, with all the preoccupations, distractions, and surprises of some known war, being re-created. All this is possible because the forest is sufficiently large, covering several square miles. All the buildings, fields, and activities are the responsibility of the boys after they have received their instructions. They must live in these towns, work the fields, and carry on all the activities of normal tribal life, at the same time preparing to defend their possessions or to make attacks according to the assignment which they have received and the account which the instructors have given of the previous war. Sometimes a lapse of two or three months may occur before the plans can be executed. This makes the situation all the more genuine. The defenders are informed of the errors in judgment and tactics which were formerly committed in actual combat, and the battle is conducted upon the basis of the previous life-situation. Then the entire war game is replayed, the defenders having learned what the shortcomings were and how to correct them, and the "enemy" making special effort to succeed in the face of the new improvements in defense. In these bat-

tles all the obstacles with which the people were once confronted in such crises are re-created. Some of the boys play the roles of women and children who must be guarded and defended, who constitute the impediment of a human cargo. The "enemy" attempts to capture and enslave these "women" and "children" just as is done in normal warfare, for it is not the custom to kill women and children in military combat.

Thus, although the "bush" school is conducted in a special environment—i.e., in one which is differentiated from the general social milieu—the degree of artificiality is not so great as it often is under the conditions of formal education among peoples of European and American cultures. The greatest amount of dissimilarity between the school situation and that of native life in the towns and villages would seem to be the absence of certain distractions in the school—the removal from normal family ties, from the direct influence of mothers and kinsmen, who tend to condone the frailties of the youths. This does not seem to constitute a disadvantage or to seclude the activities in an ivory tower. In fact, there is a general notion among these people that there should be some form of counterbalance to the intimate association between children and their immediate parents (those of the simple or biological family), for under such conditions they will be cajoled, indulged, and petted too much and in this way not prepared for the sacrifices incidental to normal social life beyond this narrow circle. For this reason, children are distributed often among the more distant relatives for various periods of time. The requirement that life in the "bush" school must involve withdrawal from such contacts appears to be an application of this fundamental principle. Indeed, a child is not expected to enter a "bush" school in which his close relative has a position of authority.

Life in the secret society is a complete *rite de passage* from the helplessness and irresponsibilities of childhood to citizenship in a world of adults. Thus a youth acquires a new name in the *bêlì*, according to his rank in the group and his achievements. He retains this name for life, and it is always applied to him by those who have been initiated in the school. Uninitiated persons may not use it. This latter form of life, it may be seen, is developed gradually within the confines of the institution. Entrance to the society is a symbolic death for the young, who must be reborn before returning to family and kin. Those who die from the strenuous life are considered simply not to have been reborn, and their mothers are expected not to weep or grieve for them.

It may be seen that life in the "bush" school is not a tranquil experience but rather a thorough physical, mental, and moral test in which unsuitable traits are eliminated, the individual either undergoing profound modification or meeting his death. It is said that abnormal characters experience no rebirth; weaklings, freaks, and homosexuals do not return. This has elicited some disturbance among the missionaries and humanitarians, but it should cause no lack of elation for the Hootons,[6] for the natives feel that those who cannot endure the test are no loss to society.

Yet a boy is proud of his "bush"-school days, and he reflects over them with fond remembrances. At the completion of the session the chief is informed privately, and he then (as during the whole period) visits the society only in the role of a private citizen. A day or two after his return he sends his representatives to meet the leader and the authorities in a highly ceremonious manner. The boys make a number of demonstrations, covering a day or more. Then there are various examinations administered by the representatives, after which they return to the chief and elders, who are informed of the impressions received. At this time preparations are made for the ceremonial return of the boys to the town. This is usually considered to be of great tribal, and in some instances intertribal, importance.

A type of pavilion is erected within the chief's compound for the reception of the

boys; or, if the chief's court is sufficiently large, it may be decorated elaborately for the purpose. After all these preparations have been completed, the chief and his retinue meet with the leader and the officials of the society, when the formal presentation or return of the forest to the ruler and elders is made. This does not usually occur in the forest itself, and only responsible male citizens are present. Great speeches are made, and sentiments of appreciation are expressed to the leader. After these ceremonies the leader rises, thanks his chief and elders in a brief speech, and finally kneels before the chief (the boys of the school following his example) and, with the palm of his right hand resting on the ruler's knee, makes a statement somewhat as follows: "I pledge loyalty to you and to my tribe. Now I give back your forest. Here am I, and here are your boys." This is followed by great shouting, rejoicing, and the sounding of drums. The chief, sitting in his official chair of state (formerly a stool), lays hands on the leader and replies, "Thank you. I bid you rise." Following this, the chief is escorted to his compound with all the pomp and circumstance befitting a great ruler.

By this time the parents and relatives of the boys, the general public, friends and acquaintances from far and near, have assembled in the town in order to witness the arrival of the boys. The latter, having been ceremoniously washed and having rubbed chalk or clay on their bodies, splendidly clad in their "bush" uniforms, each bearing a long staff, are lined up near the town awaiting the signal to enter. Suddenly the report of a musket or sound of the tribal drum is heard, and amid great shouting and rejoicing the boys begin rushing immediately into all parts of the town, gazing furiously in all directions as if they were warriors anxiously in search of booty.

According to tradition, the boys have the right at this time to beat to death any animal which may be encountered as they rush about the town. Some parents deliberately leave such animals as sheep, goats, and fowl at their doors so that the boys may kill them

[6] See Earnest A. Hooton, *Apes, Men, and Morons* (New York, 1937), e.g., as well as his studies of criminal behavior.

in this manner. Wealthier people may leave even cattle for this purpose. There are at least two native explanations for the custom. One is the idea that the boys, as warriors and adventurers being permitted to enter the town, have the freedom to plunder therein, while the other notion is that they must be given the privilege to demonstrate publicly their manly and courageous spirits. It is said that at present animals other than fowl are rarely left exposed to such destruction.

After this period of license the youths are lined up again and led to a stream, where they take baths and dress in their best clothing. Then they are taken back to the "bush" quietly and secretly by way of a different route. Next they march in orderly and peaceful manner, to the accompaniment of the native guitar, drum, and singing, applauded by the jubilant and anxious spectators, to the pavilion erected for them. In this place they are met once more by their relatives and friends and enjoy the companionship of the distinguished men of the tribe. Gifts are bestowed upon them by relatives and friends. While quartered in this pavilion, they are not permitted to raise their hands to their mouths, but each is fed from a dish by a special servant, for they are considered to be babies, newly reborn. They are retained in the building for four or five days, during which time there are great feasts and much rejoicing. They have many great privileges and may call for and receive the best that can be afforded. This may constitute a burden on their proud parents, who, if they are poor, even incur debts in order to please their boys. In some instances years of preparation are required before a boy can be initiated, so heavy is the cost. This may delay the time until the boy almost reaches full manhood, or even later. However, this expense is connected entirely with the aggregation rites, as there are no fees for attendance in the school.

After these rites have been concluded and sentiments of appreciation have been expressed to the leader, chief, and elders, the boys are returned without ceremony to their parents and are finally taken to their respective homes. They are now full citizens of the society, with legal rights and responsibilities equal to those of all adults. Before being worthy of great leadership, however, a youth must have further experience in the civic and political societies, of which there are five grades.

The elaborate ritual of aggregation fulfils the function of giving effective public expression to the social sentiments associated with the cultural values which the school preserves, enlarges, and passes on to the young people. These rites are therefore educative, for it is through public expression that the sentiments are kept alive and made contagious. The behavior has inherent motivation, as it is bound up intimately with certain basic elements of human nature, such as pride, display, and heroism. Thus the activities of this group are contiguous with those of the general social order, and the *bêlì* may be regarded as an effective educational institution—judged of course, in the light of its cultural setting.

Attention may be directed now to the sister-organization. No great detailed consideration of it seems necessary here, for in organization and operation the *sàndì*, or "society for girls," is parallel to the *bêlì*. However, it is not conducted so far from the town or in so great a space as is the latter. The inclosure for the *sàndì* consists of a large fence constructed of giant forest wood, neatly plastered on both sides with clay and surrounding a spacious campus. It is usually built near one end of the town and, if possible, near a river, so that the girls may wash and bathe without having to go very far and expose themselves to public gaze. Within are constructed several temporary buildings, according to the number of inmates; and, as in the case of the school for boys, the entire structure is burned at the close of the session. The buildings and campus are the *bòndò* proper, indicating privacy, while the society itself is the *sàndì*.

The heavy construction work is done by men, after which everything is given over to the women and the men may have no further concern with the institution. It is considered to be a capital crime if a man should gain knowledge of the activities or interfere with the deliberations.

At the head of the society is the *zó: bà,* "the big *zó:,*" whose position, as that of the chief official of the boys' group, is hereditary. She represents the spirits of the female ancestors, who have left the institution and all the cultural values to their descendants and who are with the latter in the school. She is usually a woman of more than middle age, established in the society, and in position to break her ties with the home and domestic responsibilities during the term of the school. As a representative of the ancestral spirits she may undergo a metamorphosis and become what has been called by Europeans "the dancing devil," due to the fact that she, or a younger substitute, dances on certain occasions completely concealed by a large mask and special dress. There may thus be two persons with this title—the one who rules the school and the other who dances in the form of the spirit. The division may be necessary because the leader may be too old for the strenuous exercise required by the dance. In any case the identity of the masked dancer can never be revealed, as she is symbolically a spirit. There is a special attendant who follows the dancer, continuously praising and giving thanks to the spirit for the benefits which have accrued to the group. This attendant carries a mat, as the dead are wrapped in mats for burial. The active leader is merely the spirit having taken corporeal shape. In all these respects she is similar to the leader of the boys' society.

Next in rank to the leader is an official called the *lèĭ gbà* (with open *e*), who holds the position of vice-leader or assistant leader. Then comes the *lèĭ gbà kpó kpó* (with open *o*). These constitute the leadership of the group and are called "mothers" by the girls. In addition, there is another woman, the *mámbáĭ* (with closed *i*), who supervises and is responsible for the cooking, washing, and general domestic affairs. Among the girls the oldest or first initiated also holds an official position. She is a type of student leader, who calls the girls together for various activities; decides, in consultation with the adult women, the program of work and recreation; and assigns the girls to various groups for these activities. She must be highly respected by her fellow-members, and she takes the lead in every important affair.

There is some uncertainty as to the time during which this society holds its session. It may very well be that the period is practically the same as that of the society for boys (which is the notion of our female informant, who herself was initiated but did not remain for a complete term). She estimates the term as varying from three to seven years, but her figures for both groups are higher than those of her younger brother, who says: "In no case do girls remain in the *sàndĭ* or *bòndò* for more than one year; this term has from ancient times never changed." By way of comparison, Westermann's figures for the Kpelle groups may be cited. He states that the *pórò* in this tribe has a term of six years, while the *sàndĭ* term is only three years.[7] The differences between the social responsibilities and status of males and females may constitute an argument in favor of a briefer session for the latter.

There is not much ceremony at the beginning of the *sàndĭ,* although the girls must undergo clitoridectomy. It appears that the age for entrance is about the same as that for boys and that the actual time of joining likewise may vary according to circumstances.

This institution is very clearly maintained for the purpose of preparing a girl to assume her place as a wife and mother attached primarily to the domestic unit in the social order. The girls are said to be spirits, as all unborn children are, and they smear their faces with a preparation of white clay so as to simulate spirits. This clay must be replenished and replaced when washed off until the session is concluded. It is symbolic of membership in the *sàndĭ,* along with a necklace consisting of a small horn-shaped fruit shell in which a red berry is placed and a

[7] *Op. cit.,* pp. 234 and 256.

string of beads made of cylindrical pieces of wood and worn around the waist. These are removed at the ceremonial washing of the novices at the end of the term.

The girls are instructed in all domestic affairs, such as cooking, the various ways of preserving food, the collection of nonpoisonous mushrooms, medicinal herbs and lore, the preparation of cosmetics, spinning, embroidering, the care of children, and the elements of being good mothers and capable wives, as well as in dancing, singing, storytelling—all that which a native woman is expected to know. Like the boys, they receive new names according to their position and accomplishments in the society; and, like the boys, the weaklings may not experience rebirth.

The aggregation rites are very much the same as those at the close of the society for boys, including the special reception hall, the feasting and rejoicing (except, of course, that the girls do not rush about the town and "plunder" it as the youths do, nor do they bear staffs or wear "bush" uniforms). Upon graduation, in most instances, they are ready for marriage, although in the case of very young girls the marriages may not be consummated physically for some time. Also the girl, unlike the boy, until she has reached middle age or thereabout does not venture to offer her hand in greeting the leader of the school in which she was initiated, even for years after the session has closed. She usually bows in deep respect, resting the palm of her right hand on her knee. The leader responds by placing her hands lightly on the subordinate's shoulder.

The sàndì, which so closely parallels the bêlì, seems to possess the same educational characteristics and suitability as the latter, and both may be rated on equal terms.

It may appear that much of what has been described more closely approaches the ideal native cultural pattern than what is carried out in actual practice. This is no doubt true; but it would not seem to invalidate the conclusion that these institutions, considered in relation to the cultures of which they are a part, are more genuinely educative and efficient than many of the formal schools of occidental culture. There are no cultural lags and "useless knowledge" stored in symbols remote from the contemporary social order. Some of the activities and subject matter of the "bush" school may be rejected on the basis of the standards of modern civilization, but the system should be considered with sympathetic appreciation before missionary or other efforts are made to modify it fundamentally; for no criticism so severe as that which has been made of the French educational system of the recent past (and which seems largely applicable to many of our present-day schools) can readily be made of the native youth trained in the pórô or of this institution in relation to its cultural milieu. It has been said of the French system that

the primary danger of this system of education —very properly qualified as Latin—consists in the fact that it is based on the fundamental psychological error that the intelligence is developed by the learning by heart of text-books. Adopting this view, the endeavour has been made to enforce a knowledge of as many hand-books as possible. From the primary school till he leaves the university a young man does nothing but acquire books by heart without his judgment or personal initiative being ever called into play. Education consists for him in reciting by heart and obeying.[8]

The experience which is gained in the "bush" school would seem to be far less spurious.

[8] Gustave Le Bon, The Crowd (London, 1908), pp. 103-4.

EDUCATION, CHILD-TRAINING, AND CULTURE

SCUDDER MEKEEL

ABSTRACT

This paper discusses the implications of a total cultural approach for what is termed "education," especially for peoples of an alien cultural background. It treats the effects on the individual of the education imposed by his own culture and of one foreign to his culture, discussing the pertinence of these findings for action programs in the education of culturally alien peoples.

Within recent years we have begun to appreciate culture as a totality. The implications of this approach have already started to affect not only those who are studying the individual as a person but also those who are workers in such fields as public administration, social work, and education.[1] Here we shall discuss the implications of the broader psychocultural approach for the field of education, particularly as it affects the education of culturally submerged peoples.

First, let us try to gain some perspective on education in relation to our own society. For us "education" has come to mean that formalized process of knowledge-and-technique transmission which is the special burden of a particular set of institutions we label "educational." In other words, we have isolated from the totality of our culture certain knowledge, techniques, arts, and ideals and have put the primary responsibility for their transmission upon a group of institutions known collectively as our educational system. Not all societies have precipitated out of solution the same parts of their culture, nor have they turned them over to the same type of institutions. Some societies, for instance, have chosen the time of puberty and only the male sex for an intensive period of training in certain aspects of their culture. Stratified societies have often limited formal education to a particular class, as a class of nobles or of priests. As we compare one society with another we find great variation in the material that is selected from a culture to be formally taught, in the age at which the individuals are taught, in the reasons why they have to be taught, in the method of selecting them for learning, and in the type of institutions which are given the educational responsibility.

From this viewpoint, then, we see that formal education does not necessarily influence directly and overwhelmingly the whole culture of a people, nor can it be used to maintain or change every aspect of culture effectively. Quite often, when we become acutely conscious of social and economic problems, we begin to think about the possibility of education as a cure-all; or we agitate for a law to put an end to the difficulties by fiat. We forget that education is only a segment of our entire culture, as is law. Both law and education, to be effective, must first be geared to the actual cultural behavior of individuals and to the particular social structure before either can turn the wheels of change to advantage.

The true place of education as a formalized process in our culture can most readily be grasped by examining the history of the application of our educational system to culturally alien peoples, such as the American Indians. With them the first concerted attempt was made during the latter half of the nineteenth century. At this time boarding-schools were built away from the Indian reservations. In order to fill these schools the children were almost kidnapped. The idea behind the boarding-school program was that if the Indian children were separated from their parents and their Indian environment for a few years and exposed instead to

[1] Scudder Mekeel, "A Social Science Approach to Case Work with the American Indian," *Family*, October, 1937; "Social Science and Reservation Programs," *Indians at Work*, November 15, 1936.

American white education, they would become American whites in their behavior and could then be safely sent back to their reservations. Strangely enough, it was found that by far the majority returned to Indian ways, or went "back to the blanket," as it was called.

The reasoning of the administrators of this policy had evidently been that, since American white children were educated in school, Indian children would become like American whites if subjected to the same influences. Two extremely important factors had been overlooked—factors which we are only beginning to consider in our educational programs. The first was that the Indian children had already been subjected to training during the most formative period in their lives—that is, the first six years.[2] Furthermore, this training had been in their native language and by their native techniques and ideals. The second neglected factor was that, regardless of how much or how little of American white culture had penetrated while they were in boarding-school, the Indian children with extremely few exceptions returned to their own communities, which, aside from language, upheld institutions, standards of behavior, and ideals different from those supported by the boarding-school education. Even if white standards had made a deep impression, it never occurred to anyone to ask what an Indian youth would have gained by acting like an American white among his own native people. He certainly would have been cut off from all human contact within his natal community. It was not "savagery" that sent him back to the blanket, but rather the yearning, which we all share, for contact with our own kind. The boarding-school experience merely cut into, and interrupted for a time, the main stream of an Indian child's education.

Therefore, without questioning the potent force of education, it can be stated that, in so far as producing or maintaining a cul-

ture is concerned, it is only one such force. Education cannot be expected to carry the whole burden of cultural transmission or change. We have come to an appreciation of this fact within the past decade.

Next, from the standpoint of culture as an operational totality, we shall have to reexamine other assumptions in the educational field. For example, in those instances where we apply the educational system of our society to peoples of a differing culture, we sometimes attempt to select choice bits of that culture for preservation as it begins to change. In fact, we often think rather sentimentally of the "cultural heritage" of immigrant groups or of preliterate peoples. By "cultural heritage" we may mean anything from art forms to a folk or tribal costume. We think that there must be some way of preserving the "best" of the "old" and of adding it to the "best" of the dominant cultural environment. This view would be justified if each culture were made up of separate pieces which carried intrinsic and absolute values and which could be interchanged indiscriminately with pieces from other societies. Unfortunately, every culture has a matrix, a configuration, into which the pieces fit. Actually, the "pieces" are not pieces at all but are mainly our own abstractions.[3]

For education, as well as for other action agencies, a better approach to this particular question of change in submerged cultures is to look on culture as an attempt to solve the problems which every society faces —problems of getting a living, problems of easing human relationships, and problems of orientation to life.[4] An immigrant group or a preliterate people swamped by Euro-American influences must revise its customary solutions in the face of a changed environment. For such groups the problems go

[3] Scudder Mekeel, "Beaded Necklaces [and Culture]," *Indians at Work.*

[4] See Robert Redfield and Lloyd Warner, "Cultural Anthropology and Modern Agriculture," *Farmers in a Changing World: Yearbook of Agriculture, 1940* (Washington, D.C.: Government Printing Office, 1941), pp. 983–93.

[2] Scudder Mekeel, "An Anthropologist's Observations on Indian Education," *Progressive Education,* XIII, No. 3 (1936), 151–59.

far beyond a moral or an aesthetic "best" in choice of cultural material for their solution.

Even the problem of preserving its identity may become acute to a submerged people. Such a group may seize on one or more of its older cultural forms as a symbol of its distinctiveness from the surrounding peoples. This may be a varying bit of dress taken over from the older costume, a special way of preparing food, or a particular economic pattern. Thus, a rural nationality group within the United States may insist on certain agricultural techniques even though they are inefficient. The county agricultural extension agent, who knows of more practical methods, tackles the problem with confidence of success. But in spite of his urgent advice the people are obdurate. They tell him that they farmed that way in the old country, or that their way is all right. The county agent ends by feeling that he has to deal with an obstinate, stupid group. However, the situation is far from being purely economic. The very identity of the group appears to be at stake, because these farming methods are its symbol of distinctness. Their former country has quite likely advanced in its farming techniques, but the immigrants think of what those techniques were at the time they left. Hence, in such instances, new farming methods cannot be taught merely in terms of their efficiency. The total situation must be understood.

Of course, some peoples attempt complete and rapid submergence of themselves as a group in the dominant society, rather than preservation of identity. Here, also, certain aspects of culture are seized on; but in this case it is those of the dominant society, and especially those aspects that symbolize that society for the submerged group. Or these two tendencies—to preserve group identity and to lose it—frequently occur in a single community. Then there occurs a polarization of the old way and the new way for the same segment of culture. For instance, on the Pine Ridge Indian Reservation, South Dakota, the Teton-Dakota Indians feel the necessity of following a re-

spectable wedding with a feast. The host, however, has the alternative of a Christian or an Indian feast. One symbolizes the American way and the other the Dakota. The main criterion seems to be chicken for one and dog meat for the other, whereas Indian pemmican and American pie could both be served at either. The two latter, pie and pemmican, have not been singled out as symbolically Indian or American. In other words, only certain cultural items were selected to carry the burden of meaning.

Thus culture is not an index of easily movable items. It must be viewed as a meaningful whole, just as the particular situation in which a group of people carrying a culture find themselves must be looked at in its totality. Broad educational plans must be adjusted to the situation and the culture as they are and then be carried on from that point. We cannot yet predict just what aspects of culture will be retained in a particular acculturation situation. We know only that there are processes involved, both psychological and cultural, which preclude our calling them haphazard or accidental in nature.

So far I have tried to relate education and its problems with alien or folk peoples to culture as a dynamic entity. Now I should like to shift the emphasis to the impact of culture on the individual. How does society impose its culture on the new individuals born into it, and what part does education play in this process? For our society it is becoming increasingly apparent that cultural conditioning of the individual begins at an early age and involves a rather severe and deep-set modification of the impulse-life. This was first brought to light in systematic fashion by Sigmund Freud, although the cultural implications have only recently become clear.[5] We have next to examine what happens to the growing individual in other cultures. This phase of the work is only in

5 Scudder Mekeel, "Clinic and Culture," *Journal of Abnormal and Social Psychology*, XXX, No. 3 (1935), 292–300; "A Psychoanalytic Approach to Culture," *Journal of Social Philosophy*, II, No. 3 (1937), 232–36.

its beginning. In so far as our society is concerned, formal education is but one process for conditioning individuals to the culture within which they will operate as adults. The most fundamental conditioning has already occurred during the early period before a child enters school for the first time. The molding of the child's personality is done primarily by the parents, who are an infant's first representatives of the culture into which he has been born. This parent-child transmission of culture for our society is no new fact, but the specific processes by which such transmission takes place are still not completely appreciated. The significance for education—especially for education of culturally alien peoples—is far reaching. For there appears to be a definite relationship between child-training and the culture which a child must eventually assume as an adult. If this is so, then our educational system, which is part of our culture, may not work on the child who has already been trained in a differing cultural situation and by different methods and standards. For, even in changing cultures, older child-training methods may persist long after the adult culture to which they were originally related has radically changed. This also has its implications for educational procedure with such groups.

It may be well at this point to examine a specific people. Let us take the Western Sioux, or Teton-Dakota tribe. These Indians, in the old days, were characterized by feather war-bonnets, skin tipis, sign language, buffalo-hunting, and the Sun Dance. To us and to Europeans the Plains Indians, of which the Dakota were a part, have come to represent *the* American Indian. At the present time the Sioux Indians, aside from the physical characteristics of race, present to outward appearance, in terms of clothes, houses, utensils, and tools, a picture not very divergent from that of the surrounding whites on a low economic level. In spite of the superficial likeness, however, one is struck by the different attitudes, thought patterns, and behavior. After over a hundred and fifty years of fairly constant white

contact the socially "full-blooded" Teton-Dakota still retain behavior patterns which are at variance with those of American whites. For example, the old prestige value in the *release* of wealth, instead of its accumulation as with us, still persists. A man who saves for a rainy day is looked down on by his own people, and even his children[6] may be ostracized by the others in school. This attitude toward wealth is so antithetical to ours that it has caused much trouble to educators who have been trying to inculcate our ways of life in terms of frugality and thrift. However, in spite of the persistence of many behavior patterns and attitudes, the Dakota culture as such is gone, just as has the buffalo, which was its economic base. Why is it that the supporting attitudes and values have not disappeared as well?

The answer lies primarily in the methods of child-training. Several years ago the writer had the opportunity to arrange a field trip with a child analyst among the Sioux. In the very cursory study of child-training which we made, it became apparent that a relationship existed between present-day methods and the old adult culture, in so far as it could be reconstructed.[7] In fact, the particular type of child-training current seemed to have changed far less than had the culture. Not having realized its full significance, neither the government nor the missionary educators had paid much attention to the particular methods used in bringing up the children.

Several features of Teton-Dakota child-training stand out in contrast to our own patterns. For instance, parents rarely, if ever, threatened their children directly with punishment. If they did not behave, they

[6] Scudder Mekeel, *The Economy of a Modern Teton-Dakota Community* ("Yale University Publication in Anthropology," No. 6 [1936]); "Teton-Dakota Acculturation," unpublished paper read before the American Anthropological Association, December, 1931.

[7] Erick H. Erickson, "Observations on Sioux Education," *Journal of Psychology*, VII (1939), 101–66.

were threatened by being told that someone would get after them or take them away. This might be either a mythical character or an old man in the community who had assumed the role of frightening children. Nowadays the "white man" is also used as a bogey. The Dakota parent also rarely strikes a child. Thus the Dakota child is not estranged from his parent by fear of punishment, as is often the case in our own society.

It was further observed that the Sioux child was not systematically estranged from the functions and desires of his own body, as is the case with our children. Sphincter and anal control were not made an issue. The child really worked the problem out by himself at an age when he was capable of doing so. In addition, the Dakota parents attempted to make their children feel self-reliant and secure. Psychoanalytic psychology has shown that the particular attitudes of parents toward the child, the child's body, and its functions appear to have a direct relationship to the retentive and eliminative modalities in the child's developing character. Not only are such factors in child-training connected with adult character, but also they seem to be related to the general tenor of adult culture as well. Certainly the eliminative-retentive modes that would be engendered by the particular type of Dakota child-training fit, as a character pattern, the Dakota emphasis on generosity and the prestige-value placed on wealth-release. This is further reinforced by the great respect of Dakota parents for a child's property.

Material in Abraham Kardiner's *The Individual and His Society* lends support to this conclusion.[8] For instance, certain factors of Tanalan culture in Madagascar appear to be bound up with aspects of Tanalan child-training. Unlike the situation among the Dakota, excretory control is imposed severely and at an early age. Adult Tanala character definitely presents features which we not only have come to associate with such early and severe training but which also are recognized

[8] New York, 1939.

as important for proper adaptation to Tanala culture. Such features include, particularly for the younger sons, a premature development of responsibility, a sense of obligation, conscientiousness, and unswerving loyalty.

It is becoming increasingly apparent that in every culture individuals are psychologically modified for participation in their culture. The primary milieu for such training during the individual's early years is the family and its extensions. However, there is great variation from culture to culture as to what methods are used for conditioning the individual, as to who does the conditioning, as to how deeply controls on the impulse life are imposed, and as to what aspects of the developing personality are seized upon either for stimulation or for repression. Psychologically, the problem needs to be studied among varying cultures from the viewpoint of specific character formation in, and individual adjustment to, specific cultural environments. For education it would be very helpful to know the genius of personality configuration in an alien culture so that objectives and classroom methods could be adjusted accordingly. In its relation to education this is as important as the totality of the culture itself.

Therefore, if we are to employ our educational system intelligently and successfully among peoples who differ culturally from ourselves, we shall have to keep several problems in mind. The first and most important is for us to be absolutely clear in our own minds as to what we as the majority group are trying to accomplish, and why we have certain special objectives. For example, up to fifteen years ago we tried to make all immigrants and Indians into "Americans" in thought, action, and language. We have recently become uncertain of this attempt and have started to talk about the enrichment of American life through cultural contributions of immigrants and Indians. Now we talk less about the complete blotting-out of all alien cultural characteristics. Yet, as our ideals and objectives change, so must our action programs. And it is always the better part of wisdom to know not only what our values actually are but also what are the underlying causes of those attitudes which motivate our action programs for the "aliens" in our midst.

The second problem, after we are certain of our objectives, is to plan a realistic action program. Part of such a program is to relate education directly to the actual lives of the immigrant or folk group. Education should help to strengthen and guide the transplanted culture. Therefore, we should understand such factors as the prevalent methods of child-training how these methods are related to both the contemporary submerged culture and the adult personality configuration, and how these factors differ from those in our culture. Again, we should understand the alien culture in terms of its "wholeness" and be conversant with the ways in which its institutions are adapted or not adapted to carry on in the American scene. We should know not only what the economic resources are, but what the habit patterns for exploiting them are; and, finally, what are the capabilities and interests of the people, especially those which can be developed for their well-being and support. It is only at this point of understanding that we can really begin to plan and put into effect an intelligent and successful educational program, in terms of objectives, values, curriculum, budget, and personnel.

University of Wisconsin

EDUCATION FOR SURVIVAL: THE JEWS

LOUIS WIRTH

ABSTRACT

The strong emphasis and high valuation which the Jews have historically placed on learning created a common consciousness and coherence which assured their survival as a separate group despite their wide dispersion. Jewish education until the Enlightenment consisted mainly of rote learning and casuistic interpretation of sacred texts. It remained medieval in spirit longest where the opportunities for participation in capitalist secular culture were most restricted. In more recent times the increasing migration of Jews to the urban areas of advanced capitalistic nations has tended to weaken the influence of religious education with all but the nationalist groups. For the most part, Jewish learning now serves only as a supplement to the secular public education. The contrast between the highly urbanized, sophisticated Jews and the Negroes is great. Nonetheless, as minority peoples they have many common problems of adjustment and orientation.

It is one of the occupational psychoses of schoolmen to be afflicted by a school-centered conception of the world and of education. There is perhaps more reason for imputing a great significance to the school in the case of the Jews than with most other peoples, for to speak of the Jews as "the people of the book" is more than a mere euphemism. Similarly, to ascribe a high value to education as a social function in the Jewish community is not just a historical exaggeration, for there is ample evidence to show that, from biblical days on, education, whatever variable content may have been given to the term, has been extraordinarily highly esteemed in the Jewish community.

EDUCATION AND SOCIAL CONTINUITY

If we think of education as part of a process by which societies keep themselves alive and renew themselves in the face of changing membership, changing locality, and changing circumstance, it is pertinent to ask what education has contributed to the survival of the Jews; for, despite the fact that even before the Nazis' massacres there were fewer than twenty millions of Jews out of a total of about two billions of human beings, they are still very much alive. It is futile to ask why a social group seeks to survive in the face of threats to its existence from without and disintegration from within. We do know that everywhere societies do manifest this tendency, which they seem to have in common with living organisms. We must leave it to the theologians to determine whether men are immortal, but there can be no doubt that societies are immortal. They cannot die even if they try, for, though the entire membership of a group be exterminated, some remnant, at least, of the culture that made them a group will make its influence felt, if on no one else but their would-be exterminators.

There are, indeed, human aggregations that are not societies, or that were societies but have ceased to be peoples distinguished by a body of heritages, values, and attitudes which bind them together into a social entity. The Jews, despite their changing fortunes throughout their long history, have never ceased being such an entity. Whether they would have it so or not, certain individuals were treated as Jews and hence regarded themselves as Jews. On the other hand, the few millions of Jews who have survived the travail of history represent only a remnant of the stock that must have descended from their ancient forebears. As the saying goes, if we go back far enough, we will find that we are all kin to one another. Even Hitler, anthropologically speaking, might, upon genealogical analysis, turn out to be a non-Aryan, reluctant though the Jews are to press the claim. In determining who is a Jew, even he went no further in his genealogical test than the non-Aryan grandmother; and it is said that Goering, when reproached by his fellow-Nazis for employing a general of undoubted partly Jewish ancestry for a leading position in the German air force, said: "In this country I determine who is a Jew."

There are varying theories as to the role education has played in the life of the Jews. As we examine the historical record, we find that many different kinds of activity have been called education, and still more widely different activities not called education have been truly educative. Looked at from one point of view, all there is to a society is its self-perpetuation, the most important part of which, even more important than physical procreation, is the communication among its members in time and in space. If by education we mean not only that communication by which we transmit an experience from one individual or generation to another but the process by which we arrive at common experiences and values, then we must conclude that all life is educative to the extent that it is social. It is this, I take it, that Dewey has in mind when he says:

Society not only continues to exist *by* transmission, *by* communication, but it may fairly be said to exist *in* transmission, *in* communication. There is more than a verbal tie between the words common, community, and communication.[1]

Since the Jews, from the days of the dispersion on, have been scattered throughout the world, the criterion for determining the scope of their society is the extent of their intercommunication. Indeed, in the absence of a concentrated settlement, of political unity, or of racial identity, it was only through communication that the widely dispersed remnants of Israel ever held together. We must add, however, that the frequent interchange of communication among the distant Jewish settlements in the East, in Africa, in the New World, and in the various parts of Europe did more than merely preserve the cohesion of a religious and ethnic community; it furnished the bases of the peculiar economic and intellectual advantage which the Jews enjoyed in comparison with their indigenous neighbors. This constant traffic of men, of goods, and of ideas provided the source of the continuous renewal of the culture and prevented it from lapsing into the parochialism and stagnation so characteristic of the Dark Ages in Europe.

EDUCATION AND SOCIAL CHANGE

Every system of education must be seen against the background of the social order of which it is a part. The social milieu in which Jewish education has operated has been highly diverse. And yet the educational objectives, institutions, and methods which may be called Jewish have persisted and have been cherished as sacrosanct virtually as they were molded in a milieu as alien to the world in which the Jews now live as Scholasticism is incongruent with the spirit of modern science and secular, free, empirical inquiry. Every system of education inevitably molds the individuals who come under its influence according to a pattern. It seeks to create a definite human type. The Jewish educational system of the Middle Ages did this as effectively as any system, even that of the Jesuits, ever seems to have done.

The type that it produced was the hairsplitting dialectician equipped to quibble about the meaning of texts culled from the Bible and overlaid with the pronouncements of the rabbis as compiled in the Talmud. The *Yeshiva Bachur*, who was the end-product of this educational formula, even prided himself on his impracticality. The world of actual human social life was extraneous to him. The community conspired to shelter him from its storms and its mundane problems. The wife to whom he was married at a very early age labored to support him while he browsed over the books, his body, by the time he reached adulthood, being so unfit for the physical rigors of life that he was little more than an invalid. But, in the measure that he immersed himself in the sacred books and mastered their contents by sheer rote learning, he shed luster upon his

[1] John Dewey, *Democracy and Education* (New York, 1916), p. 5.

family, his community, and, indeed, upon Jewry everywhere.

The saving grace of this type of education was that it only indirectly touched the majority of the able-bodied males and even more remotely the women. It deliberately set out to educate men for an order which was long past if it ever truly existed—an order which was the product of a romantic leap into an imaginary past and a utopian future. It was indeed education for futility. And yet this ceremonial form of education served a very important function for the community even though it made sacrificial victims of the individuals who were subjected to it. For the masses of Jews it made an otherwise miserable existence more endurable. It kept alive and insured the continuity of a tradition and thereby welded a scattered, haunted people into an enduring unity capable of holding intact its cultural identity in the face of overwhelming odds.

HISTORICAL PERIODS IN JEWISH EDUCATION

The principal imprint of education upon the Jewish people was made by the educational system which developed in their European communities during the Middle Ages. The education which was dominant during the Middle Ages, however, rested in part upon the foundations that were laid during the biblical period, extending approximately to the second century B.C. The core of education during this period consisted of the Torah. The emphasis laid upon education in the biblical period is too well known to warrant exposition.[2] The duty that evolved upon the parents to instruct the young in the Commandments is indi-

cated by the injunction, "And thou shalt teach them diligently unto thy children" (Deut. 6:7), and the corresponding duty of the young to seek this instruction may be indicated by, "Hear, my son, the instruction of thy father and forsake not the teaching of thy mother" (Prov. 1:8). Isaiah assumed reading and writing to be common in Jerusalem in 680 B.C. Education in the biblical period was so intimately involved with religion that a distinction between these two spheres of life can scarcely be made. It may be said that, without the inculcation and transmission of the religious heritage which was so central a part of Jewish social life in biblical times, the fate of the Jews after the dispersion would certainly have been different, for, as Saadya ben Josef (born in Egypt in 892) said, "Our people is a people only because of the Torah."

The second period in the history of Jewish education, overlapping in part with the biblical period, was the talmudic era, extending from approximately the fourth century B.C. to the end of the fifth century A.D. To a large extent the content of education in this period was colored by the nostalgic longing for a return to a homeland. The development of the Talmud itself, consisting as it did of commentaries on and interpretations and codifications of the Law, illustrates the extent to which the life of the Jews in the Diaspora was woven into a unity by an appeal to sanctions and loyalties which found their way into documents. The unity thus achieved was fortified by a belief in common descent. The Torah became a "portable fatherland" in exile, and the Talmud served as a fence around the Torah. The creed of the Jews in the period of dispersion was not so much connected with a city or a land as with a book. The emphasis upon the sharing of the content of that book, therefore, became an understandably powerful device in molding a common consciousness among people living under widely varying circumstances in widely scattered territories.

It was expected of the father during this period that he would teach his son the Law

[2] Israel Abrahams, *Jewish Life in the Middle Ages* (2d ed.; London, 1932); Salo W. Baron, *A Social and Religious History of the Jews* (3 vols.; New York, 1937); Georg Caro, *Sozial- und Wirtschaftsgeschichte der Juden im Mittelalter und in der Neuzeit* (2 vols.; Frankfurt, 1908, 1920); Simon M. Dubnow, *History of the Jews in Russia and Poland* (3 vols.; Philadelphia, 1916); Moritz Güdemann, *Geschichte des Erziehungswesen und der Kultur der abendlandischen Juden während des Mittelalters und der neueren Zeit* (3 vols.; Vienna, 1880–88).

and the Commandments as well as a trade, and it is even reported that where circumstances allowed he was to teach him to swim.

Study combined with a secular occupation is a fine thing, for the double labor makes sin to be forgotten. All study of the Law with which no work goes, will in the end come to naught and bring sin in its train.[3]

The actual practice of teaching, however, did not always conform to this talmudic injunction. Often it overemphasized the inculcation of conformity to dogma and ritual—a dogma which must frequently have seemed archaic, considering the difference between the time and condition of its genesis and the mode of life for the control of which it was invoked.

In the talmudic period, as in the biblical period, there existed a noticeable difference between education for boys and education for girls. It was the men rather than the women who were the responsible members of the religious community and who, hence, were given the benefits of formal instruction. Girls were rarely trained in anything but the domestic occupations. Even in the family ritual and ceremonial the male was dominant. Filial piety, however, was encouraged; and, even though the mother was not the responsible head of the household, she enjoyed the respect and reverence of the children and often imbibed the group heritages and learning through oral rather than written mediums.

The medieval period of Jewish education extends from approximately the sixth to the end of the eighteenth century, for the end of the Middle Ages for the Jews did not come until the culmination of the Enlightenment in Europe. Progressively the Jews in the Middle Ages found themselves more widely dispersed throughout the Western world and at the same time more isolated in their local communities. Their life took on more and more the character of a transitional stage torn between the memory of a glorious past and a messianic belief in an equally bright future. Their world was becoming more and more fictional. As Benjamin Disraeli put it: "A race that persists in celebrating their vintage although they have no fruits to gather, would regain their vineyards."[4]

THE SOCIAL EVALUATION OF EDUCATION

Indicative of the increasing importance of education in this period are the many rabbinical pronouncements extolling the virtues of education. "As long as the voices of children are heard chirping the words of the Law in the houses of worship and learning, the Jewish people are safe against all foreign aggressors."[5] "Take heed of the children of the poor, because from them will issue forth the Torah."[6] Upon the extensive store of book learning was piled a rich layer of lore. Whereas the former was transmitted through the school, the latter was communicated through the channels of intimate family living in the cramped ghetto communities.

The violent waves of persecution which frequently swept down upon the scattered communities of Jews in the Western world tended to accentuate the nostalgic intellectual feeding upon the past and the romantic elaboration of the hopes for the future. Dreams turned a gnawing sense of inferiority into visions of triumph and certainty of survival. The survival of the remnant of Israel was regarded as essential for the realization of the messianic hope. The solidarity of a widely dispersed society became more and more evidenced by the voluntary obedience to the edicts of distinguished rabbis—distinguished not through their worldly power but through their reputation for learning. Many of these rabbis enjoyed a wide territorial authority extending far beyond the village or town where they had their seat.

The domestic, the communal, the reli-

---

[3] B. Talmud Abot 2:2, quoted in G. F. Moore, *Judaism* (1927), II, 128.

[4] Disraeli, *Tancret or the New Crusade* (London, 1894), p. 388.

[5] Talmud Babli, Gen. r. 65:16.

[6] Talmud Babli, Ned. 81a.

gious, and particularly the educational aspects of the life of the Jewish communities combined to furnish not so much an escape from the hostile world as a compensation for it. In his learning, be it ever so useless and archaic, the outcast and despised Jew could inwardly rise above his untutored persecutors. Since the Jews came to Europe as strangers and to a large extent remained strangers by virtue of their different descent, culture, and occupations, they found both the necessity and the opportunity to develop a distinctive educational system. Their way of life differed radically from that of their neighbors, and their religion was the central criterion upon which their differentiated way of life rested. Often they had good reason to be convinced that they were the bearers of a civilization more advanced than that of their Christian neighbors.

The Jew was tied to his Christian neighbor, however tenuously, almost exclusively by the bonds of *commercium* rather than by the bonds of *connubium*, which ultimately are required to blend the many into one both biologically and culturally. In the Middle Ages the Jews had to contend not only against the general xenophobia of the population but also against a state religion from which they were excluded as infidels. Perhaps if the Jews had gone (and to the extent that they have gone) to countries on a higher level of civilization than their own, they would have been (and have been) disappearing as a distinct group. If the Jews had pursued the path of *connubium*, which their religion forbade, as did other strangers, there would probably be no hatred of the Jews today. But there would also be no Jews. In addition to whatever internal factors of cohesion operated upon them, of which their education was perhaps the most important, it was the xenophobia of their neighbors, their exclusion from full participation in the life about them, and their persecution that insured their survival. As the founder of modern Zionism put it: "We are a people—the enemy makes us a people."[7]

The recognition that education has been

one of the prime forces making for the survival of the Jews is amply recorded in educational history.[8]

As Dr. Isaac Landman says:

The primary function of the Synagogue, even before it became a *Beth Hatfillah*, a house of prayer, is a *Beth Hamidrash*, a house of study. Now, if we are to seek an aim, a purpose, an objective for religious education without channeling these into a prime definition, we seem to have them here: to *educate for survival.*[9]

The education in the case of the Jews designed to bring about this survival was an education in a way of life, changing with the changing circumstances in which the Jews found themselves in different times and places, but rooted in the Torah and the Talmud (which literally means "teaching") and in the accumulated lore of centuries.

Not only during the period when the ghetto was the characteristic mode of communal life of the Jews, but even after partial emancipation, when the winds of secularism began to disintegrate the isolated Jewish community, education among the Jews was primarily religious education. The obligation of the individual to seek this education and of the community to provide the facilities for it is emphasized time and again in

---

[7] Theodore Herzl, *A Jewish State* (London, 1934).

[8] See Isaac Landman, "Survival Values in Jewish Religious Education," *Religious Education*, XXXIV (July–September, 1939), 135–42. Landman quotes, among others, Elmer Harrison Wilds, who stresses that "education has been the prime force in their national and racial existence. . . . . The greatest lesson to be drawn from the history of the Jews is that a strict adherence to an educational system based upon a peculiarly high religious and moral ideal has preserved the unity of the race in a way that no political system could approximate. The salvation of this people has been due to its education" (*The Foundations of Modern Education*, pp. 60–77). Landman also cites Thomas Davidson to the effect that "one lesson, above all, Jewish education has to teach us, that the most important element in all education is moral discipline. The Greek with his art and his philosophy, and the Roman with his law and his statesmanship have vanished from the face of the earth; but the Jew, with his moral discipline, with his Torah, and his Talmud, is still with us, as strong and ready for life's struggle as ever" (*A History of Education*, p. 85).

[9] *Op. cit.*

the codes and edicts of the rabbis as well as in the fundamental law which centuries of dispersed Jewish communities embraced as a living entity. Maimonides, one of the best representatives of rabbinic Judaism in the twelfth century, stated this individual obligation as follows:

Every man in Israel is obliged to devote himself to study, be he rich or poor, of good health or afflicted by diseases, a youngster or a doddering elder; even if he be a beggar living on charity or a father burdened with a family, he ought to set aside time for study by day and night. . . . . Among the greatest scholars of Israel there were wood-pickers and water-carriers, even blind men, and they nevertheless studied the Torah by day and night. . . . . Up to what age is one obliged to study the Torah? Unto the day of death. . . . .[10]

And those who were not able to study were enjoined to provide the means whereby others could do so. Maimonides may be taken again as the example of the rabbis who declared it to be the duty of the community to

appoint elementary school teachers in every state, district and town. A town which fails to send children to school shall be excommunicated until it appoints school teachers. If it persists in its failure, it shall be outlawed, because the entire universe is maintained only by the breath of school children.[11]

In the medieval Jewish community, while wealth conferred prestige and power, it

was effectively counterbalanced—indeed, more often than not far outweighed—by the influence and social dignity of descent (*yihus*), piety, and especially learning.[12]

But piety and learning did not

create any distinct, superior class of charismatic priests such as existed in the contemporary privileged Catholic clergy. . . . . We may readily discount some of the widespread exaggerated notions of the rabbi's position in the ghetto

community, as fostered by both the predominantly rabbinic orientation of extant sources and the romanticizing modern scholarship. We must nevertheless admit that at least until the rise of the early modern *parnasim* who ruled the communities of Holland, Germany and Poland with an iron hand, the leadership rested principally with scholars and men distinguished by good deeds or renowned ancestry, which itself was largely estimated on the basis of scholarly or pious deserts.[13]

The emphasis upon rabbinic studies to the disadvantage of biblical and linguistic studies was accentuated as the status of the Jews in medieval society was lowered and as their segregation became more complete. At times the dialectical method of talmudic instruction, especially in the north, was carried to absurd extremes. This was particularly unfortunate in view of the fact that the general overemphasis upon intellectualism in the ghetto already tended to produce unbalanced types of personality.

There were wide variations both in the esteem in which learning was held and in the methods of education as between the different regions of Jewish settlement. On the whole, the rabbinical tradition was strongest in northern and eastern Europe, and weakest in the south and in the west. Where the Jew had the opportunity to participate in the rising secular culture, the sciences and the professions, trade and commerce, the educational content and methods of the ghetto community were forsaken for the richer opportunities without.

CONTEMPORARY JEWISH EDUCATION

The advance of capitalistic civilization in Europe, associated as it was with the rationalization and secularization of life, did even more to undermine the traditional Jewish communal life than that of European society in general. The new liberal atmosphere opened the door to assimilation and weakened the ancient and once-powerful religious sanctions without giving the Jews a virile national culture to fall back upon. What is more, in more recent times the trend of Jew-

[10] Salo W. Baron, *The Jewish Community*, II (Philadelphia, 1942), 169.

[11] *Ibid.*, p. 170.

[12] Salo W. Baron, "Capitalism and Jewish Fate," *Menorah Journal*, XXX (summer, 1942), 128.

[13] *Ibid.*

ish migration has been overwhelmingly in the direction of the most advanced capitalistic countries and in these countries into the most urbanized areas. The proletarianization of the Jews and the associated influences of socialism, trade-unionism, and class consciousness have further weakened the force of the old religious tradition and with it the religiously sponsored education. A notable exception is found among nationalist, particularly Zionist, sections of the Jewish population, where a distinctly Jewish education continues to be provided for the young.

The traditional type of school among the Jews from medieval times on was the *cheder*, which, if it became imposing in size, somewhat like a modern consolidated school, was called a *Talmud Torah*.[14] Instruction consisted in reading and writing Hebrew and in memorizing texts by means of mechanical repetition and rote learning. By the time the boy reached the age of ten to fourteen he graduated to a secondary school, or *yeshiva*, where he studied the Talmud and was subjected to dialectical drill. This teaching was a unique medium for continuing the Jewish religion unchanged—embalmed—from generation to generation and for maintaining the Jews together as a separate cultural unit in a hostile world.

This form of teaching, which until recently was continued virtually unchanged in eastern Europe and in some of the cities of the United States, concentrated on literary knowledge to the exclusion of science and art. It had no place for sport or recreation, which among pious Jews, as among the Puritans, were regarded as distractions from the serious business of life and learning. The place of games in these schools was taken by intellectual acrobatics, which were thought

[14] For a summary account of contemporary Jewish education see Arthur Ruppin, *The Jews in the Modern World* (London, 1934), chap. xix; *Jewish Education*, now in its fourteenth volume; Israel Chipkin, "25 Years of Jewish Education in the United States," *American Jewish Yearbook*, XXXVIII (Philadelphia, 1936), 27–116; Samuel Dinin, *Judaism in a Changing Civilization* ("Teachers College Contributions to Education," No. 563 [New York: Columbia University, 1933]).

to be conducive to the further development of the mind in the subtleties of talmudic casusitry. When it is recalled that until approximately the eighteenth or nineteenth century compulsory education was virtually unknown to Christian children and that, in contrast, the Jewish boy was confined to the *cheder* from approximately the fourth or fifth year on, during most of the day virtually every day in the year, the long-run effect upon the differences in personality of the respective groups must have been serious. The ideal product of this system of education was the *matmid*, or the young man who devoted himself to the study of Hebrew literature day after day without intermission. While such a person was stamped with the gravity of a joyless youth, he was a person who entertained no doubts about his moral and intellectual convictions and loyalty to his people.

In addition to these elementary and secondary educational institutions, there were higher educational institutions or seminaries devoted to the training of advanced scholars. It was in these institutions that the most serious rumblings of the secular influence were felt, and it was these that were most ready to make the readjustments to a changing world situation. It is generally among the emancipated intellectuals who have intimate contact with the outside world that we must expect the critique of the established dogma to be most vocal. Thus, for instance, it was men like Moses Mendelssohn and his circle, who were moving along the margins of the European world of the Enlightenment, who accomplished some of the outstanding modern reforms in Jewish education. From the higher institutions in turn there reverberated in our own time upon the elementary and secondary institutions the more modern and scientific ideas concerning educational content and method. In the larger cities of America and of Europe today and, to a lesser extent, in the smaller communities Jewish religious education is proceeding along lines not so far different from the most progressive educational methods of the country at large. Increasingly the teachers and administrators in these institutions are trained according to modern principles, and, if they lack the fervor of old, they have at least mastered the techniques of the new day.

Whereas the Jews of western Europe and the United States have generally replaced their parochial schools with public education, in so far as the latter was accessible to them, and have supplemented this by religious schools, in other sections of the widely dispersed Jewish settlements the Jewish community has by choice or necessity maintained a complete and separate educational system.

In the typical American community Jewish religious education shows decided variations, depending upon the structuring of the community. In general the oldest settlers and economically the most successful part of the Jewish population belong to the *reformed* religious congregation. Jewish education in that part of the community is not unlike the Sunday school training given in modern Christian churches, supplemented occasionally by the study of Hebrew and by Jewish history and contemporary problems. It is supplementary religious education facilitating or at least not seriously obstructing assimilation.

A second form of religious instruction is found among the *conservative* part of the community, generally comprising the second-generation eastern Europeans. In this part of the religious community customs and rituals have only been partly modified to conform with what are regarded as the necessities and conveniences of life and retain most of the religious tradition of the community from which the settlers originally came. To a large extent this section of the Jewish community is Zionistic in its political orientation. The religious education in this group consists of supplementary week day and Sunday school. It lays more stress than does the reform group upon Hebrew, upon indoctrination in Jewish traditions, and upon a nationalistic outlook.

The most recent settlers (excluding the bulk of the refugees from Germany) represent the *orthodox* section of the Jewish community and are composed largely of first-generation eastern European immigrants. Until recently this group had deviated least from the educational pattern represented by the *cheder*, the *Talmud Torah*, and the *yeshiva*. The emphasis in Jewish education among this group is upon the preservation of the cultural and religious integrity of the Jewish community.

A fourth group is the secular, moderately nationalist, and sometimes politically radical proletarian section of the Jewish community emphasizing Yiddish as a folk language. It is upon this group largely that the Yiddish press continues to rely for its existence. In many respects this group conceives of itself as an American ethnic minority, whose future is bound up with the problem of other minorities, but particularly with the problem of the wage-earning masses.

In many American cities the religious education of most or all of these groups is administered by a centralized body known as the Jewish Board of Education, assuring the maintenance of high standards of teaching, of teacher-training and selection, and of school administration. While allowing for a wide range of difference in religious beliefs, the general policy of these boards has been to maintain the continuity of Jewish traditions and the basic tenets of the Jewish religion. However modern their educational policy may be in other respects, the general objective has been to maintain the Jews as a separate social and religious group and to rekindle a waning loyalty to the Jewish people.

It should be noted that in the contemporary American and European Jewish communities the school is supplemented as a solidifying agency by Jewish social centers, philanthropic institutions, recreational agencies, religious institutions, burial societies, clubs, lodges, and a host of other agencies, including the press. Together with the schools they are in part the product of past isolation and tend, though inadvertently, to perpetuate this isolation.

EDUCATION FOR INDIVIDUAL ADJUSTMENT VERSUS COLLECTIVE SURVIVAL

The anxiety which most Jews—not only those under direct attack by the organized forces of naziism and anti-Semitism—feel about their future has reduced the estrangement of the younger generation from their elders and has given impetus to a revival of orthodox forms in religion and in formal Jewish religious education. The sense of liberalism and cosmopolitanism, which was given impetus by the Enlightenment and which through the *Haskalah* movement even penetrated to the more provincial sections of eastern European Jewry, has suffered a setback with the rise of political anti-Semitism in our time.

The survival of the Jews has probably depended more upon the segregation and internal solidification of the Jewish community as a response to exclusion and persecution than upon toleration by the outside world. In the light of the history of the Jewish people up to the rise of naziism, the adaptability of Jewish life to changing situations is scarcely subject to doubt as a powerful factor in survival. But the will to live is perhaps more convincingly manifested in the adjustment of Jewish education to changing needs and circumstances than in any other phase of Jewish social life. While it has been concerned with the transmission of knowledge and skills of a sort, it has been primarily designed to nurture a consciousness of a common past and a common destiny. The most important part of the education which the Jewish family and community has provided its members, especially the youth, has served to inculcate in the individual a sense of belonging to a historic people with deep roots in the past and of sharing the future of that people despite the seeming discrepancy between the fortune of the one and the fate of the many.

It should be noted, of course, that in all the countries of the Western world except those under the dominance of Nazi doctrines the education of the Jews, except for the religious education, is part and parcel of the general educational system of the country. The disproportionate crowding of the Jews into the professions in the past few generations has to some extent repeated what their concentration in business and finance

had done in an earlier period: It gave rise to a reaction expressing itself in Jewish quotas in many higher educational institutions, if not complete exclusion in the case of some. Incidentally, it may also be noted that the quota system in higher educational and professional institutions has mainly resulted in intensifying the individual struggle for admission and advancement.

The fascination which higher education and professional careers have had for the Jews may be traced to at least three factors: (1) the traditionalist scheme of learning cultivated as a social value for centuries and now translated into secular terms; (2) the relatively high degree of urbanization of the Jews; and (3) the lack of interest in or opportunity for entering other occupations. It is a striking fact that agricultural vocational education (except in the retraining of refugees in an emergency like the present or as stimulated by nationalistic enthusiasm, as in Zionism, or as a deliberate policy by philanthropic and resettlement agencies) has failed to attract more than a trivial segment of the Jews.[15] In the higher brackets of education anti-Semitism has frequently generated a personal sense of frustration and embitterment. Among the Jews, as among other minority peoples, discontent is not confined to the lower strata but extends on up into the top reaches of the social hierarchy and is perhaps most acute among those who, despite their abilities, have found their path to advancement or acceptance barred.

THE JEWS AND THE NEGROES: CONTRAST-
ING EDUCATIONAL PROBLEMS

The experience of the Jews may well stand as the classic example of the survival of a people and the perpetuation of a culture from which others similarly situated may draw appropriate inferences for their policies, both positive and negative. There

[15] See Ruppin, *op. cit.*, chap. x. For an account of the chief experiment in agricultural education and settlement see Gabriel Davidson, *Our Jewish Farmers and the Story of the Jewish Agricultural Society* (New York, 1943).

probably is no people more unlike the Negroes than the Jews. The latter have long been sophisticated, urbanized, and literate. While immersed in the stream of Western civilization, the Jews have retained a profound consciousness of their separate identity and past. The Negroes in these respects are virtually exactly opposite. The Jews, for instance, have no need for an urban league as do the Negroes, for the Jews, having grown up with the city, find urban life their natural milieu. Whereas the Jews on many occasions faced their supreme problem in resisting assimilation, the Negroes only rarely have been permitted to assimilate. Whereas the Jews have inherited their communal organization, the Negroes have had to build up their community structure painfully and laboriously. The Negroes have no minority language, ritual, religion, and culture to speak of, for which they must seek toleration as do the Jews. It is interesting to speculate how much of the anomalous status of the Jews today is due to the progress of the industrial revolution and how different the contemporary position of the Negroes would be if they had been permitted to share in the industrial, commercial, and professional roles which the Jews have played. Despite the obvious differences between the Jews and the Negroes, however, none can perhaps profit more by the historic experiences of the Jews than the Negroes themselves.

We already see in the crystallization of schools of thought among Negro leaders striking likenesses between the issues and the strategy of adjustment. Assimilationism and nationalist separatism are the extreme poles in both instances. Intermediate between these lie a series of variant policies which have close resemblances in the two peoples. Accommodation, submission, and sublimation are three distinctly recognizable intermediate forms of proposed adjustment. The Jews have perhaps more of a recognizable will to live as a people and as a culture than have the Negroes. Moreover, the Jews, as a historic people, have a core of cultural traditions to knit them together and enable them to face a hostile world with an inner sense of equality and with equanimity despite their dispersion. The greater visibility of the Negroes, on the other hand, furnishes a not always welcome basis of racial identity from which the individual cannot, even if he would, escape

The fact that the Jews have, through the centuries of their dispersion and their struggle for recognition and survival, acquired certain unmistakable successes within the framework of Western civilization no doubt gives them an advantage over the Negroes, who have had to traverse the road from African folk culture to Western civilization more recently and in a much shorter time, which did not permit them to share even those opportunities which the Jews until recently thought they could take for granted as permanent gains. On the other hand, it is the very success of the Jews in surmounting the obstacles put into the path of their progress which has made them the object of envy, hate, and persecution and which makes them vulnerable to the propaganda of organized anti-Semitism.

Despite the momentary and, we hope, temporary vicissitudes of history which have allotted to the Jews a more precarious prospect than there was reason to hope would face them in the age of liberalism, it is not unlikely that they will continue to enjoy in the long run certain advantages over the Negroes which even the aftermath of naziism cannot completely cancel. There is no doubt, however, about the fact that large masses of Jews who thought they were well along on the road of assimilation have, through their setbacks incident to the advent of racism and anti-Semitism as political weapons, come to a point of seeing themselves and their fate with a greater feeling of kinship and sympathy for the Negroes. For both peoples the goal of a happier adjustment to the world in which they must live is seen to be further distant than either had expected. They have the consolation that they can travel at least part of that road in companionship.

UNIVERSITY OF CHICAGO

THE EDUCATIONAL PROCESS AND THE BRAZILIAN NEGRO

DONALD PIERSON

ABSTRACT

Although the class distribution of Brazilian Negroes is not dissimilar to that in the United States, the differences in implication are profound. Whereas in the United States the rise of the Negro and of the mixed-blood has been principally within the limits of the Negro world, in Brazil the Negro competes freely with all aspirants, white or black, to the same class; and, if he gives evidence of personal worth, his racial antecedents will be to a considerable extent overlooked. Blacks, mulattoes, and whites are to be found participating together on all educational levels. Segregated schools are unknown. African customs and rituals, practiced on the lower-class level and partly fused into the culture even at the upper levels, are gradually losing their hold on Negro youth because of disparagement by prestige-bearing members of the European community. This process facilitates the education of Negro youth in European habits and ideas.

When considering the educational process in its cultural significance as observed among Negroes in Brazil, one should perhaps first of all define what is meant here by "education." By "education" we have in mind the series of communications by means of which a cultural heritage is transmitted from an older to a younger generation—in other words, the entire round of human interaction which enables a culture to renew itself and to maintain its existence.

Education conceived in this way obviously is not limited to the formal schooling of a generation which, in due course of time, will be left alone to perpetuate the culture in question; in fact, cultural transmission is perhaps only to a limited degree obtained by such rational attempts to extend the range of transmitted skills, ideas, attitudes, and sentiments and to insure their accurate reproduction as the school represents. It is probably trite to say that, without human association from infancy and the free play of interaction between the younger and the older generations, societies would disintegrate and cultures disappear, except in so far as written records might continue to furnish a link between the past and the future. It is perhaps not so obvious, however, that a considerable measure of this interaction is of a nonverbal character; that, in other words, the play of facial muscles, the movements of the eyes, slight shifts of the shoulders, the tensing or relaxing of the whole organism, the manner of responding to a specifically put or implied question—indicating, as these gestures all do, approval or disapproval of given acts—play significant roles in transmitting that body of meanings which constitute a culture.

THE BRAZILIAN NEGRO

During more than three centuries, from approximately 1532 to 1856, large numbers of Africans were imported into Brazil as a labor supply, particularly for the sugar plantations of the northeastern coastal belt and the diamond and gold-panning regions of the interior. By the latter year probably more Negroes had entered Brazil than were ever imported into the United States or the West Indies. The burning of official records following emancipation in 1888 leaves in doubt the precise numbers. But anyone familiar with the five present centers of Negro concentration—the port cities of Bahia, Pernambuco, Maranhão, Rio de Janeiro, the interior state of Minas Geraes—and with the unfavorable conditions for survival, particularly during the colonial period, is readily convinced that the total must have reached millions.

The exact number of Negroes in Brazil today is perhaps equally unknown. The last attempt to enumerate the population according to race was made in the census of 1890, or fifty years ago. This enumeration gave 2,097,426 blacks and 4,638,495 mixed-bloods (including both mulattoes and Indian-white *mestizos*), equivalent to 14.6 and

32.4 per cent, respectively, of the total population. More recent vital statistics which take account only of color indicate that in the city of Bahia, for instance, 14.3 per cent of the children born in the thirty-one years between 1903 and 1933 were black and 49.4 per cent *pardo*, or brown.[1] A comparatively recent study made at the National Museum by Roquette Pinto estimated 14 per cent of the total Brazilian population to be black, 22 per cent mulatto.[2]

Although these statistics are probably subject to grave question regarding their accuracy or adequacy, especially from the point of view of racial conceptions in the United States, one may safely say that Negroes represent a considerable part of the present Brazilian population and that, with the exception of areas in the south where relatively few Africans were originally imported and large numbers of European immigrants have come in during the past century, probably at least a majority of the population has some African blood. To consider, then, the educational process as observed among Brazilian Negroes is to deal with education among a major portion of the Brazilian people, especially if one conceives of the term Negro as it is ordinarily employed in the United States.

It should be pointed out, however, that the significance of the term Negro in Bahia, for instance, where I have known rather intimately Brazilian Negroes from the various classes of society, varies in marked degree from that common to the United States, where any individual descended from African forebears, even though he may be, to all appearances, white, is considered a Negro, provided, of course, the facts of his origin are known. In Brazil a man is a Negro if he looks like a Negro, and particularly if there is added to these physical marks social characteristics ordinarily associated with the Negro in the Brazilian mind. In other words, numerous individuals whose ancestors were in part, at least, African are classified in official statistics as "white" and are so considered by their associates.

A still more significant fact is that color, hair texture, and facial characteristics are in the Brazilian society of perhaps no more importance as indices of social classification than certain other indices, such as family connection, education, "breeding," professional competence, economic status, and cultural identification. The result is that numerous individuals are considered "white" who not only are descended from African forebears but who carry in their physical makeup unmistakable marks of such origin. In other words, the possession of social characteristics ordinarily associated in Brazil with upper-class standing tends to take a given individual out of color, as well as racial, categories. For instance, an English visitor at Pernambuco in the early part of the nineteenth century was surprised to hear a mulatto official referred to as "white." Upon pointing out to the speaker that the man in question appeared to the eyes undoubtedly to be a mulatto, he received the paradoxical (but, as far as the Brazilian racial situation is concerned, illuminating) reply: "He *was* a mulatto, but he is *now* a white; for how can a mulatto be a *capitão mor?*"[3]

---

[1] Official records, city of Bahia, on file at the Secretaria de Saude e Assistencia Publica. The recording of births is admitted by public officials to be incomplete, many deliveries among the lower classes (principally colored) going unrecorded by attending midwives. During the same period 24.6 per cent of the deaths in Bahia are recorded as occurring among blacks, 52.1 per cent among *pardos*. Data on births are not available for the years 1911, 1915, or 1919; no deaths for 1910, 1911, or 1917–20.

[2] E. Roquette Pinto, "Nota sobre os typos anthropologicos do Brasil," *Archivos do Museu Nacional*, XXX (Rio, 1928), 309; *Ensaios de anthropologia brasiliana* (São Paulo, 1933), p. 128. Artur Lobo da Silva, in a study of 30,000 recruits for the Brazilian army, found 10 per cent to be blacks, 30 per cent mulattoes "and other mixed bloods" (Coronel Artur Lobo da Silva, "A anthropologia do exercito brasileiro," *Archivos do Museu Nacional*, XXX [Rio, 1928], 19). Lowrie recently estimated the population of the southern state of São Paulo, which has received large numbers of European immigrants in recent years, to be one-sixth colored (Samuel H. Lowrie, "O elemento negro na populacão de São Paulo," *Revista do Arquivo Municipal*, XLVIII [São Paulo, 1939], 5–51).

[3] Henry Koster, *Travels in Brazil, 1809 to 1815*, II (Philadelphia, 1817), 175–76.

CULTURAL TRANSMISSION AMONG
THE *Africanos*

Although assimilation of the Africans and their descendants has been proceeding at a gradually accelerating rate and has now reached an advanced stage, identification with Africa and with African cultural forms, in such centers of Negro concentration as Bahia, still marks off rather noticeably a portion of the population. Differences in dress, in food and food habits, in music, in forms of religious expression, in sacred specialists, in attempts to exercise control over personal destiny and over other human beings, and in credulity in folklore and, to a limited extent, differences in language describe different worlds which still coexist at Bahia: one largely African in derivation, the other European. Although most of the blacks have now to a considerable extent sloughed off their former cultural identification with Africa and been more or less completely incorporated into the European world, a remnant of *Africanos* still lives, in spite of symbiotic relations with the European group, to a considerable extent culturally apart.

Among those individuals identified with the African tradition, most of whom are Negroes but some of whom are whites, the *candomblé*, or fetish-cult ceremonies, which are serious, dignified, and carried on according to fixed, traditional forms, furnish informal instruction in the use of African musical instruments and ceremonial costumes, in songs, dances, and other ritualistic practices, and in the nomenclature and "behavior" of the *orixás*, or deities, who under favorable circumstances visit assembled worshipers. The four or five hundred adults present at a ceremony of this kind ordinarily bring with them the children and young people of their families, mothers with infants in their arms being not uncommon. Instruction in ritual and belief may be had informally outside the *candomblé* from relatives or friends who participate in the ceremonies or from sacred specialists, while for the important *filhas de santo* (literally, "daughters of the *orixás*"), or ceremonial dancers, formal instruction is provided. Thus, on the first "visitation" of an *orixá* to a prospective *filha de santo* she must immediately enter upon a period of rigorous training. After surrendering all her garments so that, in symbol of the new life which she is about to begin, they may never be worn again, the initiate, or *yauô*, as she is now called, submits to a ritualistic bath, at dusk, in water scented with sacred herbs. Her hair is cut, her head shaved,[4] and dots and circles are painted in white all over the head. The *yauô* is then escorted to the *camarinha*, or sacred instruction chamber, where she remains for a period of six months to a year to be taught by sacred specialists the various rituals of the cult, the songs, dances, the beliefs and sacred traditions. The more adequate her eventual knowledge of these cultural forms, the greater her prestige among the *Africanos*. Negroes (and whites) among this portion of the population will say with pride, "She is very learned in things African."[5]

But this portion of the population, as has been indicated, is proportionately small. Most Negroes in Brazil have now come to be identified primarily with the European culture.

EDUCATION, RACE, AND CLASS

From what has previously been pointed out about the Brazilian racial situation, it will probably be clear that, among those Negroes whose close approximation to the whites in pigmentation, facial characteristics, and hair texture identifies them with

[4] Formerly, all hairy parts of the body were shaved.

[5] For detailed information on African cultural forms still to be observed in Brazil see particularly Nina Rodrigues, *Os africanos no Brasil* (São Paulo, 1932) and *O animismo fetichista dos negros bahianos* (Rio, 1935); Artur Ramos, *O negro brasileiro* (2d ed.; São Paulo, 1940) and *O folk-lore negro do Brasil* (Rio, 1935); Manoel Querino, "A raça africana e os seus costumes na Bahia," *Annaes do 5° Congresso Brasileiro de Geographia*, I (Bahia, 1916), 626; Edison Carneiro, *Religiões negras* (Rio, 1936) and *Negros bantus* (Rio, 1937); Donald Pierson, "A Study of Racial Adjustment in Brazil" (unpublished Ph.D. thesis, University of Chicago, 1939), chaps. x and xi.

the white portion of the population, the educational process proceeds in a manner fundamentally identical to that among Brazilian whites. With children from the upper classes it ordinarily involves the assimilation of a cultural heritage composed predominantly of Catholic European and Moorish cultural traits modified by transplantation to a virgin continent; by vicissitudes attendant on the formation and growth of a new society upon what in reality constituted for a long time a European cultural frontier; by a fusion, to some extent, with native Indian elements and, more extensively perhaps, especially in areas like Bahia and Pernambuco, with African cultural forms. With children from the lower classes outside the *Africano* group it involves the taking-over of a cultural heritage which, although essentially European in character, has been influenced to a greater extent than the culture of the upper circles by native Indian elements and, especially in centers of Negro concentration, by African cultural forms.[6]

Among the lower classes cultural transmission, with the exception of the instruction of the *filhas de santo* by the *Africanos*, proceeds largely in an informal manner. Illiteracy among this portion of the population is, in Bahia, for instance, almost universal. The educational process proceeds here, then, primarily by way of social interaction inside the family, the clan, the play group, and the work group; by way of the light, color, odor, and sound of the Mass and other Catholic ritual and, to varying degrees with different individuals, of the ceremony and ritual of the *candomblé;* and, to a limited extent, by way of the cinema and the radio. On the other hand, white children from the upper classes

[6] Direct connection between Bahia and Africa was perhaps more intimate and was maintained over perhaps a longer period of time than any similar connection elsewhere in the New World. Even after the extinction of the slave traffic vessels regularly plied between Bahia and Lagos, repatriating nostalgic emancipated Negroes and returning with West Coast products much prized by Africans and their descendants in Brazil. This contact did not cease until approximately 1905.

ordinarily receive elementary and secondary instruction of a quite formal character, together with professional training in a school of law, medicine, or engineering. Regular access is had to one or more daily newspapers and to a limited number of magazines, journals, and books, as well as to radio broadcasts, including short-wave programs from other countries in Portuguese or in foreign languages, with one or more of which they may be familiar; they have also occasional contacts with visitors from other lands. They may also travel in Brazil or abroad, particularly in Europe, and perhaps study for some time in France, Germany, or (only recently but increasingly now) the United States.

Not only is the education of those Brazilian Negroes who are identified with the white group in no way different from that of the whites in both the upper and the lower strata of society, but also the education of the children of those Negroes of darker pigmentation and more negroid features whose possession of other indices of social status (e.g., an adequate education, "good breeding," professional competence, outstanding public service, or wealth) admits them to advanced social position. In the case of the latter children, cultural transmission may even proceed in the bosom of exclusive clubs or other organizations with limited and carefully selected membership.

The facts so far presented indicate perhaps the difficulties involved in considering the education of the Brazilian Negro as one would consider the education of the Negro in the United States; that is, they indicate the difficulties involved in treating Brazilian whites and Brazilian Negroes as distinct groups sharply set off one from the other. As far as Brazil is concerned, it is more feasible to trace the educational process among the lower and the upper classes, in each of which appear in varying proportions both whites and blacks; or, with reference to the principal centers of Negro concentration where African culture forms still persist, to consider the transmission from generation to generation of the European and the African cultures, in each of which both whites and blacks, in varying numbers, participate.

One finds today at Bahia, for instance, a freely competitive order in which individuals compete for position largely on the basis of personal merit and favorable family circumstances. Consequently, individual competence tends to overbalance ethnic origin as a determinant of social status. Since, however, the darker portion of the population has had to contend with the serious handicap that their parents or grandparents or other immediate ancestors began at the bottom as property-less slaves of the white ruling class and since they now bear constantly with them, by reason of color and other physical characteristics, indelible marks of this slave ancestry, it is not surprising to find that the unmixed blacks are still concentrated in the lower classes, that they gradually disappear as one ascends the class scale, and that in the upper levels they are to be found only in limited numbers. The mixed-bloods, however, demonstrate a strong tendency to advance in social position and are at present concentrated in the middle ranks, while a considerable portion, especially of very light mixed-bloods, or *brancos de Bahia* as they are sometimes called, have penetrated into the upper strata. The whites, as might be anticipated, are concentrated in the upper levels. Their numbers, both absolute and relative, diminish sharply as one descends the class scale, appearing only in small percentages in the lower tiers.

One might note that this racial distribution in the classes at Bahia is not greatly dissimilar to that in the United States. In other words, the Negro, either pure or mixed with the white, has slowly but steadily advanced both in Brazil and in this country until today he is represented in all the classes. Even the relative numbers in the different levels are somewhat similar in the two cases.

The differences, however, are profound. Whereas in the United States the rise of the Negro and of the mixed-blood has been principally *within the limits of the Negro*

world, in Brazil the rise has been with reference to the *total community;* that is, the Negro in Bahia not only competes freely with all other individuals of his own color, but he can and does compete with all aspirants to the same class; and, if he has ability and gives evidence of definite personal worth, he will be accepted for what he is as an individual and his racial antecedents will, at least to a considerable extent, be overlooked.

These facts are reflected in the structure of the formal educational system. Table 1 indicates that blacks, mulattoes, and whites are to be found participating together in all educational institutions. Segregated, exclusively Negro schools as well as exclusively white schools are unknown. There seems never to have been in Bahia any deliberate attempt to limit racial contacts such as occurs where races have been embittered for a long time.[7] Table 1 also reflects the relative numbers of the different ethnic groups in the various classes; for instance, the blacks are best represented in the elementary schools, especially in those which are state supported, attendance at which is free and hence more accessible to children from the lower economic groups. They gradually disappear, both numerically and proportionately as one ascends the educational ladder. Mixed-bloods, however, are to be found in increasing numbers throughout the educational system, even in the superior schools.

The Public Library at Bahia is patronized

[7] This is what one might expect, considering that in large areas of Brazil the descendants of Europeans and of Africans have since colonial days been closely associated in an intimate, personal way and that no serious threat to the relations which grew up normally between the races in contact has ever appeared. A Bahian student once wrote: "From his earliest years, a child in Bahia is accustomed to associating with all racial types without any distinction being made between them." Even since emancipation, it is rare to find a white family without a Negro cook, maid, or houseboy; and most upper-class children are still reared by Negro nurses. The laundress in all probability is a black, as also, if the family owns an automobile, is the chauffeur. This close association over a long period of time has resulted, quite naturally, in the development of personal attachments which have tended to undermine formal barriers between the races.

by individuals from all the different ethnic groups, although blacks appear among its frequenters in rather limited numbers. For instance, of 560 persons observed using the

tions. Ethnic distribution here also follows rather closely ethnic distribution in the classes. A number of instructors, particularly in elementary and secondary institutions,

TABLE 1*

SCHOOL ATTENDANCE AT 38 SCHOOLS, CLASSIFIED BY ETHNIC ORIGIN, BAHIA, 1936

SCHOOL	No.	WHITES		MULATTOES		BLACKS		TOTAL	
		No.	Per Cent	No.	Per Cent	No.	Per Cent	No.	Per Cent
Faculty of Law............	1	97	80.8	22	18.4	1	0.8	120	100.0
Faculty of Medicine.........	1	273	79.1	63	18.3	9	2.6	345	100.0
Engineering School..........	1	45	76.3	12	20.3	2	3.4	59	100.0
Normal School..............	1	157	55.1	83	29.1	45	15.8	285	100.0
Public *ginasio*	1	196	73.9	45	17.0	24	9.1	265	100.0
Private *ginasios*	2	93	67.4	37	26.8	8	5.8	138	100.0
Parochial *ginasios*	2	101	84.2	17	14.2	2	1.6	120	100.0
Manual Arts................	2	43	17.7	114	46.9	86	35.4	243	100.0
Public Elementary..........	22	385	29.2	496	37.6	438	33.2	1,319	100.0
Private Elementary..........	8	175	56.1	97	31.1	40	12.8	312	100.0
Parochial Elementary........	7	318	72.7	88	20.2	31	7.1	437	100.0

* Criterion: physical appearance. Data obtained by analyzing in each case groups present at the school in question on a given data and at a given hour.

TABLE 2*

TEACHERS IN SECONDARY AND SUPERIOR SCHOOLS, CLASSIFIED BY ETHNIC ORIGIN, BAHIA, 1936

SCHOOL	WHITES		*Brancos da Bahia*		MULATTOES		BLACKS		TOTAL	
	No.	Per Cent	No.	Per Cent	No.	Per Cent	No.	Per Cent	No.	Per Cent
Faculty of Law.....	22	91.6	1	4.2	1	4.2	0	0.0	24	100.0
Faculty of Medicine.	98	66.7	28	19.0	21	14.3	0	0.0	147	100.0
Engineering School..	17	77.3	3	13.6	2	9.1	0	0.0	22	100.0
Normal School.....	52	84.0	7	11.2	2	3.2	1	1.6	62	100.0
Public *ginasio*.......	20	60.6	6	18.2	7	21.2	0	0.0	33	100.0

* Of 30 elementary teachers observed in state elementary schools, 3 were blacks, 11 mulattos, 6 *brancos da Bahia*, 10 whites.

library facilities on different days and at different hours (1936), 9.6 per cent were blacks, 35.9 per cent mulattoes, and 52.7 per cent whites.

As indicated in Table 2, individuals of Negro descent are to be found among the teaching staffs of all educational institu-

are mixed-bloods, although the greater number are whites. Black instructors are still rare and are limited, with few exceptions, to the elementary ranks.

The instruction of white children by colored teachers and professors is not uncommon. For instance, in a private elementary school a class of boys ranging in age from seven to eleven years were observed being taught by a black. Among the group were two whites, one *branco da Bahia*, one mulatto, and three blacks. Several substantial white citizens had received their early training under this man. In intellectual circles one often hears of a dark mixed-blood of distinguished appearance who organized some years ago one of the more important secondary institutions at Bahia and whose two sons are today well known and highly regarded educators. Several whites now prominent in local and even national circles speak with pride of their schooling under this distinguished man. A similar attitude is not infrequently shown with reference to other colored teachers and professors: for instance, a prominent medical specialist and noted lecturer at the Faculty of Medicine in Bahia; a legal "authority" and author of textbooks in law, now a justice of the Brazilian Supreme Court; a prominent nerve specialist; a noted surgeon; and the city's ablest and most-quoted literary critic.

As in the United States, professional training has been an important means by which both blacks and mixed-bloods have risen in economic position and social status. Recently, at the graduating exercises of the Faculty of Medicine in Bahia, a dark mixed-blood, upon receiving his diploma, was given by his fellow-students (chiefly whites) a vigorous round of applause, he being one of the few graduates so honored. "He is a fine man with a brilliant mind," remarked a white colleague. "We are proud of him." The development, after independence in 1822, of institutions for professional training offered to the more able blacks, and especially to the mixed-bloods, possibilities not previously attainable. Since, by reason of their mental alertness, this vanguard of the Brazilian Negro excelled in pursuits wherein intellectual ability is an essential to success, the development of these centers opened ready access to the rising professional classes, especially as *doutores* or *bachareis*.[8] Many

[8] Graduates of the Faculties of Medicine, Law, and Engineering.

promising young mulattoes were aided to a professional training by indulgent white fathers or other relatives and friends among the dominant class. For instance, of a prominent Brazilian intellectual, whose father was a white planter and whose mother was a Negro slave, we are told:

Theodoro was very intelligent as a boy, and showed remarkable ability in his studies. It is said that when a very young child at Santo Amaro, he used to slip away late at night, after his mother's master had gone to bed, to study by the street lamp on the corner near the house. When his father discovered this, he was much impressed, and other signs of Theodoro's intelligence and his ability to apply himself multiplied the interest which his father took in him, and he supplied all his needs. When his father left Santo Amaro to come to Bahia, he brought Theodoro with him, and here Theodoro went to primary school where he had as white playmates his father's nephews and others. Later, when his father went to Rio, he took Theodoro with him. The boy never left his father's company as long as his father lived.[9]

Theodoro was a dark mixed-blood with kinky hair. He grew up to be a prominent citizen, noted not only for his distinguished bearing and personal charm but also for his intelligence and professional competence. He had a noted career as an engineer and intellectual, representing Bahia in the Federal Senate, and for years was head of the Instituto Historico e Geographico da Bahia. At one time he was a close friend and confidant of a recent president of Brazil.

EDUCATION AND ACCULTURATION

As has been pointed out, cultural transmission at Bahia ordinarily results in the continuing fusion in the minds of the younger generation, both white and black, of cultural elements from the different cultures in contact. With many individuals from the lower classes the subtle influences emanating from association with persons identified with either of the two cultures—one European, the other African—provided they rep-

[9] From a letter to the author from a man reared in the same community as the individual in question and long acquainted with him.

resent in their eyes relatively equal prestige, seem quietly but inevitably to result in cultural fusion. Among the upper classes contact with the ideas, attitudes, and sentiments of other peoples, particularly those of European origin, by way of newspapers, magazines, books, foreign visitors, and foreign travel leads to less noticeable perhaps, but nonetheless real, cultural fusion. Hence, the educational process at Bahia often becomes intimately bound up with the process of acculturation and even to some extent identical with it.

The education of the Negro in European habits, points of view, and philosophies of life began with almost the first contact between Africans and Brazilians. It proceeded primarily in an informal way, although it was at times aided by organized attempts at instruction. One of the first of these was the instruction in catechism which took place in the homes of the masters, in the chapels attached to the great landed estates, or in the church itself. Education within the households of masters during the Brazilian colonial period is a subject worthy of detailed study. Certain it is that, as association between members of the master's family and his slaves became more constant and intimate, instruction in European habits and traditions increased, aided, of course, by the efforts of the church and, to a much lesser extent, the school, until today the task of educating millions of persons of African descent in the habits and skills derived from Europe has proceeded a long way.

One should point out, however, that this process has seldom operated unilaterally; that is, it has seldom happened that the descendants of Europeans, in teaching Africans and their descendants European ways, have not themselves been taught, in an unconscious, if not conscious, manner, many of the attitudes, sentiments, ideas, and even skills imported with African slaves. The *ama*, or Negro nurse, well beloved in Brazil and widely renowned in poetry and song, and the *mucama*, or maid, were the primary agents of this instruction. Great numbers of Brazilian children, particularly those of the upper classes, learned even their first words of Portuguese from black and mulatto women and in the course of this close contact quite naturally took over numerous African words and phrases, some of which have become universally employed throughout Brazil. African folklore, African ideas, attitudes, and sentiments, were in many cases also taken over and are to be found today deeply imbedded, particularly at Bahia, Pernambuco, and other centers of Negro concentration, even in the upper classes. Africans are said also to have introduced, during colonial days, iron-working into Minas Geraes and cattle-tending skills into the pasture areas of the north.

Unfortunately, we still know too little about the mechanisms involved in the process of acculturation. It seems clear, however, that, among other things, fusion proceeds only as long as, and probably to the extent that, each culture in contact enjoys prestige in the eyes of the individuals concerned. A Bahian lower-class Negro once remarked, "This *candomblé* stuff! It ought to be done away with! Only a backward people tolerate such nonsense. Why, the English have driven it out of Africa,[10] but here in Bahia these old customs still hang on." Clearly, this individual no longer cares to identify himself with the culture of his African forebears—a shift in attitude all the more remarkable when one considers that his uncle is probably the most competent leader of the *Gêge-Nagô* fetish cults at Bahia, a wise old man of some eighty years, widely known and respected throughout the lower-class world not only at Bahia but also at Pernambuco, where he occasionally goes to perform African rituals for which there is no competent local individual.

Upper-class Brazilians tend to look upon the beliefs and the practices of the *Africanos* as matters for ridicule, disparagement, and, at times, condemnation. African forms of behavior are thought of as queer, bizarre, unintelligible, inferior. They represent an-

[10] Reference is here made to Lagos, with which West African port Bahian Negroes were long in direct contact.

other world to this element of the population.

The general disposition, however, is to tolerate these practices as long as they are not too obviously indulged in, particularly in public places, and as long as they in no way interfere with the European habits of the major portion of the population. Upper-class Brazilians act in this respect with somewhat the same leniency which an adult exercises toward the immature conduct of a child, in the confident expectation that, as a Bahian once put it, "time and education will do away with these evidences of backwardness."

Thus, because of constant, although ordinarily tolerant, disparagement on the part of most prestige-bearing individuals in the European portion of the community and of such institutions as the church, the school, the newspaper, and the political organization, most of the younger Negroes now tend to be weaned away from the beliefs and practices of their ancestors, to forsake, for instance, the *candomblé* and the body of ideas and sentiments identified with it, and to look upon these customs and traditions as evidence of "ignorance," "backwardness," and "retarded mental growth." Older leaders of the cult often complain, as did one in 'my hearing, that "the *candomblé* isn't what it used to be. The young people today don't learn *Nagô* like we used to and so they don't know how to carry on and—what is worse—they don't want to learn."

The children and grandchildren of the *Africanos* are at times in more direct contact with the schools and other instrumentalities of European cultural diffusion than their parents and grandparents; and, in many cases, they have now come to take toward their immediate relatives the same attitudes which the Europeans take toward

them. This behavior on the part of their children as well as their European associates is developing in the *Africanos* themselves an increasingly acute sense of inferiority.

By reason, then, of the fact that not only cultural fusion but also cultural conflict is taking place at Bahia, the educational process becomes quite complex. The loss of prestige on the part of the African culture in the eyes of Negro youth often places insuperable barriers in the way of the transmission of that culture from the older to the younger generation. The extent to which communication is inhibited may, and often does, reach the point where the two generations become virtually isolated psychically from each other, even though they may continue to live in the same household and even to participate in certain common activities. In other words, the antagonism directed toward African cultural forms on the part of individuals identified with the European culture, especially on the part of those connected with the school, the church, and the local political organization, tends to shake the confidence of the younger generation of Negroes in the efficacy of the cultural forms of their parents and thus to inhibit and eventually to block altogether the re-creation of the African culture in the minds of the new generation. This blocking of communication, this damming-up, so to speak, of the free flow of ideas, attitudes, and sentiments between individuals from different generations, may result—and, in fact, is in Brazil today resulting—in the gradual but persistent disappearance of a culture, namely, that transported from Africa with imported Africans. At the same time, it facilitates the education of Negro youth in European habits, ideas, attitudes, and sentiments.

Escola Livre de Sociologia e
   Politica de São Paulo

EDUCATION AS A SOCIAL PROCESS: A CASE STUDY OF A HIGHER INSTITUTION AS AN INCIDENT IN THE PROCESS OF ACCULTURATION

HORACE MANN BOND

ABSTRACT

The Fort Valley State College is a social institution. The members of the college provide subjects for the study of the process of acculturation. Preliminary studies suggest the development of attitudes which individuals use in part to compensate for deficient environments. These attitudes have some resemblance to a religious faith. Equipped with the apparatus of faith, a "permanent minority" enjoys a peculiar stimulation in its intellectual life. The parallel with the early history of the Jewish minority is provocative.

I

During the last two years I have been engaged, as an active agent, a participant, and something of an observer, in what is at least designed to be a series of educational processes. In our four-year college we make a systematic effort to "educate" more than 300 young men and women of the Negro race. A high school enrolling 225 students, an elementary school enrolling 652 students, and a nursery school enrolling 25 small children are also under the immediate direction of our institution.

At our institution, when we are trying to impress certain persons with the immensity of our task and with the number of human beings upon whom our salutary and beneficial work is being lavished, we frequently quote these figures. If this symposium were our local Chamber of Commerce, I would also give stress to the fact that we are spending more than one hundred and fifty thousand dollars a year and that we give employment to eighty-two adults in the community; in short, that, second not even to the local bus manufacturer or to the local peach-crate factory, ours is the largest pay roll and the largest industry in Fort Valley.

There are better reasons for attaching significance to this enterprise. The twelve hundred human beings we are trying to "educate" and the eighty-two adults whose assistance we employ in effecting the "education" of these twelve hundred younger persons provide a fascinating field of inquiry

for that person who would inform himself with reference to such a theme as that set for this symposium. Beginning with the youngest child in our nursery school and ending, if you will, with the president himself, these twelve hundred human beings are, in the mass and individually, tremendously interesting human beings. Each has a most complicated personal history; and each in his own right deserves the studied inquiry, analysis, and understanding that the keenest tools of scientific social inquiry might provide. Beyond the twelve hundred students there are thousands of other human beings equally fascinating, though more remote from our range of concern, who must be included in the estimation of such an educational institution as the Fort Valley State College. Our students come from families; they have fathers and mothers (or foster-fathers and foster-mothers) and sisters and brothers and aunts and cousins without number.

Each of the teachers, staff workers, and employees of the institution also has a personal history that, if we understood it adequately, would help us understand him adequately. In our local school constituency we have Negro and white ministers, physicians, storekeepers, bankers, lawyers, farmers, day laborers, W.P.A. workers. On our controlling board we have lawyers, newspaper editors and owners, educational leaders, statesmen, and politicians—especially politicians. Over and above all these persons whom we meet directly are the thousands and hundreds of thousands of black and white inhabitants of the state of Georgia who represent our clientele.

What we are, as an educational institution, is what a composite of these students and teachers and directors and trustees and constituents would be. It is a complex picture; and I have only suggested its complexity to say that this paper can be merely an introduction to what, if it is ever written, will be a much more detailed account of the educational process as it is conducted in such an institution as the Fort Valley State College. I intend here, then, only to sketch the merest outlines of the subject.

II

I began by saying that our interest was in education as a social process, a social process illuminated by the particularities of the institution with which I am connected. Description requires preliminary definition of the terms employed. We may agree with Dr. Robert E. Park, in his abstraction of a definition from John Dewey, that "formal education is merely a rational procedure for further carrying on and completing, in the schoolroom, a task that began with the child in the home."[1] In the same book from which this summarization was derived, John Dewey defines education further as the "communication of ideals, hopes, expectations, standards, opinions,"[2] from one generation to another.

While Fort Valley includes a number of formally organized educational institutions, we realize, as Dewey does, that education as a social process may be incidental and indirect. In our formal efforts we agree upon certain objectives, and we press toward their achievement by establishing appropriate procedures and structures. Outside of our formal efforts and, indeed, within them, incidental education of a kind that may or

[1] "Education as a Social Process" (Nashville: Fisk University, 1941). (Mimeographed.)

[2] *Democracy and Education* (New York: Macmillan Co., 1923).

may not be consistent with our formally stated objectives is proceeding apace.

And this is so because we cannot escape regarding all affecting forces and institutions as true educational instruments. Each individual, white and black, lives in a series of overlapping social orders to which adjustment in various degrees must be made. It may be agreed that judgments as to the propriety or social usefulness of these learnings are dependent upon a hierarchy of values as to the ultimate vitality and importance of the social sphere in which a set of social learnings or adaptations takes place. The formal educational institution established and supported by a political state is one in which the objectives pursued as desirable goals have received the sanction of this political over-world in which the students live. Formal education then becomes, indeed, a "rational procedure for carrying on in the schoolroom" not *all* tasks begun in the home but those particular tasks which the over-world—what we might call the "official social order"—has selected out of the many that are being carried on in the home and which are adjudged as having a functional value for the persistence and self-renewal of the forms and structures of that "official world."

We need here to make a distinction that is of importance and that, when made, avoids a paradox, especially in the consideration of educational structures for a minority group. The home may initiate many types of learning which the school must uproot. Entirely contrary learnings, or modifications thereof, must be substituted. The ideal homes of which this is not true are rare.

Take the example of language. The average Negro home from which our elementary-school students at Fort Valley come does begin, with the child, the important task of transmitting to that child the language of the over-world in which that child may some day live. The families carry on this task with numerous imperfections. In the smaller social area—the plantation economy, or the small town of Fort Valley—the corrupted grammar which these children learn at home could be regarded as a functional learning with adaptation values. A Harvard or Oxford accent has definite disadvantages in our small world—the Negro and the white world—of Fort Valley. At the same time the corrupted usage these children learn as an incident to their home life must be modified in our formal educational efforts. One of our greatest difficulties is to modify in the formal educational institutions—elementary schools, high schools, and colleges—these habits of speech which were begun in the home and which are continually being reinforced outside of the schoolroom.

Now this example illustrates a vital point suggested in Dr. Park's article for this symposium. He referred to the conflicts that arise in the process of socializing the second generations of immigrant families in this country. The conflict is sharpened where the educational tasks begun in the home (and entirely appropriate to the original social order in which the family lived) are found to require modification or substitution in the new setting. The formal educational structures and the informal contacts sustained by the youth of these culturally nonstandard homes actively effect such modifications and substitutions.

This is the nub of our problem at Fort Valley, although, as I hope to be able to show, our particular situation is immensely more complicated. The immigrant family finds in the American school a place where the standard American culture is communicated to the new generations. To the extent that the ordinary American school teaches the children of native whites, immigrants, and Negroes standard English, the use of figures, the general facts of nature, some simple manipulative skills, and the elementary facts of personal physical survival, it is within the bounds of objectives which the entire community generally recognizes as fit and necessary tasks for all. This is the standard cultural heritage to which all children are admissible with hardly any constraint or public feeling of impropriety. In

itself this fact is a significant index to a profound change in public opinion, especially in the South. Within the memory of living men the admission of Negroes to the most fundamental of these social heritages was denied by force of public law and opinion.

III

The immigrant child of the second generation lives in a dual world, at home and at school, of ideals, hopes, expectations, standards, and opinions. Our Negro children live permanently not in two but in several different worlds. What this situation means for personality and other difficulties in immigrant children is known to us all; and the implications for Negroes are just beginning to be sensed. Unlike the immigrant, the Negro child is a member of what, at present, seems to be a *permanent* minority.[3] This fact we have frequently remarked but have been slow to accept in its implications for our educational philosophy. As Dr. Park has again reminded us, the similarity between the status of the Jewish people and that of the Negro is provocative, at least. As the Jewish people throughout the world today appear for various reasons to be a permanent minority, so the Negro in America is likewise a permanent minority. Those of us who have followed the history of this ancient people in such a book as Sigmund Freud's *Moses and Monotheism*[4] will remember, with renewed interest in the similarity, that once the Jewish race was a permanent minority in Egypt.

It is membership in a permanent minority —about which I will admit reasonable argument—that raises the most far-reaching questions regarding the education of Negroes as a social process in the United

[3] When this paper was first read at the Fisk University Symposium, the phrase "permanent minority" (greatly to the surprise of the author) provoked strong dissent from some, who saw in it implications for the passive acceptance, by Negroes, of long-time patterns of racial segregation and discrimination.

Two alternate forms descriptive of Negro status in America are "caste" and "minority." The term "permanent minority" is preferred by the author.

[4] New York: Alfred A. Knopf, 1939.

States. At Fort Valley, as elsewhere, our formal educational efforts are bent in the direction of realizing the aims and objectives of that which we have called the "official social order." It is sometimes astonishing to find official and unofficial organizations, indeed, bending every effort to aid us in realizing these aims. Not long ago, in a Louisiana village where I lived, a representative of the American Legion asked for permission, on behalf of the local Post, to award a medal to one of our pupils who had written the best essay on "The Principles of Americanization." The occasion was provided, the representative came; and with sincere tears in his eyes and an honest catch in his throat, he exhorted us all to live up to the proud privileges of American citizenship, with all its rights and its responsibilities.

On occasion we have welcomed to our platform several of the more prominent religious leaders among the white people of our state. These gentlemen—and, indeed, the great masses of our white constituents—far from placing any obstacle in our path, would gladly forward the achievement by our minority, through the organized formalities of our school, of the fundamentals of a standard American culture.

I might here stress the word "fundamentals," without underestimating the vast gain which even tentative sanctions, extended to admission to the bare threshold of the culture, imply. For all of us—white and black—understand perfectly the private world within which we are to constrain ourselves, or be constrained. It is this private social world of a permanent minority that is frequently described by that pregnant phrase, "knowing your place." Negroes in Fort Valley "know their place." White people in Fort Valley—and in Nashville—"know their place." That "place," for either racial group, has an attendant set of ideals, hopes, expectations, standards, and opinions, that are the stuff of a continual incidental education in the family, in the entire community, and, indeed, in the pattern of the school as it is formally organized.

It is in this sense that we may agree that the school in any social order—even where there are two distinct and apparently opposed social orders—is both formally and informally, directly and incidentally, "a rational procedure for further carrying on and completing in the schoolroom, the task that began with the child in the home." At Fort Valley, as elsewhere in the South, we are organized formally to carry on and complete, modify and correct, the tasks that were begun with the child in the home—or that should have been begun in the home—as far, at least, as the fundamentals of the standard American culture are concerned. But we are also organized, formally and informally—as elsewhere in the South—to carry on and complete, to modify, correct, or establish, the fundamentals of a subculture which has set aside the Negro in America as a permanent minority; and these fundamentals were also begun in the home.

IV

We have been collecting a number of case histories at Fort Valley. They include histories of members of the faculty and of the staff; of students and of parents; and of patrons, white and black, of the institution. They are done without the benefit of psychoanalytical interpretation; they are, to date, merely testaments to the existence of social and economic worlds—and a private racial world—which throw into sharp focus several primary facts of differences between education as a social process for standard white American elementary, high-school, and college students and for Negro elementary, high-school, and college students from a substandard economy. This is not to say that psychoanalysis is despised or underestimated as a technique; if we had the resources, it would be applied, and to our advantage. Of course, there is some doubt that the new knowledge would indicate a major point of difference between our Negro population and any other American population. Our histories are suggestive in particularly one direction, without any presumption for closer analysis. They show for our faculty—and in lesser degree as one descends the scale to the nursery school—the dominance of the matriarchate in the composition of the Negro family. One might almost generalize that the Negro teacher typically comes from a family in which the mother has been for a longer or shorter period the chief economic support of the family, the person with the best education, and the most important source of inspiration to the individual as he remembers it. This is also true of our college students, and it is true of our elementary-school students only in less degree. Whether one believes with Frazier[5] that the matriarchal Negro family is a product of the generally inferior status of the Negro in America, or with Herskovits[6] that it is a cultural inheritance from Africa, it is a fact that may be of psychological importance. One is reminded of Park's[7] old description of the Negro as the "lady of the races"; a description that may have more in it than meets the eye. Certainly no one who (even with disbelief) has followed Freud's psychological interpretation of the history of the Jewish people can fail to be impressed with the possibilities of further inquiry.

This is a brief excerpt from the life of a teacher:

I believe that some people have something in them that enables them to do anything they make up their mind to do. Whether they come from the lowest depths, if they have this quality, they can educate themselves, and teach themselves anything. When I was a child, I wanted to walk like a soldier. I wanted to walk straight. I was sickly—perhaps that was why.

I made up my mind to walk straight, and I did so. I told my mother once, "I'm going to do big things—I'm going to make you proud of me." I was born in Louisiana, and my mother always had to work hard. My father was trifling, and I never forgave him for some-

thing he did when I was twelve years old. We were on a farm, and I had a calf that belonged to me. My father took the calf, and sold it for twelve dollars. Then he took the money and left my mother and myself and my sister, and went up north. Then my mother began to cook for a railroad gang. You know that is about the roughest life a person can live. We travelled from place to place with the section gangs until I was fifteen. In spite of going from place to place, I finally graduated from elementary school. My mother encouraged me always. Then my father came back to see us on a visit. He urged my mother to join him and to go back with him. I told my mother, although I was just a lad, "No! He left us when we needed him, and we don't need him now." So he left us, and we decided to go on our own. We saved up twenty-seven dollars, and when we got up north we had just three dollars left. I got a job in two days, and from then on I supported my mother and educated myself.[8]

In its detail this is an astonishing document as the background for a college teacher. And yet document after document retells the same story: a pitifully low income with which to finance any kind of education; usually a tremendous personal drive that impels the individual to make any kind of sacrifices in order to pursue the somewhat vague objective of "getting ahead"; a starved social milieu during childhood, with poor, or no, cultural or intellectual stimulation; a childhood which, even when lived in the bosom of a family in "polite" society, is replete with contacts with the children of the very poor, with their irregular sex and other attitudes and habits; in short, the story of self-made men and women who have arisen from the depths of poverty—and of being a Negro.

It may be that similar accounts of white teachers would tell similar stories; and yet I doubt that there would be as much of privation and denial and sacrifice—and of inner drive. With our very youngest generation of Negro teachers we are coming to a social inheritance of literacy and income that permits the leisurely and ordered acquisition of

---

[5] E. Franklin Frazier, *The Negro Family in the United States* (Chicago: University of Chicago Press, 1939).

[6] Melville J. Herskovits, *The Myth of the Negro Past* (New York: Harper & Bros., 1941), pp. 173 ff.

[7] Robert E. Park, "The Bases of Race Prejudice," *Annals of the American Academy of Political and Social Science*, November, 1928, pp. 11–20.

[8] From the Fort Valley State College manuscript collection.

higher and graduate instruction without the terrific miseries and deprivations that now appear in memory as a bright and comforting badge of courage, but which have left their scars in mind and soul and body. A human being who has done so much and suffered so greatly is likely to be a tough-minded realist, indeed, in a world that calls for realism.

Here is the account of one of our young men students, who is currently being exposed to the process of education in our institution:

My grandfather was killed by white men, when my father was a little child. Later my grandmother married again. She had seven children by her first husband. My mother's parents were born in Telfair county. Grandmother died when my mother was ten years old. My mother's father has been married twice since. The second wife left him for another man. My mother has seven sisters and eight brothers living.

My mother was married when she was eighteen years old. The first three children were boys. One of these boys died. The next child was a girl and then I came and after me another boy and then another girl, but the girl died.

We had an income of about $100 a month until 1930, which was very much better than most of the other people around us. We lived in a good home. My father was a skilled mechanic with the waterworks until the depression came in 1930, when he was laid off due to prejudice, and a white man put in his place. My father tried to make ends meet by doing a lot of things. He peddled on the streets. We finally moved to a farm and my father and the family made twenty bales of cotton and we had just enough clear to get my two older brothers a suit apiece. The rent from two houses we owned in town enabled us to eat.

When we came back to town after that bad trial on the farm my father started to run a grocery store. He sold whiskey, also, which was illegal. The sheriff covered up for him by staging fake raids, and they split the proceeds. One day the sheriff cursed before my mother, and father told him not to do so. He called father a "smart nigger," and said he was going to get him. My father got out of the business and stuck to his grocery business. The sheriff framed him anyway by planting some whiskey in the backyard, and then having some fellow "tip him off." . . . .

During my elementary school life I was quiet and good. I suppose this was because I hadn't been around much and I didn't know what it was all about. As I grew older I began to run with the boys all over town, and I began to learn my way around. Girls didn't take effect upon me until I was about thirteen. I hadn't had any experience with girls, and so I was greatly interested. The boys would often tease me about not having any sex experience. I had my first real sex experience when I was fifteen, and I didn't have another until I was seventeen. . . . .

We are not living, but existing. I hope, and am working for the day I can help my people to live as I think they should live.[9]

I know that any group of white college students could yield a similar document. And I will say for our Fort Valley State College population that comparative data from other institutions in the South show that (principally due to limited dormitory space) we have a relatively high selection of students from the upper social and economic brackets among the Negro population. But such figures universally show for all our institutions that our student populations are drawn, in far greater measure than white colleges, from the children of the poor; that, even when the families represented are middle-class families, the circumscribed ghetto of the Negro community from which they have come has brought them almost without exception into close and constant contact with the seamy side of life. Class residential segregation among white persons sets the middle and upper classes which fill the colleges apart from the low-income and the disorganized white populations. There is not enough economic self-sufficiency in any Negro population in America to provide the Negro child, and the prospective college student, with insulation from the raw and ugly "facts of life."

•Let me repeat what seems to be a most significant aspect of all these documents. It is the constant reiteration of high ambition for personal and for familial security. Each of these students and each of these teachers has a cause; a reason for struggle and for "getting ahead," for persisting in the grim

[9] *Ibid.*

struggle with life. One would expect, in such a population, an immense amount of defeatism, of the subsidence of the human spirit under the crushing load of economic and racial inequalities. But you find little if any of such a spirit.

One is reminded, in re-reading these documents, of a statement from an autobiographical account by DuBois.[10] He was thunderstruck one day, he says, to hear a young Bostonian—wealthy, handsome, of good family—confess that he was puzzled over what he should do as a life's work, because there was "nothing in which he was interested." It had never occurred to DuBois, he says, that a person should have any doubt regarding what he should do; as for himself, the pathway of duty and of service to the Negro people, as an imperative necessity, lay clear before him. At Fort Valley our young men and women exhibit—in the midst of poverty and the evidences of human exploitation—an unconquerable resolution and, indeed, an utter faith and conviction in their sense of having a mission to perform in the elevation of themselves and of their people.

V

The summarization of our problems might be given in statistical form. Our studies show that children in our elementary school are retarded in their learning of reading and arithmetic by approximately one year in the third grade and two years in the sixth grade—a variation from standard American expectations which does not increase through high school and college because of a more rigorous selection. One of the members of our staff has recently completed a study which shows that the children of skilled workers—who are few in number—in a year increase their score on standard-achievement tests by seven-tenths of the whole grade they should achieve, while the children of unskilled workers and of farmers increase their score on these tests only by sixty-four hundredths of the whole grade. The children of Baptists enrolled in

[10] W. E. B. DuBois, "The Significance of Henry Hunt," *Fort Valley State College Bulletin*, October, 1940, p. 8.

our elementary school increase their achievement index by sixty-seven hundredths of a whole grade, while the children of Methodists increase their score by only sixty-five hundredths of a whole grade. The children of parents in families with one room to the inhabitant have a slightly higher annual increase in score over the children of parents in families with three-quarters of a room to the inhabitant.

On the basis of comparisons between white and colored students in Georgia, we discover what is characteristic of such students throughout the South. Only 25 per cent of our students achieve the middle score made by Georgia white college students in standard-achievement tests. These white students similarly show relatively the same lag when compared with white college students in the North and West.

Furthermore, there is evidence, at least from our elementary school, that there are definite limits to the degree to which our children may be expected to attain standard-achievement ratings, even with the most expert teaching and with the optimum conditions provided for instruction. The culture is so powerful in its force that it seems to fix, in the learning of the standard fundamentals of the culture which are sanctioned by the society, improvability within certain definite limits. In other words, if our elementary-school children now increase their scores by a median of sixty-seven hundredths in the course of a year, the optimum provision of educational advantages could hardly be expected to raise that index above, say, eighty hundredths of a normal year of progress. The same conclusions might be drawn for students in our college. Now this would be a magnificent gain and quite enough to justify any amount of investment. The point is, the culture imposes a law of diminishing returns as far as formal educational investment is concerned. We are led to believe that the rapid comparative improvement of migrant Negro children from the South—witnessed and documented in New York, Chicago, and Washington—is not so much a testimonial to the superior formal educational advantages provided the

Negro population in those cities as compared to the South, as it is an index to the total superiority of the stimulations and advantages of incidental educational processes in those urban communities to which our Georgia—and Fort Valley—children have gone.

I have referred here to the outcomes usually expected of formal educational institutions working toward the achievement of formal educational objectives. There is another area suggested to me by the conviction that another factor, not by any means universalized but still present and, on the whole (by the evidence of the last three generations), still growing in the Negro population, deserves our very serious attention.

This paper has already suggested the possibility that the Negro in America shows evidence of developing a parallelism to the behavior and general attitudinal structure of a permanent minority. Not long ago, half in jest—but only half in jest—I remarked to a Jewish friend that I believed the Negroes were a chosen people. The friend replied wryly, "Chosen—to suffer?"

That wry suggestion has since that time, as I have reviewed the scope of this paper and the implications of the materials which I have had no opportunity, by reasons of space and time, to include therein, begun to take root and form in my mind as a most interesting speculation, if nothing else. It might be argued in all seriousness that a permanent minority is one that is "chosen to suffer," and because of this fact it is also in a very true sense a "chosen people." I have referred to John Dewey and to Sigmund Freud; I should like to add to the list of basic references for this paper William James's *Varieties of Religious Experience.*[11]

The resoluteness of conviction and the indomitable courage in the face of terrifying obstacles, found in all the documents of students and of teachers that we have collected at Fort Valley, appear to me to be nothing more or less than a variety of religious feeling, or at least of the fertile soul-stuff in which a permanent minority may

well discover a religion. Indeed, it is the stuff of which the minority may discover not only "a religion" but the "true religion" itself. The parallelisms in Negro religious folk songs to the sufferings and to the history of the Jewish people are too well known for me to do more than mention them. We have sung—and we sing now—"Go Down Moses" and "Joshua Fit the Battle of Jericho" with an enthusiasm that bespeaks not merely primitive usage of a convenient folk knowledge but intelligent and discriminating identification with the historical parallel.

I do not mean to say that our students at Fort Valley are deeply religious in the vulgar sense of the word as usually applied to Negroes. If a revivalist came there, he would be laughed at. A great many of them attend Sunday school and church in the community; but they have done so more with the sense of achieving identification with, and opportunities for service to, the humble masses of their people through an existing agency for uplift than from naïve religious feeling.

It is probably not necessary to say—except to the excessively naïve—that this paper is not a platform for solving racial problems through attendance upon Sunday school, church, and prayer-meetings. Religion has been viewed with what James called an "experiential" rather than a "spiritual" judgment.[12] The prospect for its development is seen as an effective mechanism for the permanent minority that is the Negro in the same way in which Freud, in his psychological treatment of the history and religion of the Jewish people, viewed monotheism as the essential kernel of their evident intellectual superiority and continued social cohesion and survival down through the ages.

If anyone would see what religion can do for ordinary human beings, members of majorities, who deliberately set themselves aside by their choice of new religious forms, see what Fox did, not merely for his contemporaries but for later generations of Quakers. Remember what Joseph Smith

[11] New York: Longmans, Green & Co., 1902.

[12] *Ibid.*, p. 48.

and Brigham Young did for the descendants of the rude people who embraced their faith. Go to the Shakers, the Campbellites, the Adventists, the Dukhobors; and see what transformations a religion can effect in ordinary folk—as far as the achievements of the objectives of our formal educational processes are concerned.

When, going beyond the mere addition of religious stimulation to a sector of a majority population, as in the case of the sects mentioned before, there is the combination of a permanent "racial" minority with a permanent "religious" minority, as in the case of the Jews, a combination results that may be depended upon to fertilize the world permanently with intelligence, as well as with blood and tears. Said William James:

Religious feeling is thus an absolute addition to the subject's range of life. It gives him a new sphere of power. When the outward battle is lost, and the outward world disowns him, it redeems and unifies an interior world which otherwise would be an empty waste.

. . . . In its characteristic embodiments, religious happiness is no mere feeling of escape. *It cares* no longer to escape. It consents to the evil outwardly as a form of sacrifice—inwardly it knows it to be permanently overcome. If you ask *how* religion thus falls on the thorns and escapes death, and in the very act avoids annihilation, I cannot explain the matter, for it is religion's secret.[13]

I conclude this paper with this speculation: that the Negro in America is at present in all practical respects a "permanent" minority; that as a permanent minority the process of education, both formally and incidentally, has effects upon it and results in structures different from those which might be characteristic of the standard majority; that any permanent minority, in due course, will develop feelings, attitudes, and convictions that serve indeed as a protective, but even more as a stimulating, device in contact with the majority; and that this latter set of attitudes may be depended upon to provide a powerfully compensating force to offset the ordinary effects of the environment. Were this the religious institute, and not that of the social sciences, I should be tempted to say that the Negro people are just as certain to produce a Moses and a Messiah to formulate an ethics and a religion appropriate to its status as another permanent minority, some time ago, discovered a Moses and has since sought a Messiah.

FORT VALLEY STATE COLLEGE

[13] *Ibid.*, p. 49.

COMPARATIVE EDUCATION IN COLONIAL AREAS, WITH SPECIAL REFERENCE TO PLANTATION AND MISSION FRONTIERS

EDGAR T. THOMPSON

ABSTRACT

On the basis of Wissler's analysis of American culture in terms of mechanical invention, universal suffrage, and mass education the historic culture of the South has not been American. The amount and character of education in the South, as well as the nature of the section's educational problems, must be understood in the context of its own special culture. At the basis of whatever cultural uniqueness the South has is the institution of the plantation. From the point of view of the educational process, plantation societies may be compared with agricultural mission societies. The plantation and the agricultural mission have different histories and conflicting ideologies, but they develop in similar environments; and in adjusting to the permanent elements in the environment, like geography and climate, they eventually become very similar institutions. The educational process in each goes about as far as, and not much further than, the needs of the situation require. And the needs are, or have been, about the same. The comparison suggests that education is fundamentally a process of biological adaptation and survival. But an education which has sufficed for the relatively simple world in which both the plantation and the mission developed will not suffice for competition in the more complex and uncertain order into which the world is moving.

We already are familiar with some of the more general and objective facts concerning white and Negro educational opportunities in the South. These facts are often and strikingly expressed in terms of the money spent in our biracial system of education. Thus it is pointed out that the average expenditure for every pupil throughout the nation in 1930 was $99.00. The average expenditure for white children in the South was less than half this amount, or $44.31, while the average expenditure for Negro children was only $12.57, or about one-fourth that for southern white children and about one-eighth that for the average of the United States. Those southern states with large Negro populations, where the average pupil in a rural school comes from a tenant family, show even greater discrepancies. In 1930 Georgia spent an average of $35.42 for each white child and $6.38 for each Negro child. Mississippi, with half her population Negro and more completely dominated by the plantation system than any other state,[1] spent more for her white children than did Georgia ($45.34 per child) and less for her Negro children ($5.45 per child).[2]

More important than these figures (and many more might be offered) are the attitudes in the southern social situation which they represent and presumably measure. All such statistics must be understood in the context of southern culture. A comparison of southern culture with American culture as seen, for example, by Clark Wissler may serve to suggest some of its essential features. After comparing American culture with the cultures of other societies, Wissler tells us that its dominant characteristics may be condensed into three sets of ideas and beliefs which, he says, actuate the American people. These are mechanical invention, universal suffrage, and mass education.[3] Now if the complex of these characteristics defines the American culture, then historically the South has not been a part of it, or at least has been only marginal to it. In fact, the South has differed so radically from the rest of the United States that it be-

---

[1] "There is little doubt that the plantation system is both absolutely and relatively more important in Mississippi than in any other state" (quoted from *Plantation Farming in the United States* [Census Bull. (1916)], p. 21).

[2] These figures are taken from a little booklet entitled *School Money in Black and White*, published by the Julius Rosenwald Fund and prepared by a committee of which Fred McCuistion was chairman.

[3] *Man and Culture* (New York: Thomas Y. Crowell Co., 1923), pp. 5–12.

came, by the time of the Civil War, culturally and economically almost a separate nation. The establishment of the Confederacy was intended to give these cultural and economic facts a more complete constitutional sanction.

American culture is and has been characterized "by a great emphasis upon mechanical devices." Southerners have imported and used these devices in increasing degree, to be sure, but the "amiable American hobby" of tinkering with machinery has been so little an integral part of southern life that a mechanical cotton mill is still regarded by many as a "fotched-in contraption" alien to its traditions. Economic opportunities in the North have offered a constantly increasing variety of ways of earning a livelihood, whereas the South, until relatively recently, has offered only one, agriculture, and that, a particular kind of agriculture. The mechanization of southern agriculture has, in recent years, expanded rapidly, but traditionally the southern plantation has operated mainly with hand labor and with only elementary tools and machines. Negroes particularly have been outside the American mechanical tradition.

Industry in the South, and especially the textile industry, was originally developed by local interests in a sort of crusade to provide opportunities for poor whites. It came with the recognition that the section had a poor-white as well as a Negro problem, and it was sponsored as a program for the solution of that problem. These white millworkers, recruited from rural areas, have continued to speak. the language and carry the mental images of the farm. Control of the industries in which they work has largely passed to outside interests; and these interests have succeeded, in large measure, only by bringing the operation of the factories into line with the paternalistic traditions of the plantation system.

Universal suffrage, or "the idea that what most of the people in the group approve will be as near to the correct solution as can be achieved for the time being," is, according to Wissler, another dominant trait of the American culture. Years ago James Bryce, in *The American Commonwealth*, likewise noted the disposition of the American people to refer every question to the arbitrament of numbers, confident that the people are sure to decide right in the long run. In the South, however, the mores have largely nullified the ideal of universal suffrage, which has been regarded as something imposed upon a defeated people by the northern victor. Since the rise of the southern white democracy the ballot box has become a symbol of class stratification based upon color. Recent southern opposition to the abolition of poll taxes serves to show that the old attitude toward suffrage as a class privilege and not as a procedure for the democratic determination of policy continues to possess considerable strength. The meeting and settling of all issues by means of the ballot has never been the practice in the South. In the United States rule by just one majority group occurs only in this section; elsewhere the membership of the majority changes from one issue to another. As far as the South is concerned there are two reasons for this. One is the presence in this region of an authoritarian tradition stemming from the planter aristocracy and woven into the general class and racial situation. The second reason is that the issues that appear as problems elsewhere in the nation have not been regarded as problems in the agrarian and feudal order of this region where they are settled in the mores.[4] Consequently, a large part of the southern population, including the greater part of the Negro population, has not been accustomed to resort to the ballot to change those conditions which constitute problems elsewhere but which in the South have been taken for granted as if they were a part of the order of nature itself.

American culture, Wissler continues, "is characterized by an overruling belief in something we call education—a kind of mechanism to propitiate the intent of nature in the manifestation of culture." But formal

[4] Walter Wilbur, "Special Problems of the South," *Annals of the American Academy of Political and Social Science*, CLXXVI (November, 1934), 49–56.

mass education, even for whites, certainly has never been a completely integral part of southern culture. That it is not even now is shown by the figures on the money spent in the South's educational system presented at the beginning of this paper. Upon an illiterate and agricultural laboring population in the South has rested a planter and upperclass white population whose literacy probably originated or was maintained through the necessity for keeping in touch with the affairs of the market and the city and with political and economic conditions affecting the market. With a substantial income and leisure even an illiterate planter became concerned to give an education and a certain amount of "culture" to his children. But for those who have remained more or less outside the sphere of direct market relationships no great need for education has been felt. In the past, southern agriculture has required little above a uniform grade of unskilled labor, subject to routine tasks, shaped to change on the basis of contingency alone, and one which was not required consciously to assume the risks incident to selling in a foreign market. As a result, education has not appeared to these classes as a necessity or as something having survival value, but merely as something which conferred status, and often a rather dubious status at that. For in the folk mind there was the general conviction that book learning only muddled up thinking and that ordinary gumption and common sense were sufficient for whatever problems men had to face. And to the planters and employers of labor an educated peasantry has seemed no more advantageous than an uneducated one.

The numerous towns and villages which, from the very beginning of settlement, formed a nucleus for the small farms of New England and provided favorable soil for public school education found no historical parallel in the South. Here, after the Civil War, towns and villages began to appear in greater numbers with the partial disintegration of the plantation system. The southern public school movement, which accompanied the rise of towns and villages, repre-

sented in part an adjustment to a new set of economic and social needs in a changed situation. It assumed the character of a crusade led by devoted idealists charged with pathos for the illiterate and benighted and urged on by unfavorable comparisons with the more advanced North and West. The crusade resulted in notable progress in attaining a more fundamental educational process, but, as in the educational crusades of Japan and Soviet Russia, much of the alleged advance has turned out to be spurious when the amount of rote learning it produced is considered. Learning by rote has become not only a fact but something of a tradition, especially in the rural white and Negro schools of the South.[5] The reason is that southern society, unlike a society such as that of Denmark, has not been the kind of society in which separate institutions designed for the instruction of the children of the masses were required for the integration of economic and political life. This is ceasing to be true, but the tendency from Colonial days to the present has been to regard the public school, and especially the Negro school, like the cotton mill, as a "fotched-in contraption." The schools have been tolerated and maintained by being brought into line with the class and racial traditions of the plantation system.

Accompanied by a friend, I once attended a rally at a Negro school in a Texas community. The white city-school superintendent of this community was a Scotchman from North Carolina. The rally had been organized by the colored principal acting under orders from the white superintendent, who, while making a speech, pointed his finger at the colored principal and said, "I told him if he didn't bring this school into line I would find me another principal." The setting was in a school building and there was no cotton or tobacco to be seen, but my friend and I agreed on our way home that the superintendent seemed to run the school as if it were a plantation and to regard the

[5] Robert E. Park, "A Memorandum on Rote Learning," *American Journal of Sociology*, XLIII (July, 1937), 23–36.

principal, the teachers, and the pupils as the planter regards his tenants and laborers. There was no ill will, and the superintendent seemed to have the welfare of the school at heart; but the pattern of control was the pattern of the plantation.

It should be evident from all this that we have to understand education, like almost everything else in this region of the United States, in the light of a cultural situation which is southern and not American if we accept Wissler's analysis of American culture. And it would seem that behind whatever differences there are in the southern situation lies that very quintessence of southernism, the plantation, an institution which long has ceased to be merely a large estate on which cotton or tobacco is grown but one which, like Christian Science, has become a state of mind. Within the structure of this institution and the system which has grown up around it the positions of both white and Negro education have been assigned along caste lines.

The institution of the plantation, as it developed in the South and in other colonial areas around the world, was originally and has continued to be a type of economic enterprise very unlike those other economic enterprises that developed in the laissez faire capitalism that succeeded feudalism in Europe. Unlike the "free" labor of capitalistic Europe—that is, labor free to seek and to change employers—plantation labor was sought, moved, settled, and controlled by employers. In different plantation societies the control has taken different forms, and in a single plantation society like that of the South the control has changed in form from indentured servitude and slavery to sharecropping. But always the form has served to emphasize the political, i.e., the authoritarian, character of the institution to a degree exceeding that of the economic enterprises of European and northern United States capitalism.

The plantation represents one kind of political institution which develops at points of intercultural and interracial contacts, but in the course of the long history of such contacts on the part of migrating peoples there have been many other kinds of latifundia. The state itself, according to Oppenheimer[6] and others, originated in just such situations. It would seem that the contact of peoples differing in race and culture nearly always results in some new institution, organized around the problems of control growing out of the new social relationships and furnishing a structure through which the motives and purposes of those who came to exploit the situation can in some measure be realized.

Thus along the world's frontiers have arisen such varied and interesting institutions of the land as haciendas, plantations, farms, missions, ranches, and the like. They are as varied and as interesting as are the immigrant institutions of the large city, but they cannot be passed in quick review by walking through forty blocks,[7] and so their range is not so apparent and comparison among them is not so easy. They are institutions of the land and of settlement, and, once established, they largely determine how people shall live on the land. But more important for our purpose here is the fact that they seem to lay bare the elementary processes that go into the making of the state; in them the competitions and conflicts of racial and cultural groups living in the same territory are brought down to their most elementary terms. And as obvious and as elementary as any, in the conquest and exploitation of a pioneer region, is the process whereby the land is alienated and its resources brought under the control of invading settlers, planters, missionaries, and the like. New land or settlement institutions arise as an incident in the process of extending the range of the "political formation and economic exploitation" which Oppenheimer has conceived to be basic to state-building. The land changes hands, and those who come to possess it and to convert it to new and presumably higher uses subject those

[6] Franz Oppenheimer, *The State* (New York: Vanguard Press, 1938).

[7] See Konrad Bercovici, *Around the World in New York* (New York: Century Co., 1924).

over whom they come to possess authority to new and stricter forms of discipline. To this end they make and enforce new rules and impose new conditions of life generally. The important point to be noted here is that the class which enforces the new arrangement is the same class which instructs in the new arrangement, not simply in order to indoctrinate but also to bring about a level of efficiency necessary to sustain it.

Education in a homogeneous society is normally a process of inducting the maturing individual into the social heritage. It is thus, as Dewey has emphasized, essentially a process of renewal and growth without which the group would have no continuity. As the society becomes more complex, the process by which members educate one another through their daily contacts has to be supplemented and augmented by more formal instruction in separate educational institutions, but education continues to be a matter of transmitting a tradition from one generation to another. In a situation of racial and cultural contact, however, education becomes a matter of expanding a culture from one people to another; it becomes a part of the process of acculturation. In intercultural and interracial situations, where the culture of the dominant group is regarded as the standard, the members of the lower groups must learn things from the school which members of the dominant group are presumed to learn in the home, such as rules of hygiene and of conduct. Since the adults of the subordinate group are as illiterate in these matters as their children, education often begins with the adults before it reaches their children. In any case, the task of the elementary school for the subordinate population is much more important and much more difficult than that of the elementary school for the children of the dominant group. Incidentally, it is on the elementary-school level that the education of Negro school children in the South is weakest.

The whole of European culture has never impinged equally upon the whole of a native culture. Since culture is carried in the knowledge, skills, attitudes, habits, and tools of particular individuals, European culture has worked upon native society through the medium of the purposes of trader, administrator, planter, missionary, etc. Because these purposes and programs get incorporated in plantations, trading factories, missions, and the like, the thought suggests itself at once that a comparison of the histories of these various colonial institutions, with attention to the role of education in each, might prove very rewarding. Students of southern education might in this way gain insight into and perspective toward the problems of education in a plantation society which might very well change our whole conception of them. We might, for one thing, discover just how education grows up as a natural process, how it works, how it becomes formalized and ritualized, and just why and how it undergoes change. For such a purpose no other institution of the frontier seems to promise more than a study of the agricultural mission.

Such a study is made all the more significant by the fact that the education of Negroes in the South has always had a certain missionary quality about it, even since the planter regained control from the northern missionary. The schools of the Negro in the South, unlike their churches, have always been directed and controlled from outside their own ranks. Planter and missionary have held different and conflicting points of view, but both have assumed the necessity for outside and overhead control.

In their most obvious and visible aspects the plantation and the agricultural mission appear quite similar. They both are large landed estates. They both rest upon an agricultural economy; and very often the mission, like the plantation, exports its products to foreign markets. They both import supplies from abroad. In both, the field labor is performed by a people different in cultural and ordinarily in racial origin from those who direct and manage the enterprise. The latter possess great authority, and the former may be legally or in effect slaves. But, similar as the two institutions are in their organization and in their natural interests, in their political and moral principles they are ideological antagonists. Their very different histories and original purposes have, nevertheless, resulted in a similar phenomenon.

The mission represents the working-out of motives and purposes inherent in religious proselytism. Implicit in such a religion as Christianity is the belief that it possesses a universal validity, a belief which imposes upon its followers the moral obligation to transmit its precepts. This obligation takes an organized and concrete form in the person of the missionary, who, by definition, is committed to the propagation of his faith by teaching and persuasion. And, of course, the most obvious field for propagation lies among those people most completely outside the culture in which the religion originated.

The pioneer missionary usually begins his work by carrying his message to the heathen in a direct manner. There is something typical in the picture of Charles William Eliot in early New England preaching with Bible in hand to the Indians in the snow. The Indians appeared interested in his strange behavior, at least for a while; but they did not know what he was talking about, and Eliot undoubtedly soon discovered that fact. When it is apparent that direct attempts at conversion avail little, then it is realized that conversion has to begin with civilization. Missionaries conceive of themselves as propagating a particular religious doctrine, but they are really propagating a culture. Usually coming from small communities, they soon begin to lose interest in their narrow religious doctrines and begin to interest themselves in the larger problems of cultural assimilation. What they finally seek to do is merely to educate. The immediate expression of the indirect method in missionary activity is a concentration upon agricultural, health, and domestic education as a solvent for the native's physical and mental disabilities.

There are subtle and unexpected adjustments to be made, too, in the missionaries' social relations with the heathen. What these are and how they arise is naïvely revealed in a letter written by Mrs. Lucy Thurston, wife of one of the pioneer missionaries to the Hawaiian Islands, to a friend in Boston in the year 1835. The letter was occasioned by the necessity for explaining to their supporters back home why the missionaries in Hawaii kept native servants in their households.

. . . . In our own house we have the various classes of master and mistress, of children, and of household natives. There is a native family attached to our establishment, whose home is a distinct house in our common yard. They give us their services. One man simply cultivates taro, two miles up the country, and weekly brings down a supply of the staff of life for ourselves and our dependents. Another man every week goes up the mountain to do our washing. . . . . In like manner a third man, who under the old dispensation, officiated as priest to one of their gods, now, under a new dispensation, with commendable humility, officiates as cook to a priest and his family. Then, aid in the care of the house, of sewing, and of babyhood, devolves upon female hands.

We commenced mission life with other ideas. Native youth resided in our families, and so far as was consistent, we granted them all the privileges of companions and of children. Not many years rolled on, and our eyes were opened to behold the moral pollution which, unchecked, had here been accumulated for ages. I saw, but it was parental responsibilities which made me so emphatically *feel* the horrors of a heathen land. I had it ever in my heart, the shafts of sin flying in every direction are liable to pierce the vitals of my children. . . . .

I reviewed the ground on which I stood. The heathen world were to be converted. But by what means? Are missionaries with their eyes open to the dangers of the situation, to sit conscientiously down to the labor of bringing back a revolted race to the service of Jehovah, and in doing so practically give over their children to Satan? . . . . I could see no alternative but that a mother go to work, and here form a moral atmosphere in which her children can live and move without inhaling the infection of moral death. . . . . The first important measure was to prohibit them altogether the use of the Hawaiian language, thus cutting off all intercourse between them and the heathen. This, of course, led to the family regulation, that no child might speak to a native, and no native might speak to a child, babyhood excepted. This led to another arrangement, that of having separate rooms and yards for our children, and separate rooms and yards for natives. The reason for this separation . . . . was distinctly stated to household natives. . . . . We are willing to come and live among you, that you may be taught the good way; but it would break our hearts to see our children rise up and be like the children of Hawaii. . . . .

Dear Mrs. Bishop, who was laid in her grave six weeks before the arrival of the reinforcement, longed exceedingly to see and give them a charge from her sick couch. The purport of it was this: "Do not be devoted to domestic duties. Trust to natives, however imperfect their services, and preserve your constitutions." I needed no such warning, for I had learned the lesson by my own sad experience, and when, after years of prostration, I was again permitted to enjoy comfortable health, I availed myself of the aid of natives for the accomplishment of such domestic duties as they were capable of rendering. . . . . For as one of our physicians told me, "You may as well talk of perpetual motion, as to think of performing as much labor here as you could have done by remaining in America."

As to the effects produced upon natives thus employed in our families, they have more intelligence, more of the good things of this life, more influence among their fellows than they could otherwise possess; and numbers of them, I doubt not, will be added to that great company, which no man can number, redeemed out of every kindred, and tongue, and people, and nation.[8]

A planter's wife in early Virginia might easily have written an almost identical letter to a friend in England.

Lind has shown the close affinity between the mission and the plantation in the development of the Hawaiian Islands. The early competition between them merely evidenced "the fundamental affinity between them." Later they joined forces "in urging the transition from the native system of land tenure to one more in conformity with capitalistic principles." The missionaries were among

the earliest to foresee the commercial possibilities of sugar cane, especially after financial assistance from the homeland was terminated, as a means of supporting the missions and furthering the advancement of their parishioners. The mission estate of Father Bond in Kohala formulated a fixed set of rules for the government of its members.[9]

Protestant missions not only developed agricultural estates in the past but they maintain a large number of them at the present time, or did until recently, in the Orient, in Africa, in South America, and in the South Seas. In 1920 the International Association for Agricultural Missions was organized "to promote the interests of Christian agricultural work in all lands."

But the institution of the agricultural mission was carried to its most extreme development by missionary priests of the various Catholic orders operating in what is now the southwestern part of the United States, in Latin America, and in the Philippines. Perhaps no other community in the world has been so greatly influenced by the agricultural mission as has Paraguay, in South America. In the seventeenth and eighteenth centuries the unmarried Jesuit priests in Paraguay, unlike the Protestant missionaries in Hawaii, did not encounter the problem of protecting their children as they grew up among an alien population, but other forces in the situation established them as a class apart. However, their demonstration of success in the organization of agriculture, and the example of their own efforts and production, operated to set up links of influence and dependence between themselves and the natives: links which were not established forcefully or even consciously but which gave them prestige and then authority and power.

When the power of the Jesuits extended far enough to make it possible, tribal life was forcefully broken up and the Indians were "reduced," as the friars put it, to mission-

<hr>

[8] Lucy G. Thurston, *Life and Times of Lucy Thurston* (Ann Arbor, Mich.: S. C. Andrews, 1882), pp. 125–31.

[9] Andrew W. Lind, *An Island Community* (Chicago: University of Chicago Press, 1938), pp. 147, 149, 170, and 214.

village life. These reductions grew up, Keller tells us, "in the wide regions relatively or totally unoccupied by Europeans."[10] In the missions the Indian charges were rigorously isolated from the world, and the missionary normally formed the only contact with the outside.

Bourne gives us a picture of mission life and points out what the mission came to be. Under the increasing supervision of the friars, the Indians, he says,

.... were taught the elements of letters, and trained to peaceful, industrious and religious lives. In fact, every mission was an industrial school, in which the simple arts were taught by the friars, themselves in origin plain Spanish peasants. The discipline of the mission was as minute as that of a school: the unmarried youths and maidens were locked in at night; the day's work began and ended with prayers and the catechism; each Indian, besides cultivating his own plot of land, worked two hours a day on the farm belonging to the village, the produce of which went to the support of the church. The mission was recruited by inducing the wild Indians to join it, and also by kidnapping them. Spanish America from California and Texas to Paraguay and Chile was fringed with such establishments, the outposts of civilization, where many thousands of Indians went through a schooling which ended only with their lives. In the process of time a mission was slowly transformed into a "pueblo de Indios" .... and the mission frontier was pushed out a little farther.[11]

When the mission in Latin America "had been included within the slowly expanding area of intercourse with the outside world," as the market came nearer and the mission became more and more dependent upon it, it ceased to be a mission. Like the plantation, it was a frontier institution, and when the frontier passed on the mission went with it. But not before it had accomplished a significant transformation in the culture of the Indians. It introduced new methods and standards of agricultural production, it taught new arts and crafts, and it left the Indians at least nominally Catholic in religion. However, in spite of the devoted, persistent, and strenuous efforts of the priests, the mission left no high and lasting educational tradition. The literacy they promoted only led to the charge that the mission Indians had become mere apes and parrots incapable of progress and invention when left to themselves.[12]

If the mission grew up out of a background of religious fervor, the plantation had its origin in northern European capitalism. A plantation was originally a migration, a transplantation of people to overseas territory; and, in certain frontier areas capable of producing a staple crop for the European market, the migration passed over into an institutional structure for the production of the staple. The plantation type of migration became, in these areas, the plantation type of estate. Where this happened the migration was not composed of family, community, or congregational groups intent on reproducing in the New World the agricultural economy of the Old. It did not, in other words, result in the kind of settlements that the Pilgrims made in New England or the Germans made in Pennsylvania and in parts of the South. The kind of migration which resulted in plantation establishments, where they were economically possible, was a migration made up of individual adventurers and traders seeking profitable investments. They did not come to make a home for their children or to convert the natives to Christianity, although these things occurred to them later. It is significant that, in the histories of the various plantation societies, the members of the initial planter class are recruited from the ranks of ship captains and traders. This is the sort of men who possess both capital and knowledge of investment opportunities in foreign places. They are likely to be unfamiliar with the folk agriculture of their home countries, and there is no reason why they should seek to reproduce it abroad. But an opportunity

[10] A. G. Keller, *Colonization* (Boston: Ginn & Co., 1908), p. 286.

[11] E. G. Bourne, *Spain in America, 1450–1580* (New York: Harper & Bros., 1904), pp. 305–6 (quoted in Keller, *op. cit.*, pp. 287–88).

[12] Keller, *op. cit.*, p. 293.

for profitable investment in new commodities of agriculture like tobacco, sugar cane, or rubber is in line with the commercial interests which they represent. Hence it is that the virtues of these men are not those of niceness and scholarship but of resourcefulness and enterprise, and in the areas where they operate they are too busy opening up the country and profiting from the exploitation of its resources to concern themselves overmuch with the educational welfare of the general population.[13] The South is that part of this nation where the planter has most profoundly impressed himself upon the form of society and where something of his original motives and attitudes persist.

The concern of the missionary is for the educational and spiritual welfare of the natives, but the purpose of the planter to profit through the exploitation of land and labor leads ordinarily to an unfavorable judgment of native workers. In plantation societies the native is invariably condemned as lazy and worthless. The remedy is not to improve him through education. It is cheaper and far easier to turn to outside sources. Thus the planters of the South imported white indentured servants from Europe and then Negro slaves from Africa. The planters in Natal turned to India, and those in Hawaii to China, Japan, and the Philippines. It is a frequent observation that whereas the native is not a very satisfactory laborer in the land of his birth he is highly prized when he is transported to territory strange to him.

With imported male or family-less laborers the control situation changes in favor of the planter. It is easier to fit unattached individuals into their proper places in the organization of plantation work. They are encamped upon the land of the planter's estate, held there, and prevented from scattering out over the territory generally. It is to prevent such dispersion in areas where there is free or waste land available that slavery, indentured servitude, contract labor, and other forms of forced labor arise.

Up through this stage the plantation itself is a kind of school but not one formally and consciously organized for the purpose of teaching. Nevertheless, as Booker T. Washington said, "every slave plantation in the South was an industrial school. On these plantations young colored men and women were constantly being trained not only as farmers but as carpenters, blacksmiths, wheelwrights, brick masons, engineers, cooks, laundresses, sewing women, and housekeepers."[14] In Africa it was said that the "best school for the African is a good European estate."[15]

The situation changes again when the importation of outside labor is interrupted. This happened in the New World when the African slave trade was shut off; it happened in Mauritius, in Natal, and in some of the islands of the West Indies when India refused to allow more of her people to emigrate as laborers to these plantation areas. Now it becomes necessary to find a new source of labor; and the new source is found in the children of the laborers, for in the meantime the mass of imported and assorted individuals have gradually organized themselves into family groups and have produced offspring. Born to the situation, the children tend to accept it without question; but their very presence introduces new problems of control and changes in plantation organization.

It is when the plantation reaches this stage in its life-history, the stage of Creole or "home-grown" labor, that questions of positive educational policy begin to arise. In fact, this stage in plantation development in different areas around the world is best studied in the materials on education in colonial areas because of the close relation between labor control and educational policies. In the South, before about 1800, the idea of an education for Negroes was not rejected because it was not even entertained. Be-

13 *Ibid.*, p. 11; Lillian Knowles, *The Economic Development of the Overseas Empire* (London: G. Routledge & Sons, 1924), p. 219.

14 "Industrial Education for the Negro," in W. E. B. DuBois *et al.*, *The Negro Problem* (New York: James Pott & Co., 1903), p. 1.

15 Raymond L. Buell, *The Native Problem in Africa* (New York: Macmillan Co., 1928), I, 529.

cause some Negroes, however, had been gaining a sort of informal education through personal contacts with whites and because some of these Negroes, like the slave Gabriel in Virginia, were found plotting insurrections, laws were passed aimed at restricting educational opportunities for them. After the Nat Turner rebellion in 1831 legislation became even more repressive; yet in spite of the laws individual whites, especially pious women who believed that "everyone should know how to read the Bible,"[16] continued to teach Negroes.

As long as the children of the laborers are slaves like their fathers, as in the ante bellum South, the public educational policy is to discourage or prevent any formal education at all. "Of what use will education be to them if they get it?" is the question which appears to answer itself as far as planters are concerned. But where the children of the laborers are free, either by virtue of emancipation or because they do not inherit the legal compulsion to work which operates against their fathers, the community is forced to accept the necessity for education in some form and to some degree. The question then becomes, "What kind and how much?"

Since education is both an instrument of

control in the hands of the planter class and a means of emancipation and status for the children of the laboring classes, it is easy to understand both the hopes and the fears of the employing classes when they first begin to yield the privilege of education. Stated briefly, the educational policy of the planter class is to insure that the children of plantation laborers will remain plantation laborers. If education there must be, let it be an education designed to make hewers of wood and drawers of water better hewers of wood and drawers of water. The planters' solution is therefore an occupational education; but often this is not a solution from the point of view of the working-class members of the dominant race, for whom such an education may raise up dangerous competitors.

To those upon whom it is urged, a vocational and occupational education is suspect, since it appears to lead to an intensification of occupational distinctions and to a society consisting of impenetrable caste strata. Since the status of the privileged class is associated with educational attainment in the sciences, the liberal arts, and the professions, it is natural for those at the bottom to be attracted to this kind of education, the kind of education which promises to lead them out of their traditional class into a higher one. The son of a plantation laborer in Hawaii, whose attitude seems typical, wrote as follows:

My parents always told me to study hard and become a great man and not a cane field laborer, who had to go to work early in the morning, rain or sun, and work to late in the evening. They even said that they would buy anything for me if it is related to school.[17]

Regardless of the type of education, the appearance of the school at the stage of "home-grown" labor in the plantation's history precipitates two problems. On the one hand, it defines child labor as a social problem, since child labor is any kind of labor that keeps a child away from school. The

---

[16] The laws were enacted against the categorical Negro, but it appears to have been breached by whites in the case of individual Negroes whom they knew and toward whom they were personally sympathetic. In 1853 Mrs. Margaret Douglas encouraged her daughter to teach a class of Negro children in a room in her home in Norfolk. Mrs. Douglas was arrested and convicted by the court. In conducting her defense, Mrs. Douglas pointed out that an example had been set for her by the Sunday schools of the various churches of Norfolk. Concerning the case the *Petersburg [Va.] Daily Express* for November 30, 1853, observed: "It did not appear from the evidence of any of the gentlemen called upon by Mrs. Douglas, that they had actually seen negroes taught from books in any of the Sunday schools of the city, but the fact, as stated by them, that nearly all the negroes attending the Sunday schools could read, gave rise to a violent suspicion that many of the ladies and gentlemen of our city, moving in the highest circles of society, had been guilty of as flagrant a violation of the law as could be imputed to Mrs. Douglas and her daughter."

[17] Quoted in Romanzo Adams, *The Education and Economic Outlook for the Boys of Hawaii: A Study in the Field of Race Relationships* (Honolulu: Institute of Pacific Relations, 1927), p. 15.

recognition of the large amount of child labor in the South as a social problem is a matter of recent history. Here, as in the West Indies and in South Africa, it has led to much discussion and an agitation for the primacy of the school over the demands of employers.

On the other hand, the school tends to produce a white-collar class which the industrial and agricultural system does not absorb. Even in the South the education of the Negro has developed more rapidly than have his opportunities for wider participation in economic and political life. It is in Hawaii, however, that the contest between the educational ambitions of the sons and daughters of the plantation laborers and the labor needs of the planters is most acute. In 1882 the first annual meeting of the Planter's Labor and Supply Company defined the type of labor most ideal for plantation work with the statement: "The industrial condition of these Islands requires people as laborers who are accustomed to subordination, to permanency of abode, and who have moderate expectations in regard to a livelihood."[18]

While the sugar industry was expanding, while times were prosperous and labor continued to be imported, education did not seem to be harmful. But, under the stress of a receding price, a growing burden of taxation, and a possibility that the supply of labor from the Philippines would be cut off, there developed the conviction that education makes people unfit for common plantation labor. The planters became outspoken for a fundamental change. They would place limitations upon the schools, and such schools as remained would serve merely as training grounds for plantation workers. In his address to the annual meeting of the Hawaiian Sugar Planters' Association in 1925, the president of the association said:

Why blindly continue a system that keeps a boy or girl in school at taxpayers' expense long after they have mastered more than sufficient learning for all ordinary purposes, simply to enlighten them on subjects of questionable value;

[18] *Hawaiian Planters' Monthly*, I (1882), 187.

subjects on which they could as well enlighten themselves (if by any chance their inclinations tended in that direction) and at the same time, by entering some field of employment will, besides earning wages, be gaining experience and efficiency, and above all learn to appreciate the value of a dollar by working for it. . . . . The solution as I see it, is that the taxpayer be relieved of further responsibility after the pupil has mastered the sixth grade, or the eighth grade in a modified form.[19]

In Malaya, which developed rapidly into a plantation community during the past half-century, the British pursued the policy of educating principally for the needs of the planters. A few English schools were maintained to train an adequate supply of clerks; there were some vernacular schools for the natives and for the children of the Indian workers on the plantations; but the British were frankly opposed to "any ideal of education not adjusted to local wants," as it must inevitably "lead to economic dislocation and social unrest."[20]

A committee in Ceylon, appointed to inquire into the state of education in that colony, objected to a type of education which had done nothing more than to produce

a class of shallow, conceited, half-educated youths who have learned nothing but to look back with contempt upon the conditions in which they were born and from which they conceive that their education has raised them, and who desert the ranks of the industrious classes to become idle, discontented hangers-on of the courts and the Public Offices.[21]

Similar statements from other plantation areas might be offered,[22] but these are sufficient to show that the educational problems

[19] *Proceedings of the Hawaiian Sugar Planters' Association, 1925*, p. 13.

[20] *Education in Malaya* (London, 1924), p. 15.

[21] Quoted in H. A. Wyndham, *Native Education* (London: Oxford University Press, 1933), p. 46.

[22] See, e.g., C. Y. Shepard, "Agricultural Labour in Trinidad," *Tropical Agriculture*, March, 1935, p. 63; and T. Walter Wallbank, "British Colonial Policy and Native Education in Kenya," *Journal of Negro Education*, October, 1938, p. 52.

of the South are typically those of plantation societies generally.

When the educational process in a plantation society is compared with that of a mission society, the conclusion suggests itself that, whether formal education is promoted from above, as in the case of the mission, or whether it is demanded from below, as in the case of the plantation, it achieves no higher level than the needs of the situation require. And the situation is very much the same for both institutions. The great mission establishments of the past did not develop along every frontier where missionary work was carried on. They did not grow up in New England, for instance, even though the Congregational church there had a complete monopoly of the field. The great agricultural mission estates grew up in the same kind of areas where the plantations grew up and for very much the same reason—these were the areas that could grow the *Kolonialwaren* for which there was a ready market abroad. The fact that financial support from home for missionary activities in the Colonies was not expected to last forever faced every mission sooner or later with the problem of becoming self-supporting. Thus the aims of civilizing, educating, and converting and of finding means for self-support all came to coincide; and the result was to make the mission a large landed and agricultural estate. Where there was more land than there was labor to cultivate it, where there was a favorable market for the products of the land, the mission became very much the same sort of institution that the plantation became. One traveler who had seen both institutions thought that the lot of the Indian neophytes in the California missions differed very little from the lot of the Negro slaves on the West Indian sugar plantations.[23]

The two institutions have at times become so much alike that when found together they are in a condition of competition and conflict. In colonial Brazil, planter opposition to the Jesuits resulted in the forced withdrawal of the friars as the conviction grew that the missions "were simply competing plantations worked at merely nominal cost by converts adroitly turned into slaves."[24]

To the permanent and fixed elements in the environment, elements of geography and climate, even conflicting ideologies tend eventually to make the same kind of adjustment.

Education, like other aspects of culture, is a condition for the satisfaction of the elementary needs of individuals and of groups of individuals. Like intelligence, it is in considerable measure a response to a problematical situation that requires reflection and energy and struggle. The fundamental educational process is therefore a kind of biological adaptation. As long as a group is at least maintaining its numbers at given standards it may be presumed to have an educational system commensurate with its needs. It may be that the people of the South have had about all the education they could use in the kind of world in which they have lived and competed. The situation, however, is changing radically. The star of the southern plantation is on the wane, and for the future a region of white and Negro small-farm holdings appears likely. To win their bread and protect their liberties in the new world of competition and conflict with others, the people of the South must gear their minds and hands to new levels of endeavor. New needs will bring—must bring—a new and more vital education.

DUKE UNIVERSITY

[23] Katherine Coman, *Economic Beginnings of the Far West* (New York: Macmillan Co., 1912), I, 150.

[24] Keller, *op. cit.*, p. 154.

TRANSMITTING OUR DEMOCRATIC HERITAGE IN THE SCHOOLS

RUTH BENEDICT

ABSTRACT

No educational policies can of themselves make a stable society out of our unstable one. In our changing culture it is necessary to base our teachings upon fundamental commitments of our culture if we are to avoid teaching many things the child will have to unlearn later. Transmission of our democratic heritage is most threatened at the point of transition from childish dependency to adult independence.

Controversies about education in recent years have in one way or another turned upon the issue of the role of the schools in transmitting our cultural heritage. There have been those who have blamed the schools for every "un-American" trait they believed to be increasing in our society. Some of these critics place on the schools responsibility for the decreasing religious affiliations in our cities and rural areas; some attack them for the moral relativism they see in our decade. Such criticisms assume that an educational system can, of and by itself, have such far-reaching effects as these; and this same assumption is just as basic in a very different argument: that education should shoulder the responsibility for ushering in a new social order. In so far as these critics and exhorters have argued only that some particular set of facts should be taught in our schools—American history or the Bible or Thomas Aquinas or the achievements of the T.V.A.—there is no need for further discussion; the school curriculum can easily be improved without claiming that our educational system makes or breaks the social order. But the assumption made by these critics has consequences of its own which go far beyond the changes in curriculum they urge. It is an assumption that can be examined in the light of comparative studies of other cultures, and such an examination can throw light on the whole relation of education to social change.

It is instructive to study a long series of societies, identifying those where culture is relatively stable and those where it is highly unstable. One does not find that those which are stable educate their children in one fashion and those which are unstable in another.

There are a great many different ways of rearing children: they may be treated like little adults from birth and divide their day into work and play almost exactly as their parents do; they may be little outlaws who consider the adults fair game, pillaging their fields and evading responsibilities; they may be privileged beings whose every wish is gratified, however inconvenient. But none of these or other ways of rearing children correlates with whether or not the culture is reproduced in the next generation. Stability of culture over generations is not a function of the particular kind of education that is given to children. It is a function rather of social conditions in the whole tribe or nation. Anthropologists have to study rapidly changing cultures over and over again, and usually with sinking hearts. When a Plains Indian tribe is put on a reservation, the differences between older and younger generations are very great, and transmission of culture most inadequate. The livelihood techniques the parents knew can no longer be used, for the buffalo have disappeared from the plains, and horses can no longer be raided from other tribes. The older ways of life no longer work, and with them go the religious rites that guaranteed them and the respect which the young once showed their elders. These drop out, and the tragedy is that it is hard to replace them. Then one generation is not like another: transmission of culture has been interfered with by all the external and internal conditions which are present in an unstable society. Sometimes the anthropologist can study cultural change under more favorable conditions: when incentives to activity are increased; when there is more leisure because iron tools, for instance, have been introduced; and when the arts of life therefore flourish and new developments take place.

Under such social conditions—whatever the method of education—transmission of culture is achieved only in part. But a homogeneous society faced by no new circumstances sufficiently drastic to disturb its balance transmits its culture generation after generation, no matter how it breaks the rules of education that seem to us essential. Our problems in transmission of culture arise from the rapidity of social changes in our society; and no method of education can prevent this. The choices open to our school systems are only whether they will cling to the teaching of subjects and attitudes which the child can no longer use profitably in the world in which he will live or whether they will give him equipment he can use. They cannot possibly make a stable world of an unstable one. Those critics who blame the schools for the changes they resent in our culture are making the educational system a scapegoat for vast changes in the structure of modern society which they do not take into account.

Once we are sufficiently skeptical about the notion that schools—or parents—have it in their power to indoctrinate our children so that they will maintain the status quo, we can face the crucial problem of the relation of education to the social order. All the problems in this relationship, whatever the tribe or nation studied, concern the degree to which the method of education fits the requirements of that society. It is not a matter of identifying some good educational policies and some bad ones. The "best" education can be a weakness in a society that does not give the adolescent scope to put his learning into practice; it can breed sullenness and frustration. The "worst" can be well adapted to all that will ever be required of him as an adult.

Nothing is more striking in some primitive societies than the rapid intellectual development of children which flattens out somewhere in early life so that a man of twenty, perhaps, has already all the skills and all the knowledge of a man of fifty. This fact has sometimes been read off as an inherent characteristic of simpler peoples; it is said that their mental powers are capable of only a limited development. It would be truer to say that they do not expand if the society requires nothing further of them. If men can supply their needs of livelihood and gain prestige among their fellows without adding to their skills or their knowledge, they early reach a mental plateau. This is not a characteristic of all primitive societies, for in many tribes a man must accumulate "wisdom" and special techniques throughout his life in order to take any desired position in the society. It is this continuing stimulus to mental achievement supplied by the responsibilities society puts upon its members which in any society, our own included, prevents the arrest of intellectual development.

Not only intellectual development but also training of the emotions and will-power are relative to the social order in which they occur. Life in some primitive cultures requires tough and violent people if they are to carry on; they can fill their roles with less cost to themselves and to their fellow-men if they have been reared not to expect universal kindness. Primitive people are generally more permissive to their children than we are, and their methods of child-rearing often seem to us extraordinarily attractive. They are not all of them the better for it. In some tribes where sorcery is a common practice and greatly feared, children are believed to be unaffected by black magic. They live in a charmed circle. At adolescence they become liable to all the machinations of their fellow-tribesmen, and they are unprepared. Sorcery in such tribes is a daily terror the intensity of which is possible just because the children were secure and happy in their childhood. There are other tribes where the maladjustment between education and adult requirements is quite the opposite. Life in the band is co-operatively regulated; all members share the labors and the rewards of labor. But the boy's education is, as they say, "like breaking a colt." He must be humiliated by his elders, and they send him on lying errands to make game of him. He must be chased out of bed to jump into icy water. He is taught that he has only himself to depend on. "Rely on no one. Your hands are your friends. Your feet are your friends. Your eyes are your friends. Rely on these." The education he is given does not fit the cooperative arrangements of band life; and the aggressions, the mean gossip, the bickering of tribal life, are objective measures of the lack of consonance between child-training and the kind of character structure which can operate to advantage in the culture.

In our own culture there are of course many inconsistencies between education and the world for which it offers training. I shall not discuss the curriculum, though it is obvious that in any changing society the curriculum must be reconsidered constantly. The matters which are affected when we try to make our education consonant with our total cultural life go far beyond the curriculum. They include attitudes which our children learn in the course of studying their lessons and the institutional organization of our schools. And we cannot plan without analyzing our own culture. The more clearly we see its general outlines, the more wisely we shall propose.

We are constantly in danger in our schools of underestimating the cultural changes that occur in such a society as ours. Education in our world today must prepare our children to adapt themselves to unforeseeable conditions. It must give them a basis upon which they can make their own decisions in situations not yet on the horizon. The controversies of our decade will die out or be reembodied in quite different events. The phrasing will change. In the first decade of this century the duty of thrift was one of the absolute values on which all my teachers were agreed. Starting little bank accounts was a learning activity which would bear the fruit of the good life from childhood to old age. The object was to create in school a sentiment for valuing accumulation rather than for present expenditure. My school-mates and I have lived through the nemesis of this teaching, through periods when one's whole duty was to spend and the hoarder was antisocial. Then, too, we were taught that the world was through with war and that in our day and age ethics and humanitarianism were so developed that the voice of the whole earth was unanimous for peace. We have lived through the first World War and the Long Truce, and today we do not know where the second World War will take us. The absolute values of peace which we were taught in school are something for which people are jailed.

A clearer analysis of our culture would have made it unnecessary for that generation of school children to unlearn painfully these lessons they had been taught. If, instead of trying to educate us to recognize an absolute good in hoarding, our teachers had chosen out of the cultural values of American civilization that pre-eminent one of initiative and independence, if they had been able to teach us that according to our abilities we could get somewhere if we showed initiative and independence and that we would be honored for them by our fellow-men, they could have subordinated saving money to the due place which it holds in an American scheme of things. They could have put their teaching on the ground that some attainable goals are worth saving for. If, instead of pacifism, they had taught us that peace was the dearest possession of any people and the one most worth giving one's greatest efforts to perfect, if they had taught us that war was the greatest calamity but one which, no matter what men's ethical sentiments were, would follow from certain acts, the generation they taught would not have had to unlearn the lesson.

"Transmitting our culture" in a changing society means self-examination and a certain detachment; for, unless our analyses are good, our teachings may go into limbo with the passing of some special set of circumstances. A stable society is not faced with such necessities. It can inculcate saving for generation after generation, or it can inculcate stripping one's self of all possessions.

If these are integrated in the whole economic pattern of their culture, they can be taught to each generation in minute detail. Stable societies, too, have teachings either about the glories of war or about the virtue of peacefulness; these are consequences of the state of warfare or lack of warfare in which they live, and generation after generation maintains the status quo. The great challenge of education in our changing world today is that it requires so much more of our educators than a stable society need require.

This challenge is intensified when we try to state what we mean by transmitting our heritage of democracy. Here, too, we must stress those things without which our culture would be unrecognizable. Fortunately, in America there is a certain basic agreement. In contrast to European and South American nations, the United States from the first has had a tradition of liberty and opportunity, and despotic power has been at a minimum. It is true that there are marked divergencies in current definitions of what democratic heritage we want to transmit, divergencies which turn upon whether the speaker is demanding liberty and opportunity for a special group to which he belongs or whether he is demanding these privileges for all Americans on the same terms. What is essential to all of them, however, is that they identify our way of life with adequate scope for personal achievement. All the definitions are drawn from experience in our culture where initiative and independence are traits every man wants for himself.

The transmission of our democratic heritage means primarily, then, preparing children in our schools to act as adults with initiative and independence. Our culture does not go about this with the directness that is characteristic of many tribes which set this same goal. With us, children are dependent, and yet as adults they must be independent. They are commanded as children, and as adults they command. This is in strong contrast to those societies which make no qualitative differences between children and adults. The qualities they value in grown men they boast of also in little boys even if the child flouts his father or even strikes him. "He will be a man," his father says. Such tribes do not have the problem we have in our culture: the unlearning of dependence and docility when the child reaches man's estate. Nevertheless, this discontinuity in the life-cycle is basic in our culture, and we have used it to good advantage. We greatly prolong infancy, and we define it as a period of learning. We give ourselves, therefore, the opportunity to equip our children with all that a long-continued and uninterrupted course of teaching can give them. We do not always take full advantage of our opportunity, of course, but the opportunity is there. The child on the threshold of manhood has spent years sitting at the feet of the older generation, and his teachers have had a remarkable chance to pass on to him all they know and value.

One great danger we face under this system is not that the child will be rebellious or insufficiently docile—but that he will learn his lesson of docility too well. Our schools impose the school schedule, the subject matter, the personnel, the forms of discipline; in all these matters the child takes what is offered. As long as he accepts these arrangements as the condition of his progress toward adulthood, his docility in these matters need not interfere with a later independence. But the training is overwhelmingly in docility rather than in self-reliance and independence, and many adults have obviously been overinfluenced by this training. They find dependency hard to relinquish. Progressive education, with its greater encouragement of the kind of behavior the child will need as an adult in our culture, is clearly on the right track. There are many classroom customs which could be introduced and which could give the child greater experience in responsibility and initiative. All such methods bridge the gap between school and life and lessen the numbers who find it difficult or impossible to make the transition.

The spread of progressive education is at least in part a compensation for increased restrictions on children's opportunities for independence and responsibility in our modern cities. In the earlier days of our democracy, village and even city life provided more chances for genuine autonomy. Boys shouldered their fishing rods and organized their own games and filled their free time according to their own ideas. A bully at the fishing hole was the affair of the older boys who swam there. Their chores, too, were genuine responsibilities. A boy might have to milk the cows and tend store, but his work belonged in the scheme of things. He was doing the things his father also did. Today he listens to the radio or plays in supervised playgrounds or on the street with one eye on the policeman. His father's work is away from home and he cannot contribute to it. The changed conditions in our cities make it harder for the child to get experience in the kind of behavior upon which success in his adult life will depend; and, unless our schools offer such opportunities, the persistence of childhood dependency into adulthood—our so-called "regressions"—will inevitably become a greater social problem.

Just as our system of child-rearing runs the danger of inadequately transmitting our cultural heritage because the child may learn the lesson of dependency too well, so, too, it may fall short because he learns too well the lesson of external sanctions for moral behavior. Our moral tradition is based on internalized sanctions; we do not regulate private life by constant external supervision as is the custom in some European countries and in many native tribes of Africa. Our democracy needs as many individuals as possible with the capacity for self-discipline, individuals who will subordinate immediate and shifting wishes to a chosen goal. But self-discipline is not a lesson which is learned directly by enforced discipline. In many societies the step from one to the other is never made. It is not automatic. In our culture we make the transition the hard way, and all our psychiatric discussions of the punishing superego are documentation of this difficulty. For our transition internalizes not the actual consequences of the compromising act but the outside punisher himself, a punisher who when he is internalized can be overwhelmingly inhibiting. Many societies follow a different course. From earliest childhood they inculcate genuine self-discipline, and individuals in such societies do not have to make such expensive transitions as are common in our culture. Parents in such tribes are not so afraid as we are of placing responsibility for his acts genuinely in the child's hands. If the baby sells his tanned-skin dress to a white man for a dime, no adult punishes him; they would consider that extraneous to the issue. The dress was his, and he alone is responsible for what he has done with it. But at the next feast he has no fine dress to wear. He learns the consequences of his act; he does not learn the punishing parent. Even very extreme disciplines are left in the child's hands. From our point of view these disciplines seem arbitrary and out of all proportion to the goals sought. They may be rubbing one's self with nettles or letting wads of grass burn into one's skin or drawing blood from sensitive parts of one's body. The point is that even these are readily assumed by the child himself, not imposed by an outside authority. Democratically organized societies have often fared well by giving the child experience in genuine self-discipline. They put upon the child responsibility for going out to seek a vision and for taking the initiative in obtaining his own instruction in hunting. Data from such societies make it clear that absence of enforced discipline does not necessarily mean license or laziness. This notion, so common in conventional discussions of our educational system, can arise only in a society which has systematically minimized opportunities for preadult self-discipline.

These specific points of strain in our educational system occur just because of the contrast in our culture between the child's world and the adult world, and all our problems are acute at the period of transition itself. Gradually our schools are coming to realize that it is just at this transition period where they have failed the child. Vocational training and job-placement assistance are being provided, but the problem is only partly met, as statistics in unemployment and criminology abundantly show. Primitive democratic societies which, like us, require one set of behavior for the child and another for the adult have remarkable basic likeness in their procedure at the period of transition. They have great graduating ceremonies—the conclusion of puberty rites—and automatically give the graduates as a group their new responsibilities as adults, providing them with the necessary tools and equipment. They do not leave the transition to each adolescent's fumbling attempts, and they do not put obstacles in the way of his access to the means of production. It seems fair to say that it is at this point of transition from childhood dependency to adult independence that our culture most often fails adequately to transmit our democratic heritage and that our educators must work with our social planners if our current wastage is to be lessened.

These examples of what education can do to insure the transmission of our democratic heritage are not based on "the nature of the child" or on an absolute standard of what a mature individual should be or of what a good society is. They depend upon surveying some of the major wastages in our civilization and upon citing ways in which some other cultures have met similar situations. Such knowledge of comparative cultures can often be useful; and it highlights the truth that our democracy, with its special demand for initiative and independence, is a special way of functioning as a human being that has to be learned. All that we know about the learning process we need to apply socially to this task of transmitting our democratic heritage in a changing world.

COLUMBIA UNIVERSITY

EDUCATION AND THE CULTURAL CRISIS

ROBERT E. PARK

ABSTRACT

Education, in the more inclusive sense of that term, is the process by which the cultural heritage of a society, or cultural unit of any sort, is transmitted from a preceding to a succeeding generation. The problem of transmission is complicated by movements and migration of peoples and by the rapidity of social change, due to technological advances. Cultural crises arise when the tradition transmitted, including the folkways and mores and the religious beliefs, no longer conform to the more secular interests and practices of everyday life. When the younger generation loses cultural contact with the elder, or when one section or class of the community ceases to function in conformity with the interests and ideals of the community as a whole, the problem of education is to re-establish communication and to reweave the web of intimate and personal relations of individuals, constituting the older and younger generations, as well as the diverse regions, in order to achieve understanding and revive the loyalties upon which the moral, as distinguished from the economic and political order, rests. It is the function of news and, more especially, of art, literature, and the humanities to create the understandings which make for moral unity and solidarity in the community, in so far as it can be created and maintained by art, literature, and formal education.

John Dewey introduces his notable book, *Democracy and Education*, with an impressive statement of a fact which most of us take for granted, namely, that education is a process by which a cultural heritage is transmitted from one generation to the next. It is, at the same time, a process by which a society renews and perpetuates its existence; for society, as Dewey has said elsewhere, exists in and through communication, and communication is precisely the means by which the cultural, as distinguished from the biological, heritage is transmitted. Formal education is, therefore, merely a rational procedure for carrying on and completing, in the schoolroom, a task that began spontaneously with the child in the home.

In order to emphasize the importance of this process of cultural transmission and renewal, Dewey invites his readers to consider the possibility that by some strange chance an older generation should come to an untimely end, so that there would be a complete break in the cultural succession. In that case a new, naïve, and unsophisticated generation, abandoned in the midst of this complex civilization of ours, unable to read or even to talk, would have great difficulty digging out of books, artifacts, and other archeological remains the insights that would enable it to recover its lost inheritance.

This is, in some sense and to some degree, what happens any day when young folk leave home to seek their fortunes in the city. This is what happens to a younger generation of immigrants, particularly if it grows up in an immigrant community such as exists on the East Side in New York City or the West Side in Chicago. A rather complete and informing literature, consisting mainly of immigrant biographies, has been written on this theme.

To this second generation of immigrants, because the New World, which is strange and foreign to their parents, is the only world they know, strange things happen of which they are scarcely aware; things the significance of which only a psychiatrist would, perhaps, fully understand. Strange things happen to the older generation, also, when they learn, as they sometimes do, that they and their ways seem queer to their children.

What happens in such cases is a more or less complete break in the cultural succession. The tradition which the immigrant family brings with it is rooted in a different milieu and is part of a local and national culture different from that in which the family is living in the country of its adoption. To be sure, the difference between one culture and another is not very great as long as both are European or as long as they are local cultures which are integral parts of one of those more inclusive cultural units we call "civilization."

Even so, any interruption of the cultural

process may have profound consequences which involve the whole educational process —not only that which goes on normally in the home and in the schoolroom but that which is continued outside, in the workshop and on the playground, and, finally, in all the adventures which the theater, the dance hall, and the city streets eventually provide.

When, however, the immigrant is not of European origin (as, for example, in the case of the Japanese and Chinese), then the break in the cultural succession is likely to be more complete and more devastating. Particularly is this true in a region or in a community—like that of the Hawaiian Islands —where the population is so largely made up of peoples of different racial stocks, each living in the isolation of a more or less completely closed community. There the break between the first and the second generation is likely to be much greater and its effects more profound. In Hawaii, where there is a great deal of intermarriage between the immigrant and the native population, it sometimes happens that neither parent learns to speak the language of the other and they are therefore able to communicate with each other and with their children only through the medium of English, which is, naturally, the lingua franca of the island and, like every other franca, only imperfectly understood by the people who use it.

Some of the consequences referred to are so obvious and so marked that they have produced in the second generation a recognizable personality type sometimes described as "the marginal man," i.e., the man who lives on the margin of two cultures— that of the country of his parents and that of the country of his adoption, in neither of which he is quite at home. We know, in a general way, for reasons that are not at present wholly intelligible, that this so-called "marginal man" is likely to be smart, i.e., a superior, though sometimes a superficial, intellectual type.

On the other hand, the immigrants, whether of the first or the second generation, if they continue to live in the isolation of an immigrant community, are likely to sink to a cultural level in the country of their adoption lower than that of the national or racial stock in the country of their origin. This is true not merely in the United States but also, conspicuously so, in Brazil, where European countries have attempted to colonize and to maintain in the New World environment an Old World language and culture.

We ordinarily think of the problems that arise, in the course of such cultural diffusion and acculturation as have been described, as problems of personality. They are, however, at the same time, whether they arise in the home, in the school, or in the community, pedagogical problems—problems that grow out of the difficulties of transmitting a cultural tradition from one generation to another or from one cultural unit to another. As it appears in the schoolroom, the problem is likely to be that of rote learning; as it appears in the family or the local community, on the other hand, it is that of the problem child.[1]

What we do not know is just what is involved in this process of transmission of a tradition from one generation to another and from one cultural group to another. Especially is this true where the two cultural groups are as different as are, for example, those of the American Indian and the European, where, under ordinary circumstances, the two races live together, to be sure, but in more or less complete cultural isolation—i.e., in relations that are symbiotic rather than social. One need not, however, go so far afield for an illustration as the American Indian. An equally outstanding illustration of cultural isolation is that of the Mennonites in Pennsylvania, the so-called Pennsylvania Dutch, or the so-called "Cajuns" (Acadians) of Louisiana.

In such cases as these, isolation may measuredly preserve and perpetuate an existing culture; but some sort and some degree of break or change in the culture is bound to take place in every case in the course of the educational process. Some modification of

[1] Robert E. Park, "A Memorandum on Rote Learning," *American Journal of Sociology*, XLIII (1938), 23.

the tradition is necessary to preserve not merely the form but also the content of the cultural tradition; for a tradition is not merely a treasure to be preserved, but, like the society of which it is a part, it is an organism to be renewed and perpetuated. That is why we have continually to re-write our histories; to redefine our laws and renew, in the light of a later experience, our faith in our traditional ways of life. That is why education, when successful, is a more or less creative process in which the culture is, in course of transmission, re-created in the mind of the student and of the community.

Not only do societies and cultures change, but they sometimes change so rapidly that one generation so far loses contact with the next that it is with difficulty that the cultural tradition is transmitted. This has certainly happened more than once in America. It has happened since 1914 in the case of the younger and older generations of women in the United States. It has taken place more than once in Russia. It is, interestingly enough, the theme of Turgenev's famous novel *Fathers and Sons*, written sixty years ago, and of other less notable works of fiction, dealing with European life, written since that time.

At other times and under other conditions societies expand territorially so rapidly that they are not able, even where the economic organization continues to function, to maintain cultural contacts. In fact, as we shall see later, sectionalism in a political society, like sectarianism in a religious society, is one characteristic way in which cultural crises arise. In such cases the common understandings, or mores, by which personal and political relations are ordinarily regulated and effective political and moral order maintained, are dissolved, and understanding gives way to confusion and disorder.

Society, it seems, has at least two dimensions: (1) a temporal and (2) a spatial or territorial. If it is the function of education to perpetuate the life of society in time, by renewing and transmitting the cultural tradition from one generation to the next, it is, by the same token, the function of education

(if not of the school) to perpetuate its existence in space by renewing the understandings by which different sections, classes, and races in the community not only carry on a common economy but are able to maintain a degree of political and moral solidarity which makes effective collective action possible.

Crises, it seems, may arise in several different ways and on more than one level of integration. If I speak here and now of different levels of integration, that is merely a recognition of the fact that society, as we know it, is actually a hierarchy of relatively independent levels of association—economic, political, and religious. For each of these levels of association, with their institutions, there exist distinct and more or less independent social sciences. Furthermore, with the emergence of our totalitarian states and the existence of total war it is perhaps more obvious today than ever before that these different levels of social integration are not so independent of one another as they have sometimes seemed. It is inevitable that, in a society more completely integrated, changes and crises which occur on the economic level, where human relations are relatively abstract and impersonal, must bring about repercussions on every other level, including that occupied by the family and the church, where associations are more intimate and more personal and hence more controlled by imperatives that are traditional and non-rational rather than explicit and formal.

It may not be so obvious that these different levels of societal integration represent a hierarchy in which the economic order, at the base of the social triangle, supports the political, which, in turn, supports the personal and moral, the order characteristic of familial and religious societies.

Nevertheless, when changes on the economic level are more rapid than changes on the political and religious levels, the solidarity and efficiency of society on every other level are inevitably affected. This is the phenomenon ordinarily referred to as "cultural lag." We have cultural lag when customs and creeds no longer conform to the actual functioning of the social process and no longer control or direct them. As a matter of fact, any movement of disturbance of an existing order, if long continued, may bring about a social crisis.

Since Malthus wrote his treatise on population, there has been no question of the fact that the mere increase and aggregation of populations, or their movements and migrations from one cultural milieu to another, may have consequences on every other level of integration.

One of the more remarkable instances of disintegration of the moral order as a result of migration is reported by Pauline V. Young in her volume, *The Pilgrims of Russian-Town*.[2] In this instance a primitive religious sect of German origin, the so-called "Molokons," or "milk-drinkers," migrated to America from central Russia, where they had lived for many years in more or less complete cultural, if not economic, isolation. They settled on the outskirts of Los Angeles and attempted to maintain there the religious practices and moral discipline to which they had been accustomed in Russia. The results were disastrous, not merely to the religious community, but to the personal careers of many of its members, particularly to those of the second generation.

Recently my attention was attracted to an item in the *Nashville Tennessean* entitled " 'Sudeten Problem' Has Baptists Fighting Civil War Over Again."[3] It was an account of a prolonged debate over the petition of three thousand Southern Baptists, living in California, for admission to the Southern Baptist Convention then in session in San Antonio, Texas. The petitioners had found it impossible, they said, to work in harmony with the Northern Baptists. Living in California, they were territorially northerners, but in their customs and traditions they were southerners still. The petition was received with sympathy and understanding, but it raised a constitutional question. It was opposed on the ground that it would offend the

[2] Chicago: University of Chicago Press, 1932.

[3] Tuesday, May 19, 1942.

California Northern Baptists and would, as the opposition put it, "constitute an action similar to Hitler's assumption that Czecho-Slovakia was German because some Germans lived there." However, human nature prevailed finally over logic, and the California exiles were taken into full fellowship in the Southern Convention. The case suggests the following comments.

1. It is extraordinary what difficulties a difference of local customs can make, even among Baptists. The differences between the Northern and Southern Baptists were due, it was said, to "certain practices such as open communion." However, as I recall John Steinbeck's account—in his novel, *Grapes of Wrath*—of the migration of the "Okies" and "Arkies" to the fruit farms of California, I suspect this is, to say the least, an understatement.

2. It is interesting, too, that the case of Hitler and the Sudeten Irredentists was cited as a precedent to characterize and define a constitutional issue in a Baptist convention in San Antonio. It suggests that our traditional policy of national isolation is weakening in places where we might least expect it.

3. My interest in this incident is in the fact that the trouble between Northern and Southern Baptists in California was due to a cultural conflict—a conflict which arose as a consequence of a migration. However, a migration, if one does not take its ultimate consequences into the reckoning, is no more than a change in the territorial distribution of a population. If my diagnosis be correct, the incident may be regarded as a symptom of a condition by no means peculiar to California. It is rather, I suspect, a minor indication of a condition which exists there more obviously perhaps than in most other parts of the United States, except in our great metropolitan centers like New York and Chicago.

For some years past, during a period when migration from abroad has almost ceased, internal migration in the United States, and particularly the westward movement of population, has continued. California with its glamorous landscape has been the haven toward which everything that was human and mobile, it seems, has gravitated. During the last three decades the population of California has increased more rapidly than that of any other state in the Union.

California has been at once the gateway and the barrier to migration from the Orient. When the gates were open and migration was encouraged, considerable numbers of Chinese, Japanese, Filipinos, and Koreans poured into the country, largely by way of Hawaii. When the gates were closed, they nevertheless continued to filter in.

The demand for labor to till California's vast fruit and vegetable gardens did not cease with the restrictions that excluded Japanese immigrants. The demand was temporarily supplied by seasonal laborers from Mexico. Every year, in response to the seasonal demand, the tide of immigration that crossed the border left behind in the course of its recession a permanent deposit of Mexican Indians and mestizos and formed in this way a kind of population delta extending northward from the Imperial Valley.

Later, when the combined effects of the drought and the depression had completed the ruin of the farmers on the marginal lands in the Southwest, there poured out of that dust bowl a flood of migratory laborers to recruit the army of fruit tramps who follow the harvest from the Imperial Valley to the Canadian border.

Meanwhile, to add to the cultural complexity of California's cosmopolitan population, there has been a steady drift, westward and northward to the coast cities, of Negroes from the Southwest, destined to fill in the niches in the expanding industrial organization of the West Coast cities.

All this migration has had a marked effect upon the social structure of California society. For one thing, it has dotted the Pacific Coast with Chinatowns and Little Tokyos, not to mention the large Mexican colony in Los Angeles and the transient fruit camps all up and down the valley. Here a large part of California's population, which comes from such diverse and distant places, lives in more or less closed communities, in intimate economic dependence, but in more or less complete cultural independence of the world about them.

But the disposition of racial and cultural minorities to settle in colonies and to cherish, in the seclusion and security of their own communities, different traditions and peculiar folkways is true of other sections of California's population which are also, in some sense, alien, alien at least to those who count everyone a foreigner who was not born in the state. California is celebrated for its residential suburban cities—cities like Pasadena, where the rich and retired live in a seclusion so complete and so silent that in some of the residential hotels, it is said, one scarcely hears anything but the ticking of the clock or the hardening of one's arteries.

And then there is Hollywood, where, to be sure, the seclusion is perhaps maintained but the silence is absent. Hollywood is a sort of legendary place, visible but remote, where, from the distance that the public sees them, our film favorites live like the gods on Mount Olympus, carefree and unconcerned about anything except their family troubles.

I mention Pasadena because Professor Thorndike of Columbia, in his search for statistical indices of the good life in American cities, found that Pasadena ranks first among the first 10 which have more radios, telephones, bathtubs, and dentists, in proportion to their populations, than any of the 295 others.[4] Professor Thorndike's statistics are based on thirty-seven such indices. I mention four which seem fairly representative of the values of what Professor Sorokin characterizes as our "sensate civilization." Professor Sorokin has meanwhile published, under the title *The Crisis of Our Age*, a critique of our modern urban civilization in which he says, in effect, that it is a civilization based on gadgets rather than on ideas and ideals.[5] Obviously one evidence of the cultural crisis is the fact that such distin-

[4] E. L. Thorndike, *Your City* (New York: Harcourt, Brace & Co., 1939).

[5] Pitirim Alex Sorokin, *The Crisis of Our Age: The Social and Cultural Outlook* (New York: E. P. Dutton & Co., Inc., 1941).

guished scholars could differ so widely with respect to the indices of the good life.

The fact that California, with its Hollywood, residential suburbs, Little Tokyos, and Chinatowns, has, like some of our metropolitan cities, become a congeries of culturally insulated communities, suggests that America has already measurably achieved the communistic ideal of a classless society— that is, a society without any hierarchical structure or, one might almost say, a society with no structure at all.

But this would by no means be a complete description of California, or of any of our great cities where changes have been going on at a comparable pace. California not only has its closed communities, but it has its proletariat. It has its "Okies" and its "Arkies," its mobile, foot-loose, and dispossessed—victims alike of wanderlust and the great depression, as these have affected the population in those great open spaces we used to call "God's country." With these one should include the large numbers of people from the Middle West who, before the depression and since, have gone to the Pacific Coast to enjoy the sunshine and the luxury of a suburban fruit farm where, with an automobile, one may have all the spacious freedom of the country and the intellectual emancipation of the city.

These varied elements of a population, already pretty thoroughly mixed, meeting and mingling again in the expansive atmosphere of this last frontier, have created a milieu and provided a soil in which a wild, weedy growth of political isms and religious cults has sprung up. But that is something that has always happened, it seems, on the frontier in America. It is, as Tolstoy has pointed out, one of the fruits of enlightenment.[6]

I have cited California because it is one of the conspicuous spots in which the diverse races and cultures of our cosmopolitan population have been thrown, so to speak, into the crucible: a crucible in which, perhaps, a new civilization is brewing and a new indigenous race is in the making.

One cannot, of course, be certain what will ultimately come out of the crucible, except as we are able to compare it with what has taken place in similar situations, earlier and elsewhere. Gilbert Murray, in his volume, *The Rise of the Greek Epic*,[7] has described in convincing detail the invasion and conquest by the northern barbarians of the Aegean world of 1100 B.C. This invasion was at once the source of the Homeric legends and of the ancient Greek civilization which arose on the ruins of the earlier Aegean. The time was some three thousand years ago, but the process, though it proceeded at a slower pace, was not unlike that we seem to be witnessing in the world today. "It is almost a rule of history," says Murray, "that before any definite invasion of a new territory there is a long period of peaceful penetration. In the beginning it is not an army that comes to invade. It is some adventurers or traders who come and settle; some mercenaries who are invited in."

I cannot repeat the whole story. It impresses one, on the whole, as something with which one is not unfamiliar. The historical context is different, but the consequences are the same. While there is room for both races, there is little fighting. But a time comes when there is violence: violence which terminates in confusion and chaos, "a chaos in which an old civilization is shattered into fragments, its laws set at naught." It is a time when, to state it in one of the happiest descriptive phrases with which I am familiar, "that intricate web of normal expectation which forms the very essence of human society [has been] torn so often and so utterly by continued disappointment that there ceases to be any normal expectation at all."[8]

It is the "intricate web of normal expectation" which is torn and rent likewise when peoples migrate anywhere in large numbers or when the pace of economic change is too much quickened. Professor Herman Clarence Nixon of Vanderbilt University has recently published the annals of a little com-

[6] Lev Nikolaevich Tolstoy, *The Fruits of Enlightenment* (Boston: W. H. Baker, 1901).

[7] (2d ed.; Oxford: Clarendon Press, 1911), p. 67.

[8] *Ibid.*, p. 78.

munity in the hills of northern Alabama, called Possum Trot. Since it is the story of his home town, Professor Nixon's account is autobiographical and personal, but by no means less instructive for that reason. *Possum Trot* interested me for several reasons, but mainly because it gave me a detailed historical account of another and different aspect of the migration which has been responsible for prosperity and the present condition of California and some other parts of the country that have been similarly blessed.

If the racial and cultural situation of California, as it exists today, is the result of a current of population flowing into a growing center, then Possum Trot, as it exists today, is the result of a corresponding movement of dispersion. One of the first things that is likely to strike the sophisticated reader of Mr. Nixon's description of Possum Trot is its earlier isolation. Culture, like race, is, or was originally, a local phenomenon, the product of isolation. Civilization, on the other hand, as Spengler and others have observed, is a product of the city. In the modern world of city-dwellers the rural community is a place to be born but is not a place to live. The tragedy of life in the country, we are told, is its isolation. But Possum Trot in the last forty years has been gradually emerging from its isolation, and that seems to Professor Nixon the only really tragic thing about it. This is what he says:

Possom Trot is not more isolated than it used to be. It is less isolated than it used to be. It is closely connected with the world by economic ties. It is connected with urban "5 and 10 cent" stores. It is connected with cotton warehouses in Anniston. It is connected with the government's A.A.A. office in the county. It is connected with the courthouse in Anniston, and a few Possum Trotters can frequently be seen sitting on the low retaining wall around the courthouse lawn. Sitting there and talking. Sitting there passing the time away. Sitting there waiting for bus time.

Possum Trot is no longer either an economic or a social unit, though it once was both. Possum Trot, the population of Possum Trot, the economy of Possum Trot, is now just an integral part of a larger and unpredictable economic unit.

But Possum Trot is only slightly connected in any conscious social way with the rest of the world. It is an economic part of Anniston, but not a social part of Anniston. It is an economic part of Jacksonville, but not a social part of Jacksonville. It is an economic part of Piedmont, but not a social part of Piedmont. The economic world has absorbed Possum Trot. The social world has largely passed Possum Trot by. For Anniston, Piedmont, Jacksonville, Alabama, and the United States, the Possum Trot men, to a large extent, are just economic men. Here is then a social lag. Social change is not keeping up with economic change. Economic life goes on changing; but socially something is lost and not yet replaced. The community, no longer isolated, is an aggregation of individuals who are culturally more isolated than ever.

Possum Trot is no longer isolated. It has been incorporated into the national and into the world economy. It no longer has the control it once had, or seemed to have when people were more interested in politics than they are today, over its own destiny. Meanwhile, somehow, life in Possum Trot has lost its meaning and its zest. Something new has been added, no doubt. There are more things to buy in the stores, if one has the money. That means the standard of living is higher. But, as the author puts it, socially something has been lost. The social world, the old familiar world of personal and neighborly relations, has somehow disappeared. What remains of Possum Trot is, in the drastic language of the author, "an aggregation of economic men."

Not only in Possum Trot but in every other part of the world the economic necessities of an emerging and more inclusive social order have undermined the ancient local, tribal, and familial loyalties which once bound men together. At the same time, and as an incident of the growth of a world economy, the mechanization and rationalization of what was traditional and customary have banished the old superstitions and the old creeds by which men formerly regulated their lives. Everywhere individual men, in pursuing and achieving a new economic freedom and a new economic independence in the expanding markets of the world, have measurably ceased to be persons and neighbors and have become, in Nixon's language, "economic men."

The question that emerges from this wide-ranging discussion is this: What can education do about it? What can education do about Possum Trot? What can it do about the world? This is obviously not a problem for technology. No gadgets or scientific formulas can re-create the understandings or revitalize the institutions that have disintegrated, largely under the influence of scientific analysis and of technological changes.

Institutions are not artifacts, not even legal artifacts. They cannot be created either by discussion or by legislation. On the contrary, they are the product of what Sumner describes as "concurrent action," operating over considerable periods of time. They are the product of growth and of education, assuming that education is, as Dewey described it, a process by which society renews and perpetuates itself. There is, as far as I can see, no other means by which a society or an institution can perpetuate itself, i.e., continue in some form or other to live—except as individuals acquire, as a result of their continued participation in the conscious life of the nation and of the race, the accumulated experience and traditions of the society and institutions of which they are a part.

In the new and more inclusive society which is emerging, we shall be living—particularly if it is to be a free and democratic society—in a new intimacy with all the peoples of the world, not only with our allies but with our enemies. In this situation, what will be? What is the task of the schools?

We shall need, as never before, to know human geography and, perhaps, geopolitics. We shall need to know—not all of us, but some of us—all the languages. We must have institutes, such as they have long had in Germany, France, and England, for the study of the languages and cultures of the peoples outside of Europe, in Asia and Africa. We must, in short, prepare ourselves as never before to live not merely in America but in the world.

The most important task of the schools, including high schools and colleges, has been and will continue to be, I believe, to make Americans literate—literate in a large way, of course, making them capable, for one thing, of reading newspapers intelligently. News, like other forms of knowledge, comes to us, for the most part, in little items. To read these items intelligently involves the conscious or unconscious sorting of them and integrating of them with some previous fund of knowledge, i.e., knowledge which has accumulated in our minds about some one or the other of our permanent interests.

Integration, in the sense that I use the term here, involves interpretation of the new in terms of the old. It is, in fact, only in this way that what we read becomes intelligible. To interpret the news we must supply, from our own resources, a background that will make the news and the current events it records significant. This business of sorting out and classifying the news is done for us in a rather imperfect way by the daily newspaper when it prints its items on the particular page where its readers are accustomed to look for them. News magazines, like *Time* and *Fortune,* do the same thing but do it better. They not only classify the news, but they supply, from their records of current events and other sources, a background for the understanding of news which the average reader cannot command.

One of the outstanding characteristics of the world today is the extraordinary amount of news that is published, not merely in the daily press, but in other periodicals and in what publishers designate as current books. Furthermore, writers of current books who, like Kaltenborn, are editing the news, have turned more and more to history to find materials that enable them to interpret current events. Thus a recent writer in the *Saturday Review of Literature* (Elmer Davis, I believe) announces that two books above all others— Hitler's *Mein Kampf* and Thucydides' *History of the Peloponnesian War*—should be required reading today. Current events are never wholly intelligible except as we see them in perspective and as incidents of long-term changes in social institutions. These long-term, so-called "secular" trends represent what is really going on in the world rather than just what seems to have happened.

High schools and colleges, in preparing students to live in the world rather than in their special occupations, should prepare them to read literature. Our modern world seems to be falling apart and disintegrating, largely because men—rather than women—are so profoundly interested in their vocations that they have ceased to read literature. At any rate, they have ceased to read Shakespeare and the classics. They read instead the news, particularly the news in their special fields of interest.

William James, in an essay the full import of which seems to have escaped most professional students of human nature and society, calls attention to what he calls "a certain blindness in human beings" with which we are more or less afflicted and which makes us insensible to the feelings of creatures and people different from ourselves. This blindness is due to the fact that all values are originally individual and subjective. It is only as men and women learn to participate in common enterprises, like war or the rearing of a family, and only as these common enterprises become institutionalized, that values that were individual and subjective become objective and social.

One problem of our modern world, perhaps at the moment the greatest problem, has arisen from the necessity of curing ourselves, as far as that is humanly possible, of every form of blindness which makes it difficult for us to communicate, to achieve understandings, and to act effectively with others in the interest of a common cause. That is essentially the problem of morale—national and international. If anything—except a continued, intimate, and personal association—is measurably to cure the "blindness" of which James writes, it will be done, I believe, through the medium of literature —literature and the expressive arts.

Literature and art are, in the language of Tolstoy, "forms of human activity consisting in this, that one man consciously, by means of certain signs, hands over to others feelings he has lived through, and that other people are infected and also experience them."[9] What Tolstoy's statement amounts to, it seems to me, is this. The function—perhaps I might be more specific and say the social function—of art is to communicate not ideas but sentiments, incidentally, perhaps, creating and sustaining in this way a mood in which, for a space, one's sense of individual and personal differences is lessened and one's sense of mutual understanding and moral solidarity is enhanced. At any rate, something like this is with most of us, I am sure, a familiar experience.

Implicit in Tolstoy's statement and in his creed is the notion that art no more than science exists for itself alone. It has some more important function than that of providing an entertainment, merely, or a momentary escape from reality. "Nothing," says Santayana, "is so poor and melancholy as an art that is interested in itself and not in its subject." The same thing may be said of a science that is interested in its method rather than in its discoveries.

If, then, the function of education is, as has been said, to transmit, renew, and so perpetuate the cultural heritage, then the task of the schools in a period of cultural crisis does not differ; it is merely more difficult than it would otherwise be under normal conditions of life. That task of the schools is, in any case, to prepare students to read the news at a time when news is more disturbing and when there is more of it than usual; to prepare them to read and understand literature—the literature of great writers, whose wisdom constitutes perhaps the most important part of tradition—and to read in addition the literature of contemporary life in so far as it serves to reveal what gives significance to other, and particularly other alien, lives in regard to which, as James insists, our judgments are likely to be obscure, unjust, and stupid.[10]

FISK UNIVERSITY

[9] Lev Nikolaevich Tolstoy, *What Is Art?* (New York: Oxford University Press, 1930).

[10] William James, *Talks to Teachers on Psychology and to Students on Some of Life's Ideals* (New York: Henry Holt & Co., 1914).

EDUCATION AND CULTURAL DYNAMICS

MELVILLE J. HERSKOVITS

ABSTRACT

The problem discussed in this paper concerns the role of the educative process in maintaining cultural stability and promoting cultural change. The mechanisms by means of which African custom was transmitted, in Africa, in workable form from one generation to the next are first sketched. The question is then raised as to what institutions in New World Negro social behavior are to be regarded as having preserved their African characteristics because of the educational experiences of their carriers, and what aspects of this behavior can be thought of as the result of accommodation to European patterns through the operation of the educational process.

I

The role of the educative process in maintaining cultural stability is today too well recognized to require renewed emphasis. The understanding that this experience far transcends the limits of any formal scheme of training the young has brought with it the conception that education is a conditioning process which begins with birth and does not end until the death of an individual. From this broad point of view, every experience is educational. Even if the concept is restricted to formal methods of introducing the young to their culture, the range of situations under which the ends of instruction are achieved is far more inclusive than any institutional framework could hope to cover.

This approach, however, emphasizes the stabilizing force of education, and thus tends to minimize the aspect of change. Yet it is a truism to students of culture that one of the most difficult paradoxes inherent in their materials is contained in the fact that while a body of traditions is conservative, maintaining its identity often over centuries, no living culture exists that is not in a constant state of change. In the study of cultural dynamics, therefore, it is essential, not only to determine the resistance to cultural change as against relative rate of change in societies existing under various conditions and for various aspects of given cultures, but also to analyze the mechanisms which have made for stability or have encouraged change in as many historic situations as possible.

It is here that students of education in primitive societies have made their most slender contribution. The tendency to stress the conservative aspect of education is understandable in the light of the relatively great stability of small, isolated, nonliterate "primitive" societies when these are compared with the enormous industrialized aggregates that carry the historic cultures. Statements which content themselves with pointing out that there are situations which cause a given individual to rebel against an incest taboo, let us say, or that cause a person of unstable psychological makeup to have visions which give religious patterns new turns, contribute but little to an understanding either of how new elements are taken up and retained, or of how they are worked into tribal educative schemes and thus made a part of a cultural heritage.

Negro peoples of Africa and the New World, in their institutionalized forms of behavior and in the sanctions that underlie this behavior, run the gamut from full-blown aboriginal customs to patterns which, especially in the United States, reflect a high degree of acculturation to the sanctions and institutions of the Europeans with whom, in the New World, they have been in contact. Such materials are particularly germane, since by implication, at least, the usual assumption made by students concerning the stabilizing role of education has here given way almost completely to a position holding that the opposite result was achieved. Especially is this true in the United States, where those concerned with the understanding of Negro life seem to have ignored almost completely the possibility that the stabilizing element in education, as concerns aboriginal patterns, may have retained its strength in the new situations which confronted the Negroes in this country.

The common assumption that the attitudes, modes of behavior, accepted values in life, and other fundamental parts of the non-material cultural equipment of the Negro slaves were given over in contact with the whites tends to turn its back on the educative drive to retain earlier patterns.

But it is difficult to have one's educational cake and eat it. When it is recognized that children in Africa were taught so well that they, like all human beings, in acquiring automatic responses to given situations and in reacting in terms of these accepted modes of procedure, gave continuity to their cultures, can it be assumed that these same conditionings readily and completely gave way in a new social climate? Can emphasis be shifted thus easily from acceptance of custom to rejection, from accommodation to reaccommodation, from stability to change?

The problem can be solved only in terms of data drawn from the nature of present-day institutions of these folk, and of an examination of the ways in which they are inculcated in the young. It is proposed here, therefore, to outline something of the educational processes operative in one West African society, Dahomey, which all records indicate contributed heavily to the peopling of Negro America. Some consideration can be given to certain aspects of Negro behavior in the United States which seem to reflect something of the same traditions that are found in this West African society, and the means whereby these have been preserved and are handed down. It will be borne in mind, in reading this discussion, that limitations of space make brevity necessary; and that much relevant material from West Indian and South American societies which would fill in this sketch cannot be included. Nonetheless, enough data can be given to raise the question whether or not it is ac-

ceptable, either logically or methodologically, to assume that the stabilizing factor of education in African society disappeared as promptly and as completely under conditions of New World slavery as is indicated in current hypotheses regarding the failure of Negroes to carry over any part of their aboriginal heritage into the present-day American scene.

II

The culture of Dahomey, French West Africa, has been relatively untouched by the circumstances of French political control since the conquest of the kingdom in 1894. Except in certain obvious areas, life goes on much in the way it went on in the autonomous kingdom. Slavery is no longer practiced; the cowrie shell has been replaced by French currency; a railway runs from the principal port of the colony into the interior; one on occasion sees sewing machines. Yet, in many parts of the territory of the kingdom, descendants of those who were slaves still give half their time to working in fields owned by members of the families which owned their forebears; the cowrie shell has by no means disappeared from the markets; the railroad is an inactive factor in the lives of the vast majority of the people; sewing machines, in accordance with the aboriginal patterns governing this type of work, are operated by men and not women. Thus, once the student probes beneath surface details of this kind, their superficiality becomes apparent. In Dahomey, and, as we are realistically coming to understand, elsewhere in Africa, training in aboriginal modes of behavior is a mechanism which is permitting the people to hold fast to traditionally sanctioned custom; and this, more than any other single factor, is preventing the breakdown in morale that has been the experience of so many other peoples who have made contact with European civilization.

This culture of Dahomey is a complex entity, "primitive" only in a technical sense of not having a written language. As has been shown,[1] this culture comprises involved

[1] M. J. Herskovits, *Dahomey* (New York, 1938).

economic institutions and mechanisms and numerous social structures based on relationship and nonrelationship groupings. It was marked in the days of its autonomy by a well-organized political structure that ruled the considerable population with firmness and efficiency. The theological sanctions of its religious system make up a sophisticated concept of the universe, and the supporting structure of ritualism occupies the time of many specialists and impresses by the richness of its resources. Its graphic and plastic arts take on many forms. One pattern is particularly worthy of mention as significant in aiding this people to maintain so involved a civilization without the aid of writing—the explicit recognition of all institutions. The proper verbal label can be found for each detail of this culture, and the number of individuals who easily and freely use the correct terminology in the routine of life, to say nothing of those who can give it on request, is striking.

The desire for children is a convention that drives deep in Dahomean culture. This can be traced to economic as well as psychological sanctions, since, on the economic level, children constitute a kind of insurance. In the case of the man, sons will help him till his fields and aid him in many other ways, while a man's son-in-law will likewise owe him certain duties year by year. As for a woman with offspring, she can be assured of support in time of need and when old age sets in.

The tendency to draw distinctions, to categorize, and to name is nowhere better evidenced in this culture than in the conventions which govern the naming of children. The very fact that the existence of these differences is recognized implies differing attitudes toward such children; and their reactions to this offer suggestive leads in future research toward an understanding of the shaping of personality by social convention. A person assumes various names at given critical periods of his life, but his most important designations are those given at birth. The child born with a caul or with feet foremost; the child born to members of various cult groups; or the one who survives after a series of still-born forerunners—all these are given particular kinds of names which inevitably set attitudes and aid in conditioning behavior. Extra fingers or toes place children under the protection of one of the powerful members of the Sky pantheon; and persons bearing the names indicative of this are believed to be predestined for riches, since polydactylism is held to be a sign of good luck. A four-fingered child belongs to the feared river spirits, whose priests and the diviners are consulted to determine whether it will bring riches or poverty to its parents and whether it is to be "returned" to the spirits that gave it. In this case it is exposed on the river bank, unless it "refuses to accept the verdict" by wailing, in which case it must be taken back and reared, though with what attitudes on the part of the parents can be imagined. Children having other anomalous traits, such as macrocephaly, likewise belong to this category. Twins are, in a sense, the darlings of this culture. The effect of the twin cult on twins, and even more importantly on the child born after twins, in influencing the development of children in this category must be considerable, for on such individuals are lavished all forms of special attention.

Existence in a polygamous household, or even in a monogamous establishment governed by patterns based on plural marriage, dominates the early life and training of the child. In accordance with these patterns, a wife has a dwelling of her own within her husband's compound, where she lives with her children. The common husband likewise has his own dwelling, and here each of his wives in turn cohabits with him out of this routine until her child has been born and weaned. The difference in early experience, particularly in terms of unconscious conditioning or of later attitudes in terms of relative closeness to father and mother, as contrasted to what obtains in those cultures where, for example, a man and woman and their children inhabit the same hut continuously, the child often sharing the same sleeping-place as its parents, is obvious.

Particularly in postinfantile and preadolescent years, such matters as the relative lack of opportunity of witnessing the sex act, which as we know can have such far-reaching effects in shaping the personality of the growing child, is here a factor of some significance.

The closeness of contact between mother and child in the earliest years, outstanding in the Dahomean system of child-training, is as striking as it is important, since for the first year of life the child is almost literally never away from its mother. She busies herself about the compound, with her child always in sight, lying on a cloth under the eaves of her house, shaded from the sun. If the child becomes restless, she will put it astride her back in a cloth which she ties in front, proceeding then to go about her tasks regardless of whether the child is awake or asleep, pounding meal in a mortar, or washing clothes, or cooking, while the head of the child rolls this way and that as the mother moves. If she is the favorite of a wealthy husband, she may be permitted to do lighter tasks inside the compound for a year after the birth of her child; but in the case of one in less favored circumstances, she resumes her economic obligations after a period of three or four months, working in the fields, or trudging along the roads obtaining goods to sell in the market, or making pots, with the child always astride her back, or near by.

During the first months of life little food other than its mother's milk is given the infant, though after four or five months other foods are introduced into its diet. As among many primitive folk there are no regular feeding times, the breast being presented whenever the child cries for it, or, in any event, every few hours. As soon as other foods are given the infant, however, the Dahomean tradition of discipline comes into play, and the child is fed forcibly until it learns to eat whatever food is presented to it. Dahomean mothers are busy women and have no time to pander to fastidious tastes of their children. Their methods are direct and effective. As the child lies or sits in its

mother's lap, she supports its chin on the palm of her left hand while she presses its nostrils together with the index and second fingers of the same hand, thus forcing the mouth open if the child is to breathe. When this occurs, food is placed in the mouth with the right hand. Methods of weaning are equally efficient; the mother sprays her breasts with some evil-tasting, sour substance, and in most cases the desired effect is obtained with all promptness.

It is not to be thought that the child's early existence is characterized by any lack of affection, however; for Dahomeans are extremely fond of their young, and both fathers and mothers have no hesitation in manifesting their regard. The variation in methods of training between gentleness and brutality may be indicated by considering the way in which children are taught to walk, as against the way in which sphincter control is inculcated. When a child is about a year old, it is put in charge of a young relative, who holds the baby by its hand and encourages its first efforts. When it has learned to take a few short steps, four small bells of a special type made for the purpose, strung on a cord, are tied about each foot. The child, hearing the pleasant tinkling sound made at each step, is encouraged to continue its efforts, and the delighted shrieks of small children testify to the efficacy of this device.

Training in the control of excretory functions varies from continuous teaching to a type of conditioning experience that might well, in sensitive children, result in traumatic shock. As a mother carries about her infant, she senses when it is restless; and when it must perform its functions, she places it on the ground. In ordinary cases the training process is completed in an easy fashion after about two years, but some children do not respond to this training and manifest enuresis at the age of four or five years, soiling the mats on which they sleep. In such a case the child is first beaten; then, if this does not achieve the desired result, a mixture of ashes and water is poured over the head of the offender, who is then driven into the street, where all the children run after it, shouting over and over again the words of a song especially reserved for the purpose, "Urine everywhere." Or, in the coastal area, such a child is thrown into the lagoon. If, after a second immerson, the habit is not stopped, a live frog is attached to the child's waist, which frightens it into a cure.

Between infancy and puberty, two major educational strands can be traced in the experience of the developing child. One of these comprehends the overt training he receives, particularly in those occupational techniques that must be mastered if the individual is to take his proper place in society. In this category also is included training in proper behavior toward the living and the dead and some knowledge of religious and ceremonial custom. The other strand is constituted by continuing exposure to the psychological atmosphere of the household in which he lives and which determines the attitudes he will later take toward others, especially those belonging to his own relationship group, with whom he will in the course of normal events associate throughout his adult life.

The training gained through observation and experience of the manner of life of his elders is predominant under the first category. As in African societies generally, children are encouraged to do the things done by adults and are intrusted with tasks that would seem to the Euro-American observer far beyond their years. A child of two and a half is to be seen carrying its mother's stool to the market place, or balancing an empty calabash or dish on its head. A year or two later, he is able to handle a sharp bush-knife, or cutlass, with facility. On days when work in the forges is forbidden by supernatural precept, the boys of the ironworking sib take over, an infant of three or four operating the bellows for his preadolescent brother in the same manner as this brother performs the identical task for his father, while the preadolescent hammers out red-hot iron on the anvil to make a small blade for the miniature hoe he is constructing. A little girl,

when three or four years old, goes to market with her mother, performs her allotted tasks about the house, helps weed the fields, or carries clay for pots. Boys likewise participate, the son of a farmer helping his father work in the field, the offspring of a clothworker cutting out crude patterns and stitching these designs to remnants of materials left by his father, the child of a weaver learning the intricacies of threading a loom by operating a simple one. Patterns of economic co-operation are similarly inculcated at an early age. Le Herisse tells how, in the early days of the French occupation, small boys were individually employed to bring water to the Residency. Difficulties ensued, however, and were not resolved until the boys formed a group, appointed a responsible head, and received orders "through channels."

On this institutional level, also, the child may be said to absorb noneconomic aspects of life just as effortlessly. In the main, the ceremonials that affect him directly between the first two crisis periods of his life, birth and puberty, are few in number. The many rites that mark the birth of an infant, its introduction to society, and the return of its mother to full participation in the daily round probably occur too early to affect his behavior or personality structure. As he grows older, however, observing these rites when performed in his compound for younger siblings, he soon senses the realization of the need for supernatural sanctions in all situations, a pattern that is emphasized by his contact with the larger ceremonial round of his village. Children are ubiquitous at religious rites; nor does the Dahomean pattern of proper behavior before the gods require children, as in our culture, to be small replicas of their elders. Sanctimoniousness is entirely absent, and children play as they will during the long daylight hours when rites are performed, effortlessly absorbing the drum rhythms and melodic patterns of song, imitating dances as they wish, or, finally, as night wears on, returning to their parents to fall asleep in their places. This childhood freedom during such rites operates to induce a feeling-tone in later life toward the gods that is not unrelated to the deep interest with which the Dahomean, like most West Africans contemplates the supernatural and the almost matter-of-fact attitude he takes in his relationship to deified ancestors and other gods.

On occasion, however, ceremonial life does take the child at first hand. Children who have been vowed to the gods by their parents may be called at an early age. In such cases, unless divination shows a willingness on the part of the deity to postpone the long and expensive initiatory rites, the child will be received in the cult-center by the priests for induction into the group of initiates together with its adolescent or adult members. On one occasion the participation of an infant barely able to walk was witnessed. The child was carried on the back of a priestess throughout the long twenty-eight-day ritual, and the case illuminates the effectiveness of the conditioning process. For, though no attempt was made to teach so young a child the proper dance steps before the end of the period when it had learned to toddle, this child on one occasion danced in perfect form and rhythm the basic steps of the Sky-gods to whom she was vowed.

There are a few ceremonies performed by the children during this period, such as when a first deciduous tooth works out of the gum. When this occurs, the child assembles its playmates, who dance about in a circle, clapping their hands and singing such rhymes as:

He who has lost a tooth,
  Cannot eat salt:
Come, give me palm-oil
  To eat with my cake.

I don't want the teeth of a pig,
  They're big!
I want the teeth of a goat,
  They're small!

Training is also effectuated by the evening gatherings of the children of a compound to tell stories. Here the child is intro-duced to the sanctions underlying approved modes of behavior by means of the morals drawn from the tales. These are of the familiar Uncle Remus animal type where the principal character is the trickster, sometimes, but not always, getting the better of his more powerful but less able fellows. The child thus absorbs sanctioned reactions toward the situations of later life, learning the need for proper reserve in dealing with one's fellow-men and that too great frankness in discussing one's affairs or the naïve taking at face value of another's expressed motives often leads to disaster.

The manner in which these stories are told helps to inculcate in the child the competitive drive which, as a counterpart of the co-operative patterns of Dahomean life, are of such great moment here as everywhere in West Africa. This setting has not a little of the picturesque, and the warmth of human relations involved in the situation is of some significance. The children gather in the evening, usually at the home of one of the old people of the compound. They may perhaps first listen to stories told by their elders, but eventually one of them takes charge and, as leader, conducts the rest of the session. This develops into a contest in which each child must demonstrate his story-telling ability. Riddling is an integral part of the pattern, and the losers are assigned by the leader a certain number of tales to be told the group. Each child strives to fulfil his task, so as not to expose himself to ridicule. The educational role of these stories is recognized by the Dahomeans, one of whom, sophisticated in French culture, directly compared them to the books from which European children learn their lessons.

The second strand in the experiences of these years is more important in shaping personality structure than in teaching the child to carry on the institutionalized cultural patterns. As in the case of infants, the fact of living within a polygamous compound is paramount in this context. As far as is known, no detailed study of this situation has ever been made, which is regrettable. For, despite the methodological difficulties inherent in such an analysis, the restraints imposed by these situations and the blockages to the attainment of goals are to the highest degree suggestive for an understanding of numerous problems in the culture-personality equation as this manifests itself in polygamous cultures. Factors of sexual rivalry, of jockeying for position, of attaining preference for a child, make for intrigue that goes on against a background of shifting alliances between co-wives which reveals the inner drama of such groupings. The atmosphere of such a compound cannot but affect the growing child, not only in his immediate relations with his mother, his father, his mother's co-wives and their children, but in the way in which it shapes attitudes and typical reactions in later life.

In large Dahomean compounds rivalries between wives are intense. There are in this culture thirteen different categories of marriage, which can be grouped under two large headings—those in which the control of the children is in the hands of the father, and those in which the mother retains control over her offspring. In institutional terms this means that for the first group a man has made certain ceremonial payments and accepted certain continuing obligations toward his fathers-in-law, who have approved the marriages. In the second category these obligations are not undertaken. Wives married in the same category have a fellow-feeling, and help one another when quarrels arise between co-wives. To what extent these quarrels result from the constant jockeying for position vis-à-vis the common spouse, or from the inadequacy of sexual satisfactions, or are the result of the clash of irreconcilable personalities in constant close contact, cannot be said. That all three probably enter would seem to be justified from a priori consideration of the setting. Certainly gossip and argument run rife; and the depth to which feeling goes is indicated by the songs sung by a co-wife against another with whom she has quarreled, as she works at her mortar in the courtyard of their common habitation:

Woman, thy soul is misshapen
  In haste was it made, in haste;
So fleshless a face speaks, telling
  Thy soul was formed without care.
The ancestral clay for thy making
  Was molded in haste, in haste.
A thing of no beauty art thou
  Thy face unsuited for a face,
Thy feet unsuited for feet.

In Dahomean society, where ambition runs high, the chief objective of a plural wife is that one of her children succeed his father. This means that it is important that her sons make a good appearance. Though children are whipped when guilty of misdeeds, such misdeeds are, wherever possible, kept from the ears of the child's father, and the punishment, at least for minor infractions, is carried out at the home of the mother's sister or at her parents' home.

The fundamental factor in the child's situation, however, is that while he shares his father with the children of other women, who in a very real sense constitute obstacles in his life-career, he shares his mother with his "very own" brothers and sisters. This attitude is reflected when the inheritance of an estate is involved. For it is a truism in Dahomey that, though a man's heirs quarrel without end over the distribution of his wealth, for "real" brothers and sisters to dispute concerning a mother's estate is unheard of. Personal relationships follow similar lines. Though a man may be proud of his father's exploits and feel affection for him, the warmest regard of a child is reserved for his mother, who is, to all intents and purposes, the effective parent.

Space does not allow the discussion of other educational devices which come into play in late preadolescence and during puberty. It is not without significance, however, that the stages in a boy's and girl's life are carefully noted and named, so that even a young individual's place in society is objectified. Important but too involved to permit them to be recounted here are the techniques of sex education. Particularly as regards the girls, one here finds the closest approximation to formal schooling that exists in Dahomey; though the fact that in early puberty groups of boys build and live in houses of their own, electing their own leaders and carrying on much in the fashion of adults, is also regarded by Dahomeans as educational. Especially important are the recognized mechanisms for sexual experimentation, while perhaps not less significant is the withdrawal of nubile girls from contact with boys who might cause them to become pregnant. This creates a situation which leads either to further training of young men in sex through illicit relations with older women, or to indulgence in homosexual experience, which is sanctioned for this period. The attainment of adult status, marked for the girl by the cutting of designs in her skin which later develop into cicatrized aids to beauty, is also to be noted. In the case of boys the experience of circumcision, marked at its termination by ceremonial intercourse with an old woman to "cool the heat of the knife," is likewise important in helping make a Dahomean the kind of person he is to be as an adult.

It is thus apparent that there are numerous mechanisms which operate to shape the personality structure of the individual, at the same time fitting him into his place in the community by training him to carry on its institutions in the manner approved by his society. The degree of variation in individual reactions to the learning process is not easy to determine. On the whole, however, the product can be characterized as one which accepts the stratified forms of social structure that mark the culture, manifesting at the same time ambition to attain prestige in recognized ways, and having a drive to take advantage of such avenues of social mobility as may present themselves. At the same time, the individual is trained to co-operate with his fellows and, as a result of the overt characterization of the ways of life, to have an objectively manifested affection for and pride in his people and the institutions by which they live. He shows reserve in his dealings with others, but in certain situations, particularly when dealing with those who stand in the relation of insti-

tutionalized friendship to him or with members of his own cult group or association, he manifests a warmth of regard and a willingness to aid in difficulties that compensate for these other characteristics. Certainly, whatever the stability of such a psychological type, the effectiveness of the training given in carrying on the institutional aspects of Dahomean life from generation to generation have been demonstrated by perpetuating this culture for many generations and by performing well the task of adequately adjusting those who live in accordance with its sanctions.

III

We may now turn to a brief consideration of the problem of determining the role, in the New World, of the educational process in making for the retention or disappearance of habit-patterns and of institutionalized forms of behavior, such as have been described in the preceding section. That students of the Negro tend, with few exceptions, to posit the disappearance of African modes of behavior among Negroes of this country is not so significant as it might seem on first glance, since this conclusion has been reached on the basis of little or no acquaintance with the African background. The historical processes held to have brought about this presumed great loss of aboriginal endowment are rarely investigated realistically, a fact the more remarkable when it is considered that so radical a change in the cultural habits of so many people, achieved in such a short time, would, if true, be unique in the experience of man.

This is not the place to adduce evidence as to the validity of the common assumptions, for an analysis of such matters can be presented only in extended form.[2] What is important for the major point under discussion is acceptance of a hypothesis involving an almost complete breakdown of pre-American forms and techniques of education as a method of transmitting aboriginal beliefs and modes of behavior. Yet such a position

[2] Cf. M. J. Herskovits, The Myth of the Negro Past (New York, 1941).

would seem to involve a reconstruction of the setting of slave life that is unjustified historically or logically. Can it be held, for example, that the slave mother took no part in teaching her infant to walk? That perhaps somewhat later she imparted no instruction in behavior habits, in attitudes toward elders, in etiquette? Can it be seriously maintained that no instruction in terms of any moral code was given? That the young were not taught ways and means of meeting the hardships of their life? Must it not be recognized that, however sparse the slave culture may have been, it had to be taught, and the teaching had in the main to be done by parents? And, granting the obvious affirmative answers to these questions, can it be maintained that in all this the values and traditions of African life must have been completely ignored by those concerned with training their young?

We may envisage the situation of an African-born slave, mating and having offspring. It is impossible to assume that an educational experience of the type that has been indicated in the preceding section, so strong that it has made possible the continuation of a complex civilization over many generations, should have been completely lost in all its aspects on those brought to this country. A certain dilution in African behavior resulting from his new setting would be expected, yet it is difficult to see how it would have been possible for a slave to bring up his children without inculcating in them something of the values of life and the modes of behavior that he had in Africa been taught to regard as right and proper. Some of this teaching, in all likelihood, would, indeed, be without any direction and would involve no more than unconscious imitation by the children of habits that themselves lodge below the level of consciousness in the adult—motor behavior of various kinds, such as postures, modes of walking, the use of the hands while talking, characteristic facial expressions, and the like.

The imitation of speech habits would lie on almost the same level. Controversies concerning the derivation of American Negro speech appear almost pointless in the light of an understanding of the manner in which languages are learned. Certainly, in the light of our knowledge of educational psychology, it would be difficult to maintain that African speech habits were so completely given over by adults through more or less casual acquaintance with white people that nothing of the earlier modes of expression remained to be taught to their children. The matter bristles with further difficulties if the assumption is followed through to its customary conclusion. For in this case it would appear that not only did Africans lose their own forms of expression on contact with the whites, but in that same contact they only received and never gave.

A further point must be made. In most analyses of the carry-over of Africanisms in the United States, the Negro is regarded as a passive element in the situation. In a sense this is merely a restatement of the assertion that the educational processes—education in the larger sense—that went on in slave cabins are completely overlooked. No competent student of culture could take the position that the Negroes were not affected, and deeply affected, by the new setting in which they found themselves. But few students of the Negro have recognized that, in the New World, Negro culture or white culture is not to be regarded as a unit and that, if we look at the Negroes not as a passive but as an active element in the developing situation, our perspective will be false if we do not recognize the different interests which these people have traditionally held in various aspects of their own culture, interests which carried over as they gained competence in handling the culture of their masters. In African societies, as in all cultures, certain aspects of life are of greater concern to a given people than others. This means, further, that in every culture interests tend to center on certain activities. These take the form of conscious drives which, directed toward a certain segment of the entire body of tradition, determine that area of the culture wherein the greatest elaboration is achieved in a given period of a people's history. For Negro studies, the significance of this principle lies in the fact that, under the stresses of contact with a foreign body of tradition, these interests tended to be maintained with the greatest possible tenacity and were emphasized in the teaching of the young.

If, then, we assess the acculturative situation of the Negro in the United States in the light of his differing interest in the several phases of his traditions and in terms of varied opportunities for the retention of Africanisms in the several aspects of culture, we find a certain coincidence between the two which significantly indicates a means whereby the carry-over of earlier traits not only could have been achieved but must in many cases have been consciously striven after. When we consider the operation of the slave system, it is apparent that African technology, economic life, and political organization had but relatively slight chance of survival. Utensils, clothing, and food were supplied by the masters, and it is but natural that these should have been of the type most convenient to procure, least expensive to provide, and, other things being equal, most like those to which the slaveowners were accustomed. The extension of African political institutions was also prevented by the total setting of slavery, so that only in the most secret fashion could African legal tradition find expression or African political talent be made effective.

On the other hand, in the fields of religion and magic and certain nonmaterial aspects of aesthetic life, retention by the slaves of African customs was not only possible but, in some cases, held to be desirable by the masters. One cannot read the literature of the slave period without being impressed by the number and strength of the complaints made by leaders of church groups at the lack of religious instruction given the slaves. It is difficult to suppose that the outstanding interest of the African in the supernatural, mentioned in the preceding section, could have been completely set aside by the slaves themselves. It would seem to be more logi-

cal, as well as to be better history, to argue that the slaves carried on as best they might, in secret if necessary, thus continuing earlier patterns in sufficient vitality so that when eventually they were exposed to Christianity they developed the aberrant types of religious behavior that to this day differentiate the ritual of Negro churches from that of their white counterparts. Again, the attitudes of the masters toward song and dance and folk tales varied throughout the New World from hostility and suspicion through indifference to actual encouragement. It was recognized by all slaveowners that recreation was necessary and desirable if morale was to be maintained among the slaves. African types of dancing and singing were permitted as long as they did not interfere with work or were performed on holidays; at such times, according to numerous accounts, they were enjoyed by the masters who watched them.

The field of social organization stands intermediate between technology and religion with respect to retention of Africanisms in the face of slavery. The plantation system rendered the survival of the African compound impossible, though it by no means completely suppressed various approximations of certain forms of African family life. The marriage tie was naturally rendered unstable, yet even in the United States it is far from certain that the existence of many permanent matings among the slaves has not been lost sight of in the dramatic appeal of the large numbers of enforced separations. Certain obligations of parents to children, and of children to parents, were carried over with all the drives of their emotional content intact, particularly as concerns the relationship between a child and its mother. The vivid sense of the power of the dead, and the related feeling that the ancestors are always near by to be called on by their living descendants, tended to give a kind of strength to family ties among Negroes that persists even today. And it was but natural that these attitudes and beliefs concerning kinship should have been taught to oncoming generations without undue interference by the masters, as long as they led to no action that would impede the smooth functioning of the plantation.

Traditions underlying nonrelationship groupings of various kinds likewise survived the slave regime, especially the spirit behind the numerous types of African co-operative societies which was kept alive by the very form of group labor employed on the plantations. The feeling of the importance of helpfulness inherent in this tradition must, as a matter of fact, have contributed directly toward the adjustment of the African to his new situation, for without some formula of mutual self-help he could scarcely have supported the vicissitudes of slave existence. That this formula did survive is to be seen, moreover, in the manner in which African types of co-operative agricultural organizations sprang up in the Sea Islands immediately following emancipation, and how insurance societies, a phenomenon common to West Africa, likewise came into being. To be mentioned here also is the great number of Negro lodges in the United States today. For, though these follow in their outward form conventional white patterns, they are by no means the same as their white counterparts in inner sanction or as concerns their objectives. To explain facts of this kind, however, it is necessary once again to turn to the role of instruction, which gave to generation after generation a sense of the importance of leadership that characterizes all African social institutions. Analysis on this basis must conclude that here, rather than by the lash of the overseer, was inculcated the principle of order and regularity induced by a discipline exerted through responsible headship.

To analyze the educational devices that tended to retain African elements does not mean that the problem may be neglected of how the European patterns of behavior manifested by Negroes today, and their non-African sanctions, were established. We must also consider those positive measures which, in adults, made for acceptance of the masters' way of life and were thus taught to the children, while it is likewise

essential to bear in mind the negative forces that, without conscious direction, tended to discourage the retention of aboriginal customs. The difference between these two may be illustrated by an example. As has been pointed out, the economic workings of the plantation system inhibited African material culture and technological capacities. Ironworking, wood-carving, basketry, and the like simply had no place in the new scene, and hence such techniques almost everywhere died out of sheer inanition. On the other end, proselytizing among the slaves by Christian missionaries constituted a positive drive. There is, for example, no logical reason why the African world view might not otherwise have been continued to the same degree that African motor habits in dancing were retained. Changes would undoubtedly have appeared of themselves, as they have in the dance, since some measure of innovation must result from contact stimulus. Yet, in the case of the African world view, efforts directed toward affecting change caused a premium to be placed by the whites on the overt acceptance of Christian beliefs and practices and thus accelerated the disappearance of African religion in recognizable form.

Recognizing that more intimate contact between Negroes and whites in the United States has brought about greater accommodation on the part of the Negroes here to white institutions than elsewhere in the New World, the question as to the Africanisms that have been retained may be raised. In the main these take the form of less tangible manifestations: those that are of the kind that, as has been pointed out, would be transmitted to a considerable extent on the unconscious level, in the intimacy of the household. Aside from certain curios in the cultural cupboard, few recognizable overt African institutions are to be found except for some instances in such isolated regions as the Gullah Islands or the Mississippi Delta. Beliefs like those concerning the supernatural powers of children born with a caul or with some other unusual characteristic, or certain forms of hair-braiding of children and old women, or certain dance steps, or the fact that the coiled basketry in the Sea Islands is always done in clockwise direction are of this nature. Elements in Negro funeral rites similarly persist. These range from reinterpretation of the West African custom of having partial and definitive burials in terms of the delayed funeral of this country to the part played by secret societies (lodges) in preparing the corpse, or the custom of passing a child over the body of a deceased parent.

It is not materials of this order, however, that are the most significant for an understanding of the effective role of education in permitting the carry-over of cultural values, even under conditions of most severe stress. It is more revealing to attempt to account in these terms for certain aspects of Negro social organization peculiar to this group. Thus it has been often remarked that family types found among Negroes are aberrant when contrasted to the present forms of the family among majority groups in this country. The importance of the mother as against the father, the role of the grandmother, the meticulous care with which relationships are traced, and above all, the fact that illegitimacy in the legal sense has little meaning as a sociological force in communities are some of these traits. It is rarely recognized, if at all, that a tradition stemming from the relationships within the African polygamous household might account for some of this. As has been seen, in Africa the child is closer to its mother than to its father; and this tradition can be thought of as having been reinterpreted and re-worked in the light of the American scene in terms of families where the relationship between mother and children has continued to be stronger than that between father and children. As concerns family structure accommodated to a pattern of monogamy, this results in a grouping wherein the man, in many instances, tends to play a secondary role. But the attitudes on which such a structure is based are attitudes that are the result of the continuation, through teaching within the family, of a point of view that is far more easily thought of as originating in Africa than on the slave plantation. This latter situation, viewed in these terms, can again be regarded merely as something which reinforced earlier custom.

The very manner in which the Negro children in rural communities are trained shows again the carry-over of an earlier custom. Whipping is far more prevalent among Negroes than among whites, as is evidenced by the comments of many observers. But, as has been seen, whipping is an outstanding African mode of correction of children; this has been retained and, in all probability, reinforced by the corrective patterns of slavery. Other educational devices that derive from Africa may likewise be mentioned. Teaching of techniques of various kinds on the informal level is widespread, and the greater self-reliance of young Negro children in rural communities as against those of white families is well recognized. The manner in which a child has impressed on him, through constant contact, the types of accepted behavior at religious rituals, and the absence of sanctimoniousness at these rituals in Negro churches, where children are free to go about as they will, are similar carry-overs of African educational methods.

Even more important than such traits are the attitudes of suspended judgement, of reserve in contact with others, of keeping one's own counsel, that so characterize the Negroes of this country, not only in their relations with whites, but with members of their own group as well. It may be asserted that this is merely a survival of the protective coloration developed by any oppressed minority, and there is no desire in this discussion to minimize the extent to which reactions of this kind are essential if an underprivileged group is to survive. It is striking, however, that in Africa itself, where the people are free and where the relationships between individuals are those of any normal community, the same tendency toward reserve rather than frankness, toward keeping counsel rather than revealing one's affairs, characterizes the point of view of all classes. The continuation of an approach toward life of this kind, so widespread among such a large group of people, is not a matter of chance; it has obviously been passed on, by precept and example, from older to younger members of the group as generation has succeeded generation in this country.

Another survival, only to be accounted for by teaching in the Negro slave cabin and in the Negro home after emancipation, is the great importance of proper modes of behavior. Here, again, the simplistic explanation, that this is merely a reflection of the discipline of the plantation, or copying manners observed in the Great House, is popular. Yet the etiquette of the whites who lived in the Great House, though this may have been copied, was not observed by most Negroes, who were field hands; more often the whites who could be closely observed by the slaves were the small planters, the crudity of whose modes of behavior has been remarked by traveler after traveler in the antebellum South. It is not easy, either, to see how the codes of behavior exacted of the slaves in the fields by their overseers were such as to inculcate the soft graciousness that so outstandingly characterizes the Negro's behavior. "Mind your manners" is a phrase so well known that it has become a part of the stereotype of the Negro "mammy"; and materials are not lacking which show that within the slave community the need to be well-mannered was impressed on children in such a way as to insure proper behavior on their part. Slave autobiographies again and again testify to the respectful behavior exacted of the young slave toward his elders, and the punishment he received if he did not fulfil this expectation. But the importance of proper recognition of status, respect for elders, and the like is very great in West Africa itself; and it is here that one must look when considering points of origin.

The exploration of techniques of teaching and effective results of instruction in terms of the perpetuation of Africanisms of this less apparent type might go on indefinitely, if considerations of space permitted. The point to be made here, however, is the need for students concerned with assessing the role of education in shaping human institutions and human personalities to recognize that undue stress must not be laid on the function of education either as a stabilizing element in culture or as one making for change. Each situation must be analyzed in terms of its historical past, and of the sanctions underlying the institutions involved. The essential problem is to discover what are the situations under which one aspect or the other will predominate and to recognize that predominance of change does not rule out retention, or that predominance of retention does not imply complete stability.

NORTHWESTERN UNIVERSITY

THE CHANNELING OF NEGRO AGGRESSION
BY THE CULTURAL PROCESS

HORTENSE POWDERMAKER

ABSTRACT

The Negro's resentment caused by the deprivations imposed on him by our society may be channeled in different ways, the particular form depending largely on cultural factors. The hypothesis is that over-aggression represents only a small part of the Negro's hostility. Behind the loyalty of the faithful slave and behind the meekness of the deferential, humble, freed Negro may lie concealed aggression and hostility. This hypothesis is arrived at through a functional comparison of the psychoanalytical analysis of the dependency situation of the child with that of the slave, and the psychoanalytical analysis of the problem of masochism with that of the meek, free Negro. There is no structural similarity in either comparison, but the functional comparison offers a clue to understanding the strength of the concealed hostility behind these two roles and the compensations they offer. The second role, which has persisted through today is diminishing in frequency because the cultural and psychological compensations are gradually disappearing.

We shall attempt in this article to look at one small segment of our cultural process —namely, a changing pattern of aggressive behavior—caused by the interracial situation. We limit ourselves to considering, at this time, only the Negro side of this complex of interpersonal relations; and we shall do no more than offer a few rather broad hypotheses on the relation between the forms aggression has taken during different historical periods and changes in the cultural processes at these times. For our hypotheses we are indebted to history, anthropology, sociology, and psychoanalysis; to the first three for understanding how social patterns come into being at a given point in time and how they are related to each other; and to the fourth, psychoanalysis, for a clue to the mechanisms by which individuals adopt particular social patterns. We shall concentrate on an analysis of two forms of adaptation where the aggression seems to have been concealed and, therefore, less understood. The two forms are that of the faithful slave and that of the meek, humble, unaggressive Negro who followed him after the Civil War. Since there is much more data on the latter role, this is the one we shall discuss in detail.

Education includes learning to play certain roles, roles which are advantageous to the individual in adapting himself to his particular culture. As the culture changes, so

does the role. Adaptation to society begins at birth and ends at death. Culture is not a neatly tied package given to the child in school. It is an ever changing process, gropingly and gradually discovered.[1] The family, church, movies, newspapers, radio programs, books, trade-unions, chambers of commerce, and all other organized and unorganized interpersonal relations are part of education. All these are part of the cultural process, which determines how behavior and attitudes are channeled.

The cultural milieu of the Negro in the United States has run the gamut from slavery to that of a free but underprivileged group, who are slowly but continuously raising their status. From the time slaves were first brought to this country until today there have been barriers and restrictions which have prevented the Negro from satisfying social needs and attaining those values prized most highly by our society. How the resentment against these deprivations is channeled depends largely on cultural factors. Each historical period has produced certain types of adaptation.

Much has been written as to whether slaves emotionally accepted their status or whether they rebelled against it, with

[1] For further elaboration of this point see Edward Sapir, "The Emergence of the Concept of Personality in a Study of Cultures," *Journal of Social Psychology*, V, 408–15.

the consequent aggressive impulses turned against their masters. There is no categorical answer. Aggression can be channeled in many ways, and some of these are not discernible except to the trained psychiatrist. But others are quite obvious. The fact that thousands of slaves ran away clearly indicates dissatisfaction with their status.[2] Crimes committed by the slaves are another evidence of lack of acceptance of status and of aggressive feelings toward the whites.

Many people have assumed that there was little or no crime by Negroes during the slave regime. The impression will be quickly dispelled if one consults the elaborate studies contained in *Judicial Cases concerning American Slavery and the Negro*. . . . . In these lists can be found cases of murder, rape, attempted rape, arson, theft, burglary, and practically every conceivable crime.[3]

The fact that these crimes were committed in the face of the most severe deterrents— cutting-off of ears, whipping, castration, death by mutilation—bears witness to the strength of the underlying aggression. Equally cruel was the punishment of those slaves who broke the laws against carrying firearms, assembling, and conspiring to rebel. The Gabriel conspiracy in Richmond, the Vesey conspiracy in Charleston, the Nat Turner rebellion, and others resulted in the massacre of whites and in the burning, shooting, and hanging of the Negroes. These attempts were undertaken despite the fact that the superior power of the whites made it virtually impossible for a slave revolt to be successful.

But the overt aggression was very probably only a small part of the total hostility. The punishments imposed by the culture for failure were too severe and the chances for success too slight to encourage the majority

of slaves to rebel to any considerable extent. There were large numbers of loyal and faithful slaves, loyal to the system and to the masters. It is this loyalty that we try to understand.

Psychologically, slavery is a dependency situation. The slave was completely dependent upon the white master for food, clothing, shelter, protection—in other words, for security. If he could gain the good will or affection of the master, his security was increased. In return for this security the Negro gave obedience, loyalty, and sometimes love or affection. With certain limitations the situation of slave and master corresponds to that of child and parent. The young child is completely dependent on his parents for food, shelter, love, and everything affecting his well-being and security. The child learns to be obedient because he is taught that disobedience brings punishment and the withdrawal of something he needs for security. Basic infantile and childhood disciplines relating to sex are imposed on this level. In our culture, parents forbid and punish deviations by a child, who in turn renounces his gratification to gain the parent's approval. "The parent is needed and feared, and must therefore be obeyed; but the hatred to the frustrating parent, though suppressed, must be present somewhere."[4]

We mentioned above that there are certain limitations to our analogy. Obviously, the bondage is greater for the slave than for the child. Equally obviously, while there was love in some master-slave relationships, it was certainly not so prevalent as between parents and children. Again, the child always has a weak and undeveloped ego while the adult slave may have a strong, developed one. But most important is the difference in the reasons for the dependency attitude. The limited strength and resources of the child and his resulting helplessness and anxiety are due to biological causes. But the slave's dependency is imposed on him by culture and has nothing to do with biological factors. The structure of the two de-

[2] From 1830 to 1860 about fifty thousand escaped, chiefly through Ohio and Philadelphia. In an earlier period many escaped to near-by Indian tribes, others to Canada and the free states (see E. B. Reuter, *The American Race Problem* [New York, 1938], pp. 117–18).

[3] Quoted in W. D. Weatherford and C. S. Johnson, *Race Relations* (New York, 1934), p. 265.

[4] A. Kardiner and R. Linton, *The Individual and Society* (New York, 1939), p. 24.

pendency situations is, therefore, very different. Nevertheless, functionally they have something in common. To attain the only security available to them, both the slave and the child repress, consciously or unconsciously, their hatred for the object which restricts their desires and freedom. At this late date it is impossible to determine to what degree aggression occurred in slaves' fantasies or in minor overt acts.[5] It probably varied from one slave to another, as it does for children. Neither all children nor all slaves repress their aggression all the time. Running away is a pattern for both groups. Disobedience is followed by punishment for both. Another alternative for both is open rebellion. Finally, children and slaves may accept their dependency and repress their aggression when compensations are adequate. They may even identify with the frustrating object. The picture of the faithful slave who helped the white mistress run the plantation while the master was away fighting, fighting the men who would liberate the slave, is only superficially paradoxical.

Data from psychoanalysis indicate that those children who do not permit their aggressive impulses to break through even in fantasy, not to mention overt behavior, have great difficulty as adults in entering into any personal relationship which does not duplicate the dependency pattern of parent and child. A legal edict of freedom did not immediately change the security system for the slave, conditioned over years to depend on the white man for all security. Time was needed for the compensations of freedom to become part of the ex-slave's security system. The process of growing up, or becoming less dependent, is a long and difficult one.

With emancipation the slave, from being a piece of property with no rights at all, attained the status of a human being—but an underprivileged one. Psychological dependency did not vanish with the proclamation of freedom. In the period following the Civil War the slave's illiteracy, his complete lack of capital and property, the habituation to the past, and the continuous forces wielded by the whites in power created new conditions for the continuance of the old dependency. The recently freed Negro was dependent on the whites for jobs, for favors, for grants of money to set up schools, and for much of his security. In the South, following the Reconstruction Period, it was by obtaining favors from whites rather than by insisting on his rights that the Negro was able to make any progress or attain any security. The set of mores which insured the colored man's status being lower than that of the whites was and is still firmly intrenched. The denial of the courtesy titles (Mr., Mrs., Miss); the Jim Crowism in schools, buses, and trains, in places of residence; the denial of legal rights; the threat of lynching—these are among the more obvious ways of "keeping the Negro in his place." He is deprived of what are considered legal, social, and human rights, without any of the compensations for his deprivation which he had under slavery.

The same questions we asked about the slave occur again. Did the Negro really accept his position? Or was aggression aroused, and, if so, how did the culture channel it? This is an easier situation to study than the slavery of the past; for varied ways of reacting or adapting to this situation became stereotyped and still persist today. They are therefore susceptible of direct study.

First, there is direct aggression against its true object. Since the whites had, and still have, superior power and since Negroes are highly realistic, they rarely use this method on any large scale except in times of crisis, and then as a climax to a long series of more indirect aggressive behavior patterns. The knocking-down of a white overseer, the direct attack on other whites, has occurred, but only occasionally. One of the reasons advanced by many southern white planters for their preference for colored

---

[5] I know of no accurate way of getting data on this point. The memories of old ex-slaves would be colored by what has happened to them since slavery was abolished. Aggressive impulses which may have been completely repressed during slavery could be released and brought into consciousness after slavery ceased.

share-croppers to white ones is that the former do not fight back like the latter.

A second method consists in substituting a colored object for the white object of aggression. This was, and still is, done very frequently. The high degree of intra-Negro quarreling, crime, and homicide, revealed by statistics and observation, can be directly correlated with the Negro's frustration in being unable to vent his hostility on the whites. The mechanism of the substitution of one object of aggression for another is well known to the scientist and to the layman.[6] The substitution of Negro for white is encouraged by the culture pattern of white official and unofficial leniency toward intra-Negro crime. Courts, more particularly southern ones, are mild in their view of intra-Negro offenses, and the prevailing white attitude is one of indulgence toward those intra-Negro crimes which do not infringe on white privileges.[7]

A third possibility is for the Negro to retreat to an "ivory tower" and attempt to remain unaffected by the interracial situation. But this type of adjustment is very difficult and consequently a rare one.

Another form of adaptation consists in the Negro's identification with his white employer, particularly if the latter has great prestige. Some of the slaves also identified themselves with the great families whom they served. This pattern may likewise be observed in white servants. Still another adaptation is the diversion of aggression into wit, which has been and still is a much-used mechanism. We have not sufficient data on these two mechanisms to discuss them in detail.

But we do want to analyze in some detail a very frequent type of adjustment which occurred after the Civil War and which has persisted. We mean the behavior of the meek, humble, and unaggressive Negro, who

is always deferential to whites no matter what the provocation may be. The psychological mechanism for this form of adaptation is less obvious than some of the other types, and a more detailed analysis is therefore needed. We have called this Negro "unaggressive," and that is the way his overt behavior could be correctly described. All our data, however, indicate that he does have aggressive impulses against whites, springing from the interracial situation. He would be abnormal if he did not have them. Over and over again field studies reveal that this type of Negro is conscious of these resentments. But he conceals his true attitude from the whites who have power. How has he been able to conceal his aggression so successfully? His success here is patent. What is the psychological mechanism which enables the Negro to play this meek, deferential role?

A clue appears in certain similarities of this kind of behavior to that of the masochist, particularly through the detailed analysis of masochism by Dr. Theodor Reik in his recent book on that subject.[8] The seeming paradox of the masochist enjoying his suffering has been well known to psychoanalysts. He derives pleasure, because, first, it satisfies unconscious guilt feeling. Second (and here is where Dr. Reik has gone beyond the other psychoanalysts in his interpretation), the masochist derives another kind of pleasure, because his suffering is a prelude to his reward and eventual triumph over his adversary. In other words, he gets power through his suffering. We must not be misunderstood at this point. The meek Negro is neither neurotic nor masochistic any more than the slave was biologically a child. But the unaggressive behavior has some elements in common with (and some different from) the behavior of the masochist; and a comparison of the two gives a clue to an understanding of the strength behind the meek, humble role played by so many Negroes.

First, there are essential differences be-

---

[6] This is reflected in the jokes and stories about the man who has a bad day at the office and then "takes it out" on his wife or children when he comes home in the evening.

[7] For further elaboration see H. Powdermaker, *After Freedom* (Viking Press, 1939), pp. 172–74.

[8] *Masochism in Modern Man* (New York: Farrar & Rinehart, 1941).

tween the Negroes we are describing and the masochists analyzed by Dr. Reik and others. The Negro's sufferings and sacrifices are not unconsciously self-inflicted (as are those of the masochist) but are inflicted on him by the culture. The Negro plays his social masochistic role consciously, while the psychologically compulsive masochist does it unconsciously. These two important differences should be kept in mind while the similarities are discussed.

Our hypothesis is that the meek, unaggressive Negro, who persists today as a type and whom we have opportunity to study, feels guilty about his conscious and unconscious feelings of hostility and aggression toward the white people. These Negroes are believing Christians who have taken very literally the Christian doctrine that it is sinful to hate. Yet on every hand they are faced with situations which must inevitably produce hatred in any normal human being. These situations run the scale from seeing an innocent person lynched to having to accept the inferior accommodations on a Jim Crow train. The feeling of sin and guilt is frequently and openly expressed. In a Sunday-school class in a southern rural colored church a teacher tells the tale of a sharecropper who had worked all season for a white planter, only to be cheated out of half his earnings. The teacher's lesson is that it is wrong to hate this planter, because Christ told us to love our enemies. The members of the class say how hard it is not to hate but that since it is a sin they will change their hate to love. They regard this as possible, although difficult.[9]

One woman in the same community, who plays the deferential role to perfection and who, whites say, never steps out of "her place," tells me she feels guilty because she hates the whites, who do not seem to distinguish between her, a very moral, respectable, and law-abiding person, and the immoral, disreputable colored prostitutes of the community. She says that God and Jesus have told her not to hate but to love—and so she must drive the hatred and bitter-

ness away. Almost every human being in our culture carries a load of guilt (heavy or light as the case may be) over his conscious and unconscious aggressive impulses. It is easy then to imagine how heavy is the load of guilt for the believing Christian Negro who lives in an interracial situation which is a constant stimulus to aggressive thoughts and fantasies. By acting in exactly the opposite manner—that is, meekly and unaggressively—he can appease his guilt feelings consciously and unconsciously. It is this appeasement which accounts, in part, for his pleasure in the unaggressive role he plays with the whites.

But only in part. The unaggressive Negro enjoys his role also because through it he feels superior to the whites. Like the masochist, he thinks of his present sufferings as a contrasting background for his future glory. His is the final victory, and so he can afford to feel superior to his white opponent who is enjoying a temporary victory over him. My own field work and the work of others give many examples. Dr. Charles S. Johnson, in his recent book on rural colored youth in the South, discusses the dissimulation of many of the young people studied. He says:

Outward submissiveness and respect may thus be, as often as not, a mask behind which these youth conceal their attitude. George Cator is an example of this behavior. He has learned to flatter as a means of preserving his own estimate of himself. . . . . "When I'm around them, I act like they are more than I am. I don't think they are, but they do. I hear people say that's the best way to act."[10]

Any expression of antagonism would be dangerous, but this is not the whole story. It is not just that this boy and others avoid danger by meek negative behavior. There is a positive element in that he and others are insuring eventual victory. This was expressed by a colored servant who is a model of deferential behavior when with the whites. However, to me she says, partly scornfully and

[9] Cf. Powdermaker, *op. cit.*, pp. 247–48.

[10] Charles S. Johnson, *Growing Up in the Black Belt* (American Council on Education, 1941), pp. 296–97.

partly jokingly, that she considers it ridiculous that having cleaned the front porch and entrance she has to use the back entrance. She hates having to walk in the back door, which in this case is not only the symbol of status for a servant but the symbol that a whole race has a servant status. She adds that she expects to go to Heaven and there she will find rest—and no back doors.[11]

The Christian doctrines, "The last shall be first, and the first shall be last" and "The meek shall inherit the earth," and all the promises of future reward for suffering give strong homiletic sanction to the feeling that the Negroes' present status and suffering is a prelude to their future triumph. Colored ministers give very concise expression to this attitude. A sermon heard in a colored church in rural Mississippi related

the story of a rich woman who lived in a big house and had no time for God. When she went to Heaven she was given an old shanty in which to live and she exclaimed: "Why that's the shanty my cook used to live in!" The cook, who on earth had given all her time to God, was now living in a big house in Heaven, very much like the one in which her former mistress used to live.[12]

The Christian missionaries of the pre–Civil War period emphasized the reward for the meek and their contrasting glories in the future partly because it was an important part of Christian doctrine and partly because it was only by negating the present and emphasizing the future that the evangelists could get permission from the planters to preach to the slaves. The general theme of many of these sermons was that the greater the suffering here, the greater would be the reward in the world to come. One minister, referring to the case of a slave who was unjustly punished by his masters, says, "He [God] will reward you for it in heaven, and the punishment you suffer unjustly here shall turn to your exceeding

great glory thereafter."[13] Sermons, past and current, quite frequently picture Heaven as a place where whites and Negroes are not just equal but where their respective status is the opposite of what it is here.

This fantasy of turning the tables on the oppressor is not always confined to the other world; sometimes the setting is our own world. An example of this is the fantasy of a young colored girl in a northern town who had publicly taken quite meekly a decision that the colored people could not use the "Y" swimming pool at the same time white people were using it. Privately she shows her anger and says that she wishes the colored people would build a great big, magnificent "Y," a hundred times better than the white one, and make that one look like nothing. Her fantasy of triumph over the whites obviously gives her real pleasure and allows her to carry the present situation less onerously. Another example of the same type of fantasying occurs in the joking between two colored teachers who obey a disliked white official with deferential meekness. The joking consists of one of them boasting in some detail about how he has fired the white official; and the other one, in the same tone, describing how he "cussed out" the white official over the telephone.

Another aspect of the unaggressive Negro's pleasure is his feeling of superiority because he thinks he is so much finer a Christian than his white opponent. He, the Negro, is following Christ's precepts, while the white man does the opposite. The white man oppresses the poor and is unjust; in other words, he sins. He, the Negro, is virtuous and will be rewarded. One Negro, referring to a white man's un-Christian behavior, says, "It reflects back on him."

This feeling of superiority is a third characteristic of the unaggressive Negro's pleasure and is not limited to the feeling of Christian virtue. He feels superior to the whites because he is fooling them. His triumph is not completely limited to the distant future, but he enjoys at least a small part of it now.

[11] From the author's field notes in rural Mississippi.

[12] Powdermaker, op. cit., p. 243.

[13] Revor Bowen, Divine White Right (1934), p. 111.

One of my informants in Mississippi, who plays this role to perfection, told me how he has the laugh on the whites because they never know his real thoughts. He quite consciously feels that he and the other Negroes like him have the upper hand through their dissimulation. He says very clearly that it makes him feel superior. One woman who presents an appearance of perfect meekness laughs with a kind of gleeful irony when she tells me how she really feels, and her meekness drops away from her as if she were discarding a cloak. Another chuckles when she relates how much she has been able to extract from white people, who would never give her a thing if they knew how she really felt about them. A Negro official who holds a fairly important position in his community knows that he is constantly being watched to see that he does not overstep his place, that his position and contact with whites has not made him "uppity." As he goes around humbly saying, "Yes, ma'am" and "Yes, sir," waiting his turn long after it is due, appearing not to heed insulting remarks, he is buoyed up with a feeling of superiority because he is really fooling all these whites. He is quite aware of his mask and knows it is such and not his real self. This mask characteristic comes out particularly when one of these individuals is seen with the whites and then later with his own group. One woman who has been particularly successful in the deferential, humble role with the whites gives a clear impression of meekness and humility. Her eyes downcast, her voice low, she patiently waits to be spoken to before she speaks, and then her tone is completely deferential. An hour later she is in the midst of her own group. No longer are her eyes downcast. They sparkle! Her laugh flashes out readily. Instead of patiently waiting, she is energetically leading. Her personality emerges, vibrant and strong, a complete contrast to the picture she gives the whites. These people enjoy wearing their mask because they do it so successfully and because its success makes them feel superior to the whites whom they deceive.

The deferential, unaggressive role just described and well known to students of Negro life has a very real function besides the obvious one of avoiding trouble. As Dr. Reik says in his book on masochism, "The supremacy of the will is not only expressed in open fights." It is, as he says, likewise expressed "in the determination to yield only exteriorly and yet to cling to life, nourishing such phantasies anticipating final victory."[14] Our unaggressive Negro, like the masochist, imagines a future where his fine qualities are acknowledged by the people who had formerly disdained him. This, in good Christian manner, will be brought about through suffering. This philosophy and its resulting behavior obviously make the Negroes (or any minority group) who have them very adaptable to any circumstance in which they find themselves, no matter how painful. They continue to cling to life, in the assurance of ultimate victory. They cannot be hurt in the way that people without this faith are hurt. The adaptability of the Negro has often been noted. This hypothesis may give some further clue to understanding it.

A special combination of cultural factors —namely, oppression of a minority group and a religion which promises that through suffering power will be gained over the oppressors—has channeled one type of adaptive behavior similar to that of the masochist. This behavior pattern has given the Negro a way of appeasing his guilt over his aggressive impulses and a method of adapting to a very difficult cultural situation. Because of the understanding given us by psychoanalysis of the pleasure derived through suffering, of the near and distant aims of the masochist, we are given a clue to the psychological mechanism underlying the so-called "unaggressive" Negro's behavior. This Negro is not a masochist, in that his sufferings are not self-inflicted and he plays his role consciously. He knows he is acting, while the masochist behavior springs from inner compulsion. Again, there is a real difference in structure, as there was in the de-

[14] Op. cit., p. 322.

pendency situations of the child and the slave; and again there is a real similarity in function. The masochist and the meek, unaggressive Negro derive a similar kind of pleasure from their suffering. For the Negro as well as for the masochist there is pleasure in appeasing the guilt feeling; for each there is the pleasure derived from the belief that through his suffering he becomes superior to his oppressors; and, finally, for each the suffering is a prelude to final victory.

Neither the slave nor the obsequious, unaggressive Negro, whom we have described, learned to play his role in any school. They learned by observation and imitation; they were taught by their parents; they observed what role brought rewards. Since the Civil War the Negro has likewise seen the meek, humble type presented over and over again with approval in sermons, in literature, in movies, and, more recently, through radio sketches. By participating in the cultural processes, the Negro has learned his role. This was his education, far more powerful than anything restricted to schools; for the kind of education we are discussing is continuous during the entire life of the individual. It is subtle as well as direct. One part of the cultural process strengthens another part, and reinforcement for the role we described comes from every side.

But the cultural process continues to change with resulting changes in behavior. Just as the completely loyal and faithful slave disappeared, so the meek, unagressive, and humble Negro, the "good nigger" type, is declining in numbers. In the rural South, and elsewhere too, the tendency of Negro young people (in their teens and twenties) is to refuse to assume the unaggressive role. The passing of the "good nigger" from the scene does not entail a civil war as did the passing of the faithful slave. But it does indicate a psychological revolution. For the slave the Civil War altered the scope of the dependency situation. Today, without a Civil War, equally significant cultural changes are taking place. The Negro is participating now in a very different kind

of cultural process from that which he underwent fifty years ago.

Some of the differences occurring today are here briefly indicated. There is a decline in religious faith. The vivid "getting-religion" experience prevalent in the past has become increasingly rare for young people. Today they use the church as a social center. Gone is the intensity of religious belief that their parents knew. The young people are not atheists, but they do not have the fervor and sincerity of belief in a future world. They are much more hurt by slights and minor insults than are their parents, because they do not put their faith in the promise of a heavenly victory.

Along with changes in the form of religious participation have come many other changes. The illiteracy of the past has disappeared. A lengthening of schooling and a steady improvement in educational standards tend to give the Negro the same knowledge and the same tools enjoyed by the white man and to minimize cultural differences between the two. A more independent and rebellious Negro type is making its appearance in literature, as, for instance, the character of Bigger in the best seller, *Native Son*.

The steady trek of the rural Negroes to cities, North and South, has changed the milieu of masses of Negroes from the rural peasant life to the industrial urban one.[15] Here they come under the influence of the trade-union movement, which slowly but gradually is shifting its attitude from one of jealous exclusion to one of inclusion, sometimes cordial and sometimes resigned. The shift is not anywhere near completion yet, but the trend is there. In the city the Negro is influenced by the same advertisements, the same radio sketches, the same political bosses, the same parties (left or right), and all the other urban forces which influence the white man.

The Negro's goals for success are thus becoming increasingly the same as those of the

---

[15] Between 1920 and 1930 over a million Negroes migrated from the country to the cities. The figures for the past decade are not yet available.

white person; and these goals are primarily in the economic field, although those in other fields, such as art and athletics, are not to be minimized either. The securing of these goals is in this world rather than in a future one. They are attained through the competition and aggressive struggle so characteristic of our culture rather than through meekness and subservience. The compensations available to the loyal slave and the humble, unaggressive, free Negro no longer exist or, at least, are steadily diminishing. The white man can no longer offer security in return for devotion, because he himself no longer has security. The whites of all classes have known a mounting social insecurity over the past decade, and they obviously cannot give away something which they do not possess. Thus the material rewards for obsequiousness and unaggressiveness are fading away. Gone, too, is the religious emphasis on rewards in Heaven. When the cultural process takes away rewards for a certain type of behavior, dissatisfaction with that behavior appears and there is a gradual change to another form which is more likely to bring new compensations. Obviously, one can expect, and one finds, a growing restlessness and uncertainty which occur in any transition period, when old goals have been lost. The new goals are the standard American ones. But the means for attaining these goals are not yet as available to the Negro as they are to the white. Economic and social discriminations still exist. Unless some other form of adaptation takes place and unless discriminations are lessened, we may expect a trend toward greater overt aggression.

However, there are no sudden revolutions in behavior patterns, and this holds for the patterns of aggression. They change slowly; the old ones persist while new ones are being formed, and opposing patterns exist side by side. But change occurs. The cultural process in which the Negro has participated from the time when he was first brought to this country until today has involved a constant denial of privileges. The denial has taken various forms, from the overt one involved in slavery to the more subtle ones of today. The compensations for the denial have varied from different degrees of material security to promises of future blessings in Heaven, and from the feeling of being more virtuous than the white to the feeling of fooling him. Today these compensations are fading away. Equally important, ideological fetters of the past have been broken by the Negro's increasing participation in the current urban industrial processes.

The Negro's education, formal and informal, has consisted of his participation in this ever changing cultural process, one small part of which we have briefly examined. Slavery, religion, economic and other social factors, have channeled his activities, offering him alternatives within a certain cultural range. We have examined only two of the alternatives in any detail—namely, the roles of the faithful slave and of the humble, meek Negro who was a fairly common stereotype following the Civil War; we have concentrated on the latter because he still exists and we therefore have more data on him. Both appear unaggressive. A functional comparison with the psychoanalytical analysis of the dependency situation of the child and of the problem of masochism has indicated how the aggression may have been present, although concealed, in these two roles.

QUEENS COLLEGE

THE EDUCATIONAL PROCESS AS APPLIED IN AMERICA

EDWIN R. EMBREE

ABSTRACT

Our educational system has been making progress in transmitting the tools of survival in our culture: reading, writing, and technical skills. Its increasing responsibility for the development of personality and intelligent, flexible adaptability to changing social conditions has not been so well met. The emphasis is far too much on rote learning and verbalization rather than on the handling of real situations.

I

It is not the purpose of this concluding paper to distil, from all the erudition that has gone before, the final truth about education here or elsewhere. My task is simply to apply some of the wisdom generated by discussion of education among various peoples of the world to the problems of growing up in America.

As a starting-point let me try to frame a definition of education that will take into account the chief points stressed in the preceding papers. Education in America as elsewhere is the process of "growing up," but growing up within the framework of some specific cultural milieu. This means something more than the transmission of a tradition and a cultural pattern from an earlier to a later generation, or from one cultural group to another. It is the means by which the individual discovers and adapts himself to the particular place to which his special talents or some accident assigns him. In our modern society an important problem that every individual has to solve, and solve pretty much for himself, is to find a job for which he is fitted and to fit himself for the job which he finds.

To be a little more specific, education in any society aims (a) to draw out the personality and abilities of the individual young people, (b) to prepare them for harmonious and creative living in their society, (c) to give them skill in the crafts and techniques that will enable them to be successful in their world. In any society formal schooling is only part of the educational process. That is one of the things that has been particularly emphasized in these papers and in the discussions which accompanied them. Some preliterate peoples, it appears, have no formalized training, though the boys' societies and girls' societies, the "bush" schools of Africa, and initiation ceremonies common to most tribes are more or less comparable to what the Western nations have so highly formalized in schools.

Even in Europe and America many forces not ordinarily reckoned as schooling go into the total of education: the home, the church, the pressures of social cliques, and the admonitions of the wise old men of the tribe, as represented among us by quotations from George Washington and Abraham Lincoln, from Herbert Hoover and Father Divine.

Yet in modern times schools have become so formalized, rationalized, and glorified, so detached from the acts and experiences of daily life, that Dr. Johnson, in editing this series, has divided the papers into two parts: one entitled "Education without Schools"; the other, "Schools without Education."

Of the three prime purposes of education, it is natural that one phase should be stressed in one society and others in another. Static groups, such as island peoples or tribes cut off from outside contact, naturally stress acquaintance with and acceptance of tribal customs, rituals, laws, taboos. In modern society, marked by a high development of mechanical and intellectual tools, it is just as natural to emphasize training in the use of these very complex techniques. It is futile to scorn the ancient Samoans for not including science and mechanics and writing in their educational process, for these were not a part of their life; or to criticize America for stressing tools so greatly, for these are the very basis of our culture.

In modern civilization it is proper and necessary to give much of the whole school course to learning the skilful use of our highly developed intellectual tools: reading, writing, mathematics, science. A person simply cannot live in the modern world without these techniques. All societies have taught crafts and skills as well as religious beliefs and tribal custom. American Indian tribes carefully taught the boys to hunt, to carry on warfare, to tan hides and fashion leather, as well as to take their place in the council ring. Samoan girls learned to cook and make tapa as well as how to deport themselves in village society. It is silly to become so sentimental about "the beautiful rhythms of life in primitive society" as to say—as some extreme progressive educators were saying a few years ago—"it doesn't matter whether a boy learns to write or figure; just let him grow and develop into a fine citizen." One can't be a useful or happy participant in Western civilization without knowing the techniques on which modern life rests.

II

The fault of the schools in America is not that they stress the tool subjects. The fault is that they neglect the other prime functions of education: the drawing-out of the personality and the fitting of the individual into creative relationship to his world. A part of this fault is that the tools are taught as if they were something apart from the rest of life. Not tied in with daily experiences, the techniques tend to become formalized and sterile and thus are themselves not well learned. Let me give a few homely examples from my own experience:

The autobiography of a southern country boy records that after going to school for several years he happened to pick up the family Bible. To his amazement he found that he could read it. Up to that moment, he said, it had never occurred to him that the rote drill in school called reading had any connection with something he might do out of school. Suddenly he discovered that what he had supposed was a scholastic trick was instead a generalized tool, by means of which he could gain information and pleasure from the whole realm of literature.

This seems an extreme case. Yet the tests given to the draft troops during the first World War indicated that 25 per cent of that cross-section of American youth had never made a successful transfer from the school lessons to reading. One-fourth of the whole American draft army, although most of them had spent several years in school, had not learned enough to carry over into life the ability to read simple sentences or to write their own names.

In a little school just outside Baton Rouge, Lousiana, the teacher had been hearing a class read a lesson on birds in one of the standard textbooks. To test his knowledge of the lesson, she asked a boy, "When do the robins come?"

The pupil answered promptly, "In the fall."

"Now, Jimmie," urged the teacher, "read the lesson carefully again."

After he had droned out the text a second time, she said cheerily, "Now, Jimmie, when do the robins come?"

More hesitantly and sullenly he answered again, "The robins come in the fall."

"James, James!" shouted the teacher. "Read that lesson again. Now tell me, when do the robins come?"

Almost in tears the boy finally answered, "The robins come in the spring."

And so they do—in Boston, where the text was written. But in Louisiana, just in order to avoid the northern winter, they come in the fall, as the boy well knew.

Here we had an all too frequent combination of a stupid teacher, who was intent on grinding out a "lesson," and a textbook unadapted to the region. The result must have been either to destroy the boy's confidence in his own common sense or, more likely, to break down completely his respect for book learning.

The first problem of American education is to make the tool subjects a part of life, to teach the tools for just what their name implies, not as ends in themselves but simply as means to obtain efficiently the ends we want. These ends, simply stated, are to make a living and to enjoy life.

An Oxford professor of mathematics once boasted, "Thank God, my subject can never be prostituted to any useful end." Of course, the professor was talking nonsense—trying to glorify his subject as an end in itself. Mathematics is the most practical of subjects, the very foundation stone of exact science and of all precise thinking. In an Alabama school I saw an example of this same Oxford attitude on a humbler level.

A Negro teacher giving a class "a lesson in health" said, "Why should we wash and comb our hair?" And the row of little Negroes droned back the answer, "So it will not get stringy and fall down in our eyes."

Neither teacher nor pupils seemed to think this a surprising answer from children whose hair was so kinky that it could never get into strings or hang down anywhere. This was the lesson; all that teacher or pupils had to do was to recite it. As with Tennyson's Six Hundred, "theirs not to reason why, theirs but to do and die." And in this rote learning children's minds die as stupidly and as wantonly as the members of the Light Brigade on the fields of Balaclava.

Learning for learning's sake belongs, as a principle, to the Middle Ages. For that reason this era is properly known as the Dark Age of Europe. The habits of mind generated by the educational process must be kept near the actual movement of events. The task of education cannot be achieved merely by working upon men's minds, as some philosophers would have it; it becomes effective only with action.

Happily, some progress is being made on this front. Many American children are learning to read, write, and figure with a fairly clear idea that these are tools of communication that open up vast storehouses of information and of inspiration and beauty. The sciences are also being fairly well learned as tools. In the higher professional schools of agriculture, medicine, and engineering, scientific knowledge is very skilfully presented as the basis for practical work.

III

The great problems of the American school system—still almost wholly unsolved —are concerned with education that is not technical and does not involve the use of either tools or technique. Let me simply summarize some of the problems in stark outline.

1. In ideal organization the school should be bolstered in its educational tasks by other great social institutions. But in America the whole process of education is being more and more turned over to schools and colleges. The church has lost much of its prestige and seems to be having less and less influence in molding even the ideals of young people. The home is far from the powerful institution it was in most earlier societies. Apartment living, divorces, abdication of authority, have nearly written the family out as a guiding influence in children's lives. Play is increasingly on school grounds or public parks; standards of conduct for children are set by the gang and the play group; precepts come screaming out from tabloids and comic strips or dripping from suave radio voices and glamorous movie stars. The wise old men of the tribe are crowded out by the platitudes of the latest world's champion boxer, by ambitious politicians, by advertising slogans, by best sellers on how to make friends and influence people. Whether they like it or not, schools and colleges have to assume almost the whole role of serious education in America.

2. It is unfortunate—unnatural, as Margaret Mead has so trenchantly pointed out —that our emphasis is on teaching rather than on learning. In earlier societies young people who wanted to learn some skill that they thought useful hunted up an uncle or some wise man to teach them, or they voluntarily joined a class of their fellows who were trying to learn the same thing. With us it is the other way around. A teacher has something he wants to teach, and so *he* organizes the classes or else the school system organizes classes for him and compels the children to attend. Instead of students engaging in the pursuit of learning, schools and professors are in pursuit of students! The natural and normal thing is for children to ask the questions. With us, the teachers ask the questions and the children are expected to give the answers. Too often these answers are simply rote "recitations" from a book.

The function of education is not simply to transmit knowledge. Much more important is to keep alive curiosity and zest for more learning. The period during which children are wont to ask questions and to wonder about the world does not continue long, certainly not under the influence of the ordinary classroom. Soon the world becomes familiar; children get answers of a sort and stop asking questions. The interest in the world as a whole is destroyed because curiosity has been appeased with words or phrases which did not enlighten.

3. It is scarcely possible to prepare our children for the social order in which they are to live because our society is changing so rapidly. Our schools do well to resist the clamor to indoctrinate the students in this or that phase of "Americanism." Most of those who urge this sort of thing are themselves already a generation or two behind what America actually means. But it is unfortunate that two of the basic features of American life are distorted by the very organization of our teaching and our school system.

One of these bases is flexibility. The very essence of modern life is ability to build from where we were yesterday to where we will be tomorrow. This is true in science, in social organization, and especially in international and interracial relationships. But the essence of book learning and rote teaching is to instil the idea that there are fixed answers for every question, established codes to meet every dilemma. By closing the students' minds by a mass of rote knowledge, we tend to prevent that very inquiring spirit and open-mindedness that would enable the students to build soundly from one position to another.

The other enduring base on which our society is built is democracy. As Ruth Benedict points out, while we may give lip service to the principles of democracy in our teaching, our whole school system is an absolute autocracy. No feature of American life, not even big business, gives so little opportunity for the practice of democracy as our schools. From the kindergarten through the graduate school the student is a cog in a machine.

The teacher is as much a peon of the system as the student. If we are ever to learn democracy as a way of life, we must find some means for young people to experience it and practice it during the formative years of their school life.

4. We must find better means of drawing out the personality of the student. This is a tough task. Any given personality is largely formed by the customs of his society and the techniques he must learn. Yet there is something more. The definition at the beginning of this paper refers to harmonious and creative living. The individual is not the slave of his society or of its techniques. True, he must adjust himself to the social order, and he must learn to use the basic skills. But society and science progress as individuals create new ideas, revise customs to fit fresh conditions, invent still better tools. Professor Park grapples valiantly with this problem, although he has no ready solutions. He believes in more direct human relationships, more contact with nature, and, most of all, more contemplation. He believes that teachers with some wisdom and knowledge of life, rather than with high professional technique and low personality, should be sought as guides and instructors of the young. Our society has probably done its poorest job in this delicate process of drawing out the abilities and enlarging the personalities of the students.

This criticism leads us back to the heart of the symposium on education which these papers record. These discussions are unique in that, on the whole, they present the point of view of anthropologists rather than professional educators. They view the process of education as a whole, examining it in the context of simpler and more thoroughly integrated cultures than our own.

In preliterate societies knowledge is informal and unsystematic. It is taken over almost unconsciously as a body of folkways and mores. In our educational system common sense and traditional wisdom—the knowledge that we gained in the home and by experience—are regarded as inferior forms of knowledge because they are neither scientific nor systematic. Yet the psycho-analysts are constantly insisting that what is learned in this very way by the child in his early years is probably the most important and determining of all the knowledge that he acquires.

What can we do to bridge this gap between informal knowledge, which is so effective in forming habits and attitudes, and the systematic knowledge of the textbooks? An incidental problem is that a great deal of present scientific knowledge concerns itself with everyday mechanics—electricity, medicine, and vitamins, for example—which have not yet been incorporated in the tradition and common sense even of educated people. Since we are ignorant about the principles involved, much of our modern knowledge is little more than a new and more sophisticated superstition. Meanwhile, we omit from our formal educational system the whole realm of homely experience and basic feeling: nature, sex, love, hate, prejudice, the mechanics of growth, the satisfaction of the fundamental urges of our personalities. For many students school is school and life is life and never the twain do meet.

IV

Standardization is not the answer to education in our society. Our efforts to standardize are due, in part, to a desire to conform to the democratic ideal of a classless society in which everyone, as far as his abilities permit, will have the same education. It is assumed that precisely what is good for the American child is good for every American child—is, for example, good for the American Negro child, irrespective of his background. On the other hand, if account is taken of the cultural heritage of the Negro child, the temptation is to identify that heritage with what are conceived to be the Negro's peculiar racial temperament and capacities, supposed to be basically African. This misses the point, for the truth is that the cultural heritage of the Negro, in his present setting at least, is neither American nor African. That heritage is a unique social

phenomenon which has evolved under peculiar historical conditions.

As Horace Mann Bond points out, there is something strangely unreal about the education of the Negro in the American system. It takes little account of the actual conditions under which Negroes live. As a result the educational procedures designed for general American youth often fail to fire the interest of the colored students, especially those who grow up in the special conditions of the rural South. These children, by some extraordinary quality of sheer mentality, are expected to find interest in educational content that has no roots in their own lives. An inevitable result is that the external forms are adopted with little sense of their meanings. Education becomes rote drudgery, against which both mind and will rebel. This general rebellion is evidenced in the fact that in some areas one-third of all Negro children in school are in the first two grades; that over half of them leave at the fourth grade; and that of those who survive to college few can read intelligently or respond vigorously and with decision to an idea when it is presented to them. Rural Negro pupils have gone on strike against the meaningless routine of the school system.

Today, when old forms are passing and there is much misery and uncertainty everywhere, the woods are full of solutions of "world problems"—most notably, economic solutions. Under these circumstances it is important that education should have made us familiar not merely with words but with things and ideas. What else is to protect us from those who, without experience, take over uncritically political and economic dogmas merely because they are frustrated and do not know how to think or act in a real world.

The situation of the American Negro is more critical than that of the rest of the population. Therefore he needs a greater spur to control and self-correction, in anticipation of institutional changes in progress. Circumstance turns back most of the Negro professionals and teachers to the Negro masses themselves. It turns them back to step up the process of "civilization" of the masses, as that process seems to operate in the world in which the professional leaders are successful agents. There is no more profound service to the future of America, especially to Negroes and other minority groups, than that of carrying back to the masses the learning and interpretation of experience which the masses have somehow missed in spite of or because of the schools.

The very minority setting gives a chance to prove the adaptability of education to special groups of individuals—if educators and the minority leaders themselves were willing to try it. If, for example, schools were allowed to devote themselves to the needs of southern rural Negroes—instead of to standard "courses of instruction"—that group might learn self-reliance and co-operative living, accuracy and precision in place of loose and uncertain thinking, basic technical competence in this machine age, the ability to grow with some satisfaction in this swiftly changing society.

V

Education has never been a perfect process in any society. But every society has rec-

ognized its basic importance. In America faith in our public school system has become a religion. We have school enrolments beyond the dreams—or nightmares—of any other nation. Twenty-five million children are in our elementary schools every year. Seven million children are in high school— almost 70 per cent of all the young people of that age—as compared to 15 or 20 per cent of secondary-school enrolment even in such school-minded countries as England or France or Germany. Over a million students are in colleges and universities, five times the number or percentage of any other nation.

With the increased leisure that will come from still further development of mass production, it is likely that before the end of this century all young people between the ages of five and twenty-five years will be attending school. The very future of America, and of modern civilization, hangs on our ability to get sound educational procedures into our schools.

Julius Rosenwald Fund